Conten

LIST OF CONTRIBUTORS

EDITOR:
Dr. R. Alan Smith. General Secretary, Cumberland Geological Society.
Rigg Side, Grange Park, Keswick, Cumbria, CA12 4AY

Margaret Bennet
62, Victoria Road, Workington, Cumbria, CA14 2QT.

Dr. Richard Clark
Parcey House, Hartsop, Penrith, Cumbria, CA11 0NZ

Dennis Dickins
Watch Hill Cottage, by Aspatria, Wigton, Cumbria CA7 3SB

Mervyn Dodd
Arfryn, Main Street, Frizington, Cumbria, CA26 3PH.

Margaret Fox
Mountain Ash, Spittal Square, Arlecdon, Frizington, Cumbria, CA26 3UU

David Kelly
19, Wheatclose Road, Barrow-in-Furness, Cumbria, LA14 4EJ

Fred Lawton
6, Allerdale Grove, Cockermouth, Cumbria, CA13 0BN.

Dr.Angus Lunn
32, Trajan Walk, Heddon-on-the-Wall, Newcastle-upon-Tyne, NE15 0BJ

Dr. David Millward
British Geological Survey, Murchison House, West Mains Road,
Edinburgh EH9 3LA.

Murray Mitchell
Department of Earth Sciences, The University of Leeds, Leeds L52 9JT.

Professor David Oldroyd
School of Science and Technology Studies, The University of New South
Wales, Sydney 2052, Australia.

Dr. Eric Robinson
Department of Geological Sciences, University College London, Gower
Street, London WC1 6BT.

Tom Shipp
32, Cumberland Close, Clifton, Penrith, Cumbria, CA10 2EN.

Dr. Jack Soper
Gams Bank, Threshfield, Skipton, N. Yorkshire, BD23 5NP.

THE ROCK MEN

THE ROCK MEN
PIONEERS OF LAKELAND GEOLOGY

Edited by
Alan Smith

Cumberland Geological Society

Published by
The Cumberland Geological Society.

www.cumberland-geol-soc.org.uk

General Secretary
Dr .R. A. Smith.
Rigg Side
Grange Park
Keswick
Cumbria CA12 4AY

2001

ISBN 0-9541102-0-X

Bibliographical Reference : The Rock Men – Pioneers of Lakeland Geology
Alan Smith (Editor) 2001. Cumberland Geological Society

Printed by Dixon Printing Co. Ltd., Kendal, Cumbria

Introduction

We very much take it for granted today that information on the geology of the Lake District is readily available. A range of books and pamphlets are on hand to explain the details of the rocks, fossils, minerals and scenic features of the area and explanatory field excursion guides lead us to the key sites. We have a good coverage of geological maps that are equally comprehensive and informative. The scientific literature is voluminous, well over 2000 papers on Lakeland geology having been published in the specialist journals over the last 150 years. Most recently CD Roms and Internet sites have added new dimensions to the information highway. Clearly it has not always been like this. How did it all begin? Who were the people who worked it all out and pioneered the initial researches and investigations in the district? Where did the impetus and inspiration for the early discoveries come from?

To commemorate the Millenium the Cumberland Geological Society decided it would be worth looking back and trying to answer some of these questions. A group of members and friends of the Society were asked to identify the early pioneers of Lakeland geology, research into their lives and describe their contribution to the story of the unravelling of the geological history of this complex and fascinating area. The result was that 19 separate accounts of these early workers were written and published by the Society in its Proceedings early in 2000 (*Proceedings of the Cumberland Geological Society*, Volume 6, part 3). The success of this initial project and the interest that it created has led to this present volume. With the help of a generous award from the '*Awards for All*' Lottery Grants for Local Groups Scheme, it has been possible to enhance and expand the original accounts, add to them and most particularly, illustrate them with text figures. Hopefully this material can now reach a much wider readership.

This volume presents portraits of 25 of the early 'Rock Men' – some of the significant people who set out to decipher the geology of the district from the early days of the science. At the very start of the project the decision was taken to include only people who were already deceased. Largely as a result of this, the men described span the period from the first quarter of the Nineteenth Century to around the middle of the Twentieth Century. Only six of the people featured were writing after 1960 and only two after 1970. Strikingly all the pioneers are men. In the Nineteenth Century very few women indeed worked in the earth sciences. Towards the end of the Century a few women's names appear as assistants and co-workers to the eminent academics, but essentially geology remained a male preserve. In reality even in the first part of the Twentieth Century things changed very little. Whether the relatively rugged environment of Lake and geology was the reason for continued male domination is hard to know. Few lady amateur collectors or observers existed, the British Geological Survey employed no female surveyors in the Lake District and even in academic circles geology attracted few female adherents. Things are somewhat different today, but it is beyond dispute that the pioneers were men – hence the decision to title this volume 'The Rock Men'.

No precise guidelines were issued to contributors regarding the format of the written accounts. As a result, the content, style, length and emphasis of the finished articles show considerable variation. To some extent this reflects the quality of the source material. The detail available on some of the earliest workers in particular, is very fragmentary. Personal, as distinct from professional details, of many of the pioneers has proved very difficult to come by. On balance, the emphasis is towards portraits of these 'Rock Men' as people, rather than attempts to assess in great detail their technical contribution to the science of Lakeland geology. The specialist can always go back and read the published books and papers of these early workers and make a scientific evaluation. We have tried to portray the character of these pioneers, how they worked, their backgrounds and how they approached their interest in the region. In many instances it was important to see where individuals were coming from, whether as local interested amateurs or as directed professionals. All 25 resulting articles bring together a substantial amount of original research; certainly material that has never been brought together under one cover before. We have been able to include most of the major names of Lakeland geology within the constraints we set. None of the accounts are complete, none comprehensive. We are very aware that some well known personalities do not figure in this volume. There are limits of space and time, but more particularly, a lack a data on certain individuals has prevented their inclusion.

The collecting together of this material has produced not only a picture of the research and investigation into how some of the basic detail of Lakeland geology was deciphered, but also a series a vignettes into local social history. Many of these pioneers were local people for whom geology was a leisure pursuit and a hobby, to be fitted into a life earning a living. Geology came to them perhaps through their work in the mines and quarries or through their love of the outdoors. Many were prominent figures in the local community where they were able to introduce geology to a wider group. To others, Cumbria was a posting, a place where they brought their geological expertise and earned a living by it, perhaps also becoming the local professional who could be recruited in their spare time into community and local activities. Lakeland afforded a significant challenge to any one interested in the rocks and the geological history; here was not only a spectacular and beautiful landscape to be enjoyed, but a geological puzzle of great complexity. The pull of the area is not to be underestimated. There has always been more than enough stimulus to draw people in, excite scientific enquiry and encourage people to spend their own time amongst the mountains, fells and lakes, seeking answers to questions.

Rather than present the accounts in strict chronological order they have been grouped into five sections, broadly working from the early pioneers of the Nineteenth Century and working towards the more recent contributors. The grouping is not totally coherent, at times it may appear ad hoc and arguably some of the personalities may be slightly misplaced. On the other hand the grouping does provides a broad context in which to see how the pattern of research evolved. A short editorial note introduces each grouping. To achieve some degree of uniformity of presentation, at the end of each individual account a bibliography of the individual's complete writings on the Lake District is listed. In the case of many of the pioneers they also published other geological work (i.e. on other topics and/or on areas outside the Lake District) – these have not been included in the bibliographies. All references, notes, or footnotes used by contributors in their articles appear together in a separate section at the end of the book.

Acknowledgements

Aproject of this kind relies upon the efforts of a great number of people. First I must thank the 15 contributors who have researched and written the accounts of the 25 pioneers. Without this work there would have been no book. They are members and friends of the Cumberland Geological Society, many of them being professional people who have given of their time generously.

Secondly I must acknowledge the start I inherited as Editor from Chris Thompson, the Editor of the Society Proceedings. 18 of the initial accounts were first published by the Society in the Proceedings in 2000. Chris did the hard work in collecting this material together in the first place and editing it into publishable form. I had the benefit of material on a computer file that only needed adding to and a certain amount of electronic manipulation.

I have been assisted as Editor by an Editorial board of Council members of the Society – Mervyn Dodd, Fred Lawton, Dennis Dickins and Tony Rigby. They have advised and helped in the translation of this material into book form. I would particularly like to acknowledge the unquestioning help of Mervyn Dodd who in particular has researched the British Geological Survey archive material at Keyworth, Nottingham and Tony Rigby who has handled all matters financial for us. All of the team have chased up photographic sources for us, cajoled and encouraged people into helping in a great many ways.

The Society would also like to acknowledge financial assistance from The Lottery Grants for Local Groups 'Awards for All' Scheme North West, Dallam Court, Dallam Lane, Warrington.

Other people who have assisted with this project that must be mentioned are:

Mr George Bott of Keswick for his support and answering many of my queries.

Dr David Millward, British Geological Survey, Murchison House, West Mains Road, Edinburgh for help in very many ways with material from British Geological Survey.

Dr Eric Robinson, University College, London for constant encouragement and assistance.

Graham McKenna and other staff at British Geological Survey, Keyworth, Nottingham.

Staff of the John Rylands University of Manchester Library.

Carlisle City Library

Staff of the Padgate Campus Library, University College, Warrington.

Michael Moon, Bookseller, Lowther Street, Whitehaven.

The Kendal Museum.

The Geographical Association

The Royal Geographical Society

Acknowledgement is due to many people who have loaned or taken photographs specially for this publication :

Murray Mitchell and Brigitte Hay for loan of family photographs. (Figs. 35 and 39)

British Geological Survey (Figs. 24, 25, 26,29, 32, 34, 36, 37, 38)

Department of Geography, The University of Southampton. (Fig. 43)

Centre for Continuing Education, University of Liverpool (Fig. 42).

The following have provided text figures for reproduction :

David Kelly 9, Mervyn Dodd 22, 23, 33, 55, Fred Lawton 44, 54, Roye Rutland 51, John Guest 52, Eric Robinson 21, 49, 50 Alan Smith Cover photo and 1, 2, 3, 4, 6, 7, 8, 11, 12, 15, 16, 27, 28, 40, 45. Dick Clark 41. Cumberland Geological Society 48, 53.

Alan Smith
Editor

The Early Pioneers

The Science of Geology was established little more than 200 years ago. Before that, in the Lake District, as in many other areas in Britain and Europe, collecting rock and mineral specimens, recording of fossil remains, portraying the rock outcrops and their structures and extolling the scenic wonders of the area had long been pursued. Many of the important discoveries had been made by men of leisure, by no means always eager to publish their findings, or by early miners seeking out the mineral wealth of the region. Towards the end of the Eighteenth Century and into the early years of the Nineteenth Century, however, a more systematic approach was emerging. The linking together of the disparate strands and the formulation of a more unifying 'earth history' began to take place. Gradually it was being realised that within the rocks themselves, the minerals, the fossils and the nature of the landscape was a coherent record of earth events awaiting to be deciphered.

In the Lake District four pioneers, Otley, Ruthven, Bolton and Sedgwick dominated the scene and typified this earliest phase of geological discovery. Each in their own way were true pioneers – original investigators, initiators, men who went before others and prepared the way for those that followed. Otley, Ruthven and Bolton in particular, working largely independently, pursued their curiosity and applied enquiring minds to the district. By processes of careful observation, detailed recording of what they saw around them, collecting and categorising specimens, prodigious walking of the ground and constant questioning of their observations, they initiated the building up of a picture of the earth history of the district. Most importantly for us they all took the step of publishing their observations; Otley in his Guide Books and papers, Ruthven with a geological map and Bolton with his book of *'Geological Fragments'*. As the following accounts show, Sedgwick on the other hand, played a different pioneering role. Very much the academic pioneer he built on the work of the others, painted the broader picture and put Lakeland geology into the national picture.

All four of these early pioneers were Cumbrians by birth. Otley, Ruthven and Bolton were true amateurs. All lacked formal training and instruction in geology or science and had limited early education. Through the sheer strength of their personalities they were able to make important early contributions. For all these, geology was a leisure time pursuit to be fitted around the hard task of earning a living. The Lake District was, however, profitable ground. Not only was the district geologically interesting and varied, it also offered commercial opportunities for mineral collecting and for guiding visitors and tourists who were at the time beginning to explore the scenic delights in increasing numbers.

The material on which these accounts of the earliest pioneers are based is somewhat fragmentary. As all of them left their geological observations in various published forms, so we have a fairly good picture of how they viewed the area in their day. Some bibliographical details of Otley, Ruthven and Bolton however, are yet to be tracked down, but the three accounts published here do present fairly comprehensive and hitherto unpublished evaluations of their work. The literature available on Sedgwick, however, is of a different order. Several comprehensive accounts of his life and work already exist. The account here, written by David Oldrcyd focuses on a particular aspect of his work and presents some original research on Sedgwick's notebooks and the way he assembled his findings on Lakeland geology.

1. Jonathan Otley (1766-1856)
Father of Lakeland Geology
Alan Smith

Outside Cumbria the name of Jonathan Otley is not well known and in national geological circles his contribution to Cumbrian geology is scarcely noted. In any review of the 'Geological Greats' of the district, however, he rightfully must come first. His pioneering work in the district was acknowledged by Adam Sedgwick in the 1830's and J.E. Marr in 1916 gave him the title of 'Father of Lakeland Geology' (Fig. 1)

Otley was the true pioneer; the local man who walked the ground and came to know it like the back of his own hand. He had the eye not only for the local detail but the

Fig. 1 – Jonathan Otley in later years

amazing ability, so early in the Nineteenth Century, to see the broader picture of this structurally complex region. Otley unselfishly fed this local knowledge to Sedgwick and others, and has remained the unsung hero. Otley led Sedgwick on a number of excursions around the district, starting in the summer of 1823. This was the start of a long association between the two men. Fortunately much of their correspondence remains and provides a great insight into the early geological work in the district. Otley also corresponded with many other eminent scientists of the time, including John Dalton, (another Cumbrian), G.B. Airey, the then Astronomer Royal, and the geologist Professor John Phillips, the Museum Curator at York. He also met William Smith and accompanied him in his fieldwork although their meeting was apparently not totally amicable.

Jonathan Otley was born in October 1766 at Loughrigg, near Grasmere in south Lakeland. Although he was a child from a humble family he was

Fig. 2 – 'Jonathan Otley's up t'steps' – his cottage in King's Head Yard, Keswick

encouraged to study and attended schools in both Langdale and Ambleside. Up to the age of 25 he worked with his father making wooden sieves and baskets, but he also developed the skills of watch and clock repairing. In 1791 he moved north to Keswick, where, within a short time, he had established himself in a small town centre cottage and workshop to be known locally as 'Jonathan Otley's up t'steps'. From there his business as a clock and watch repairer flourished, but, more importantly, this was the base throughout his long life for the exploration of the Lake District, and for his interests in map making, geology, meteorological observations and natural history. Fittingly the building still stands (Fig. 2) and his life and work are commemorated in a plaque alongside the old steps to his cottage door

Fig. 3 – 'The plaque on the wall of Otley's cottage

(Fig. 3). From this humble cottage workshop he produced his writings and, most particularly, in 1818, his now famous map of the Lake District and in 1823 the accompanying guide book – *A concise description of the English Lakes and adjacent mountains.* It eventually ran to 8 editions in the period up to 1849, selling over 8000 copies – all now collectors' items. Within this guide book his essay *The Geology of the Lake District* originally written in 1820, was the first published account of the rocks of the district and was undoubtedly a seminal work.

Otley was a quiet, reserved, modest man who never married. It is clear from his correspondence and from contemporary accounts that he was renowned as a listener rather than a talker, a thinker who offered an opinion only when he had thought through and grasped the whole matter. He also had the habit of very careful field observation and a love for accuracy of detail. He was not a particularly prolific writer but what he did produce was done with great care and was plainly to the point. His earliest work was a paper on the Black Lead Mine (plumbago) in Borrowdale, read before the Manchester Philosophical Society on December 27th 1816. It was a comprehensive account of what was then known about this unique deposit. In 1819 the same Society published his paper on The Floating Island in Derwentwater – the first systematic account of this feature compiled from his very detailed field observations, done over many seasons. He was able to describe how the island occasionally rises from the bottom of the lake to the surface, and how it is related to periods of dry summer conditions between June and September. He saw it was related to decaying vegetation liberating gas, which gave buoyancy to the mat of vegetation. In a letter to John Dalton in September 1815 he refers to samples of the gas that Dalton had analysed for him, and of samples of the vegetative matter that he had systematically sampled from the surface, from varying depths within the island and from the water beneath. This was typical of the thoroughness of his observational work in the field. There was a second paper of further observations of the island in the same journal in 1831, illustrating his perseverance in continuously observing natural phenomena.

It is in his guide books, however, that Otley made his great contribution to Lakeland geology. This was the medium where all his talents and interests came together and found full expression. He was a local guide, a map-maker and engraver, a person who knew the mountain routes and the topographic detail. His geological, meteorological and natural history observations gave the books real substance.

He actually published his essay on the geological structure of the Lake District in the Philosophical Magazine in 1820 and also in the first volume of a short-lived local journal, The Lonsdale Magazine, in the same year. However, it was in the guide books that the material was most read and progressively developed in the various editions up to the middle of the century. In the first paragraph of the 1830 edition of the Guide he remarks . . ." at the time this essay was first published in 1820 the structure of the mountainous district of Cumberland, Westmorland and Lancashire was but little understood, scientific travellers had contented themselves with procuring specimens of the different rocks, without taking time to become acquainted with their relative position". He goes on to point out that . . . "the greater part of the central region of the Lake mountains is occupied by three distinct groups of stratified rocks of a slaty texture". These he called the Clayslate, Greenstone and the Greywacke – remarkably perceptive descriptions of the three familiar group of rocks which we now know make up the Lower Palaeozoic inlier of the Lake District and we now term the Skiddaw Group, the Borrowdale Volcanic Group and the Windermere Supergroup. Otley had clearly worked this out long before 1820. In September 1823 he introduced Sedgwick to the rocks of the Skiddaw area in the first of their field excursions. It was not until 1831 that Sedgwick first went into print with his ideas on the structure of the district. In his address to the Geological Society of London in that year he acknowledged that it was Otley who first recognised the three distinct groups of stratified rocks in the district. Later, in 1836, Sedgwick in a paper to the Geological Society entitled Introduction to the General Structure of the Cumbrian Mountains, after describing the various subdivisions of the altered slate around the Skiddaw Granite (the location of the pair's first excursion in 1823) goes on to say "we owe our first accurate knowledge of these subdivisions to Mr Jonathan Otley of Keswick, who not merely described them in general terms but gave their geographical distribution with a very near approach to accuracy".

An examination of Otley's descriptions of the three great rock groups of the Lake District reveals not only his intimate knowledge and observations of the area but, more importantly, his insight into what these rocks were telling him of their history. The 'Clayslate' (Skiddaw Group) he recognised as the oldest group and commented on its great structural complexity. He remarks on its lithological variability, its weaknesses as a useful building material, its intrusion by complex dyke systems and its rich mineralogical associations. Equally his descriptions of the 'Greenstones' (the volcanics) were remarkably accurate. Not only was he able to describe what he saw, he also seemed able to perceive which features did not quite fit into the general pattern of things and perhaps had special circumstances surrounding them. He clearly drew the distinctions between the porphyritic lavas and what we now know are the pyroclastic materials with a strong slaty structure. But, even more intuitively, his observations of the volcanics on Binsey and of the northern Caldbeck Fells were telling him there was something rather different here. Only relatively recently has it been demonstrated that they are in fact a chemically distinct group and the product of a separate early phase of the mid-Ordovician island arc volcanic sequences (the Eycott Group). He knew of the red haematite breccias at the base of the Lower Borrowdale Volcanic Group in the Keswick area and carefully described the presence of garnets in certain volcanic horizons - a problem that was later to fill a great deal of space in the geological literature on the district.

'The Greywacke' (Windermere Supergroup) of the southern Lakes he observed with equal insight. In his guide we read . . . "The Third Division – forming only inferior elevations – commences with a bed of dark blue or blackish transition limestone, containing here and there a few shells and madrepores, and alternating with a slaty rock of the same colour; the different layers of each being in some places several feet and in others only a few inches in thickness. This limestone crosses the River Duddon near Broughton; passing Broughton Mills it runs in a N.E. direction through Torver by the foot of the Old Man Mountain, and appears near Low Yewdale. Here it makes a considerable slip to the eastward, after which it ranges past the Tarns upon the hills above Borwick Ground, and after stretching through Skelwith, it traverses the vales of Troutbeck, Kentmere and Longsleddale; . . .". To have produced such an accurate description of what has since been known as the faulted outcrop of the Coniston Limestone not only illustrates pioneeringly perceptive geological mapping but immense physical effort tramping on foot over terrain which even today is not highly accessible nor hospitable. Bearing in mind this was a time long before the existence of accurate Ordnance Survey maps his achievements are all the more remarkable.

Perhaps Otley's greatest geological achievement was his exposition of the relationship between bedding, cleavage and jointing in the Lake District rocks. Even today the fundamental differences between these properties and their structural implications are not always easy to grasp, and in many field situations in Lakeland they have to be established before the geological story can be revealed. His early observations were later refined by John Phillips and others, but Otley was the instigator.

Many other examples of his field observations and early understanding of Lakeland rocks and landscapes exist. He clearly understood the zonation in the metamorphic aureole surrounding the Skiddaw Granite and introduced Sedgwick and others to that area. He delineated the Shap and Eskdale Granite intrusions and described the Armboth Fell Dyke. Interestingly he did not differentiate between the Eskdale Granite and the Ennerdale Granophyre and says little about the Carrock Fell Complex. Surprisingly he seems to have had little interest in palaeontology, referring only fleetingly to fossil finds. He appears to have been rather unsure how to explain the existence of 'erratic' boulders. His knowledge of the pattern of outcrops and of the topography was telling him that these stray boulders needed explaining. He describes and locates many examples and saw that some powerful erosive agent had carried them, often across the topography. Some, like the Bowder Stone in Borrowdale, he rightly saw as a products of rock fall. What he described as "rounded and smoothed surfaces . . . some striped and scored in a remarkable manner" in Borrowdale and Langdale also illustrates his uncertainty about geomorphological processes. His conclusion however that "some, who have become converts to a recently promulgated theory will attribute those appearances to the agency of GLACIERS; but the action of WATER seems more intelligible to the mere English Geologist" . . . leaves no doubt where he stood on this debate.

There is doubt whether Otley ever produced a geological map of the Lake District. It is hard to believe that someone with Otley's talents for map making and his knowledge of the regional geological pattern did not at least produce some drafts or sketches of a geological map. Otley and Sedgwick clearly exchanged topographical sketch maps. A letter from

Fig. 4 – They named a road after him, but now its mainly a car park.

Otley to Sedgwick of January 30th 1828 refers to some errors Sedgwick had incorporated in a map of the Skiddaw area. More interestingly, Sedgwick in a letter to Otley dated February 14th 1847 writes . . . "Do you wish to publish a geological map of your country, on a scale of your Lake map? If so, I would most willingly help you to the best of my power; and you might use my name in any way you thought fit. I think such a map, with a short explanatory sheet, might have a sale". Sedgwick clearly seems to suggest Otley should commit his knowledge of the region on to a map. There is some evidence that Otley attempted some geological colourations of his topographic map and sold a few copies to friends, but authentic records of these cannot be located. One of Otley's 1837 topographic maps coloured geologically is in the archive of the Geological Society of London, but who coloured it is not clear.

Jonathan Otley undoubtedly laid the foundations of Lakeland Geology. He set up the framework for others to elaborate. Because he was an amateur and a Cumbrian who appears to have rarely ventured much beyond the County, he has received less recognition than he deserves. His friendship with Sedgwick was lifelong. There are records of field excursions together in 1823 and 1824 and correspondence between the two men for almost 30 years between 1827 and 1855. Sedgwick came to see Otley on his deathbed, speechless and paralysed, days before he died aged 91 on December 7th 1856. He is buried in Crosthwaite Churchyard, Keswick. It is arguable that without Otley's pioneering work in the district Sedgwick and others would not have been able to make such early progress in deciphering the region.

If Otley is not remembered much nationally in geological circles, he is certainly revered as Keswick's geologist. The Town Museum has a small section devoted to some of his artefacts and instruments. His cottage up t'steps is on the Town Trail and in the summer visitor season a local worthy emerges from his door, suitably attired, to explain his exploits. Many years ago a road close to the town centre was renamed in his memory (Fig. 4), not an honour bestowed on many geologists. At least in Keswick the geological heritage Otley established has its rightful place in the public eye.

BIBLIOGRAPHY.

OTLEY, J., 1819, Account of the Floating Island in Derwent Lake, Keswick. *Mem. Manch. Lit. & Phil. Soc.,* ser. 2, Vol. 3, p. 64.

1819a, Account of the Black Lead Mine in Borrowdale. *Mem. Manch. Lit. & Phil. Soc,* ser. 2. Vol. 3, p. 168.

1820, Remarks on the Succession of rocks in the District of the Lakes. *Lonsdale Mag.* Vol. 1, pp. 433-438 and in *Phil. Mag.* Vol. 56, pp. 257-261.

1823, *A concise description of the English Lakes and adjacent mountains*, 8vo Sinkin & Marshall, London. (This was the first edition of Otley's Guide Book.

In 1818 he first published his topographic map of the district, which was sold separately in folded form for the pocket. It was then incorporated into the Guide Books. The Guides were progressively enlarged and eventually went to eight editions up to 1849).

1831, Further observations in the Floating Island of Derwentwater, with remarks on certain other phenomena. *Mem. Manch. Lit. & Phil. Soc.*, ser. 2, Vol. 5, p. 19.

2. Adam Sedgwick (1785-1873)
The First Professional Lake District Geologist
David Oldroyd

One of the great founders of British geology was the Cambridge professor, Adam Sedgwick (1785-1873). (Fig 5). Aspects of his work have been intensively studied by Rudwick and Secord, regarding his role in the establishment of the Devonian and Cambrian Systems respectively. Earlier, Sedgwick was the subject of a two-volume

Fig. 5 – Adam Sedgwick

▲ *Fig. 7 – The plaque on the wall of The Old Parsonage, Dent.*

◀ *Fig. 6 – The birthplace of Sedgwick, The Old Parsonage, Dent.*

Victorian 'Life and Letters' by Clark and Hughes, and there is a short non-technical biography by Speakman.

Sedgwick's studies in the Lake District, which provided the conceptual and methodological foundation for much of his subsequent work, have not been closely studied. In fact, despite Sedgwick's importance in the history of geology, there has been little detailed examination of just how he worked as a young man. I have therefore examined how Sedgwick carried out his investigations with the help of a study of his field notebooks for his work in the Lake District for 1822, 1823, and 1824. From these notes, we can learn something about how early nineteenth-century geologists went about their work; and how one such as Sedgwick began to study the geology of a complex region where little systematic fieldwork had been undertaken previously.

Sedgwick came from Dent in the Yorkshire Dales, to the south east of the Lake District. His father was the local parson, and the family seems to have been reasonably well off. His birthplace at The Old Parsonage in the village now bears a plaque in remembrance of this famous member of the community (Figs. 6 and 7) Adam was the third of seven children. He went to a nearby school of some reputation, Sedbergh, and on to Trinity College, Cambridge. There he studied mathematics and theology with great diligence, and in 1808 he was fifth in the University for mathematics (5th

Wrangler). This led to a fellowship (by further examination) at Trinity in 1810, and then to the geology chair in 1818. The present geology department at Cambridge has its museum named in Sedgwick's honour, and his private notebooks and some manuscript maps are held there.

The story of Sedgwick's appointment has often been told. According to a statement that Sedgwick himself originated, there were two applicants, and although Sedgwick knew no geology he got the position since what the other candidate knew was wrong! This story cannot be entirely true. Sedgwick's fragmentary autobiography, preserved among his papers at Cambridge University Library, tells us that as a lad he became intrigued by the rocks and fossils that could be seen near Dent and he realised how the structure of the strata along the sides of the valley could be understood. Sedgwick suffered a breakdown in his health in 1813 and it is surely relevant to the present enquiry that he recuperated by taking a walking holiday in the Lake District. He was actively geologizing on the Continent in 1816, and was 'introduced' at the Geological Society that year. He was elected Fellow of the Society in 1818 and FRS in 1821, with Sir John Herschel heading the list of twelve who nominated him. No doubt the Cambridge chair smoothed the path to the Fellowship.

Immediately after being elected professor, Sedgwick began fieldwork in a serious way. He went to Derbyshire, Somerset, and Cornwall in 1818-19. He went to Wiltshire, Somerset, and Dorset in 1820, to the Yorkshire coast and Teesdale in County Durham in 1821; and in 1822 he worked his way north through Nottinghamshire and Lancashire, and into Cumberland, thus initiating his Lakeland work proper. In 1823, he went again to Yorkshire and to Cumberland; and in 1824 he spent the whole season in the Lake District. He returned in 1833, 1835, 1845, 1851, and 1857, but his major survey work in the region was done in the years 1822-24 and his later efforts will not be examined here.

Lakeland geology is difficult, compared with that of southern Britain. The terrain is tough, and the rocks are very confused, in most places quite different from the nicely layered fossiliferous strata of the Yorkshire Dales where Sedgwick had grown up. So how did Sedgwick go about his task?

First let me say something about Sedgwick's financial situation, as background to his work. His income in 1822 from his chair and his College fellowship was £407 6s 8d, but, depending as it did on Trinity's financial well being, it declined in the following two years to £283 1s 0d and £232 15s 8d, but he probably had additional income from private pupils. I have no evidence that Sedgwick obtained financial support for his fieldwork, but being unmarried he would, I think, have had sufficient money to be self-financing. He was in the field from about the beginning of June until mid-October each year.

Sedgwick travelled by carriage, on horseback, or on foot. His obituarist John Phillips stated that Sedgwick travelled chiefly on horseback when in the field, but this cannot have been the case for many of the localities that he visited in the Lakes. Sedgwick had a portable writing desk, a leather specimen bag, and an assortment of hammers, which are now on display in the Sedgwick Museum. He also used a portable laboratory, though his notes say little or nothing about the results obtained with it. No doubt he had an acid bottle though.

For accommodation, Sedgwick stayed with friends or at local inns. There is no record of his having made arrangements in advance of his arrival. So I cannot say whether he just 'turned up', or made elaborate prior 'bookings'. But one is struck with the way everything slotted into place so far as accommodation was concerned, despite the fact that he seemed to leave little time to organise his domestic arrangements, being out in the field all day and every day, except for Sundays, when he attended church. Often he was in the field for fourteen hours or more. There is a record that when Sedgwick was visited by his colleague William Whewell in 1824, both were in 'breathless haste'.

Just as Sedgwick's accommodation arrangements worked smoothly, so too did his transport. There always seemed to be a carriage waiting at an appropriate spot, or a horse. Again, I do not know whether he planned everything carefully beforehand, or altered arrangements from day to day according to the weather and the exigencies of fieldwork. I suspect the latter. However, one thing is certain: he used local people as guides at virtually all stages of his fieldwork, and John Phillips recorded that when he met with Sedgwick by chance in the field in Teesdale in 1822 he had a miner's boy with him as a guide.

Sedgwick seemed to be remarkably little bothered by the weather. There were occasional days when he did not attempt to go out because of rain, but he never mentions problems due to cloud, and he was rarely driven home by rain, despite the Lake District's high rainfall. It may be noted, however, that in 1824, which was the year that Sedgwick made his greatest effort in the field, the Lakes had an exceptionally dry summer.

The question of maps available to and used by Sedgwick is important. There was a map of the Lakeland region by Thomas Donald (2nd edition, 1810, but originally surveyed in 1771), and we know that Sedgwick possessed a copy, for it still exists in the Sedgwick Museum. But at two miles to the inch Donald's map lacked detail and Sedgwick mentions numerous places and topographic features in his notebooks that do not appear on Donald's map, or any other published map available at that time. It may be noted that Sedgwick complained in his notes on several occasions about the inaccuracy of 'the map' and once he mentions Donald by name. One can see, by comparing Donald's work with modern survey maps, how inaccurate his map was.

Significantly improved topographic maps for the Lakeland counties, Cumberland and Westmorland, were published in 1823 and 1824 by C. and J. Greenwood, having been surveyed in 1821-22 and 1822-23 respectively. But even these did not give all the detail that Sedgwick mentions in his notebooks. Therefore, much of Sedgwick's information about local topography must have been supplied by guides.

Sedgwick's geological map of the Lakes was only published as late as 1835, the paper in which it appeared having been read to the Geological Society in 1831. Sedgwick's manuscript geological map of Cumberland (only), entered on an edition of Donald (1802), is preserved at the Sedgwick Museum, it is interesting to consider how and when this was coloured in.

On his days off in the field, due to rain or the Sabbath, Sedgwick frequently mentions writing up his journal ('journalise', he wrote), but he says little about maps. He probably synthesised his Lakeland work some time in the years 1825 to 1830, and the manuscript Cumberland map probably dates from that period. Interestingly, an annotation in the hand of George Greenough to a published map of Westmorland by John Cary (1811), held at the Geological Society, states that 'a map of Westmorland on a large scale was published by Hodgson at Lancaster in 1828 coloured geologically by Prof. Sedgwick'. I have not located Sedgwick's Westmorland map, but the annotation may give a clue to the approximate date of the colouration of his surviving Cumberland map.

Sedgwick's journals for 1822-24, name no fewer than fifty-one persons in the Lakes with whom he journeyed, stayed, dined, or conversed, or who acted as his guides. These included farmers, miners, the Lakeland poets Robert Southey and William Wordsworth, and local naturalists. His most important scientific contacts were two Keswick residents: the engineer and surveyor, Joseph Fryer; and the local guide, naturalist, meteorologist, cartographer, and clock repairer, Jonathan Otley (1766-1856).

Otley was a man of many parts. Interested in meteorology and an authority on local topography, he knew the Lakes like the back of his hand. In connection with his business as a guide, he published a topographic map of the region in 1818. In 1823, he extended this into a full guidebook, which incorporated the map, and also contained information about the local mineralogy and geology. This contained a stratigraphic subdivision of the Lakeland rocks, which Otley had already published in a local journal.

Thus, Sedgwick undoubtedly learned much from Otley, besides how to find his way around in the mountains. Most importantly, there was Otley's division of the Lakeland strata into three main categories. First, there were the dark rocks of the northern Lakes, now called the Skiddaw Group, forming mountains such as Skiddaw, near Keswick, with generally rounded profiles. South of this unit, there was a more varied group, with slates of blue or green colour, forming the knobbly hills of central Lakeland. These are now called the Borrowdale Volcanic Group, but Otley called them the 'Greenstone division'. Third, there was a group forming the gentler region of the southern Lake District. The lowest member of this third unit was a quite narrow band of fossiliferous limestone associated with slaty rock; while other members of the unit (now collectively called the Windermere Supergroup) were true slates. The limestone, which Otley suggested, in Wernerian terminology, might be a 'Transition Limestone', ran right across the Lake District, roughly from west to east. Subsequently, it came to be known as the Coniston Limestone.

Otley further noted that the slates of the northern part of the middle division appeared to be generally inclined to the north and those of the southern part inclined south. It was, he said, 'as though the mountain ridge, dividing the counties of Cumberland and Westmorland, had acted as a wedge in separating them'. So virtually the first scientific paper on Lakeland geology laid down a broad stratigraphic classification that has lasted until the present. Moreover, an important suggestion about general structure was proposed. Additionally, Otley distinguished between bedding, jointing, and cleavage – features that may easily be confused in the Lakes. Sedgwick himself said that he did not at first understand the difference properly; and it was Otley who taught him.

In his published description of Lakeland geology, based on his fieldwork of 1822-24, Sedgwick described the outcrop of Otley's 'Transition Limestone' (a term that Sedgwick himself deployed in his notebooks) as if he had traced it in the field from west to east. He described how the outcrop would continue steadily for a while, and then be displaced to the north or south for perhaps up to three miles. Sometimes a large lake or valley could be found associated with the line of displacement.

On the basis of his published paper, it would appear that Sedgwick followed the outcrop of limestone, using it as a marker band. But in practice this was not what he did, as his notebooks reveal. Rather, he would stay in one spot for three or four days and range out from there in several directions. In fact, Sedgwick's 'journals' provide enough information to enable one to trace his movements approximately on modern 1:25,000 maps. When this is done, one can see how he ranged over the country so that after three years' work he had covered, albeit hastily, most of the Lakeland terrain. And when his observations were transferred to his map, perhaps back in Cambridge, the outcrop of the 'Transition Limestone', and other important features such as the granites near Eskdale and Skiddaw, or Otley's three types of slates, would have emerged as the various areas of the map were coloured in. In fact, not all the Limestone's outcrop was covered even in the same year. It is true that for some days Sedgwick would become particularly interested in the Limestone and he was evidently following its course; but he did not do so consistently. Actually, he very likely knew what to expect, for even in his short paper of 1820 Otley had indicated in words the general outcrop of the 'Transition Limestone'.

Sedgwick's notebooks contain much information about different rock types, the lines of their outcrop and the boundaries between them, and, most particularly, information about dips and strikes ('ranges' as he called them); also the bearings of principal topographic features. His interest was evidently lithological and structural, and in his early Lakeland work he gave little attention to fossils.

There is so much numerical information about dips and strikes in Sedgwick's journals that one wonders how he remembered it all. Were rough notes made during a day's excursion, and then entered up in the journal in the evenings, or did he just have a phenomenal memory? I have no means of answering this for certain, but I believe that there must have been rough notes used to compile the surviving notebooks. So we have several stages of knowledge filtration and construction:

1 Observations in the field;
2 Writing of rough notes;
3 Composition of the 'Journal' and the destruction of the original notes;
4 Preparation of geological maps from the 'Journal';
5 Composition of a paper for public presentation and evaluation, perhaps in the light of higher geological theory or some ongoing theoretical controversy;
6 Defence of the paper at the meeting of some learned society (usually the Geological Society);
7 Revision of the paper, and its refereeing;
8 Further revision and eventual publication.

Sedgwick's journal/notes contain few sketches and those there are are unimpressive. His procedure seems to have been to cover as much ground as possible in a fairly theoretically neutral or positivistic way, and fill in a map. His categories for this were very simple, but that was doubtless to his advantage in dealing with such a difficult area in pioneering fashion. By contrast with the impoverished petrographic categories, there was a wealth of detail regarding dips and strikes of beds and of cleavage. Little immediate attempt was made to draw sections (in contrast to the notebooks of his later friend, and eventual enemy, Roderick Murchison).

As said, Sedgwick's petrographic vocabulary was impoverished. He often referred in his journal to a rock type by its locality or approximate appearance. Thus we have the 'Wallow Crag' type; the 'Barrow rock'; 'the concretionary', 'the porphyry', or even 'the blue'. Interestingly, some of these terms appear in Otley's writings, so Sedgwick probably got them from him, but he did not use them in his published work.

Back at Cambridge, Sedgwick's positivism dropped away to some extent as he developed grander, theoretical pictures. For example, when his map was finished it was obvious from its outcrop that the 'Transition Limestone' had been affected by massive faults that cut across the outcrop, wrenching it into a number of severed fragments; from which it appeared that the whole region of the Lakes had been upheaved and fractured. Then the great valleys, such as those of Windermere or Coniston, had subsequently been carved out along the lines of weakness produced by the faults Later, when he published his work, Sedgwick suggested that the movements were caused by the intrusion of the great masses of igneous rock, such as the granites near Eskdale or under Skiddaw.

Since Sedgwick made no effort to squeeze the history of the district into a Biblical time-scale, there was no problem about the erosion of the lines of fracture taking an indefinitely large time. But the fractures, he thought, were produced by what were called at the time (by William Whewell) 'catastrophic' earth movements, acting for a relatively short time, before the subsequent unconformable deposition of the New Red Sandstone round the margins of the Lake District. Thus the arguments of Reijer Hooykaas, that catastrophism could be scientific and empirically based are well supported by Sedgwick's example. His catastrophism was not just a form of physico-theology. It was grounded in, and warranted by, an enormous effort of fieldwork.

Over and above Sedgwick's catastrophism, he sought to account for what he had seen in the Lakes with the help of the overarching theory of Élie de Beaumont, though with some caveats. In agreement with the Frenchman's doctrines, Sedgwick asserted that the main lines of mountain chains in the Southern Uplands of Scotland, the Lakes, Wales, the Isle of Man, and Cornwall, were approximately parallel, and were thus generated during the same epoch. The elevation of the Pennines, running N-S, could be attributed to a different (later) epoch. Said Sedgwick in his Presidential Address to the Geological Society in 1831: "The investigation of the faults and dislocations interrupting the continuity of our secondary deposits is becoming, daily, a subject of increasing importance; and we are now called upon, not to regard them as solitary phenomena, but to trace them through whole regions, and to examine their relations to each other". Further, the uplift and fracture of central Lakeland might, Sedgwick suggested, be an exemplification of the theory of 'craters of elevation' of Alexander von Humboldt and Leopold von Buch. Thus, what started off with observations about the obscure outcrops of calcareous rocks in southern Lakeland, which rocks fizzed with acid and which did not could, with the help of the maps constructed on the basis of his fieldwork, turn into grand speculations about the history of the globe. Thus it was that the endless notes about dips, strikes ('ranges'), and cleavage were used to underpin grand theoretical models. Ultimately, it seems, this was the point of Sedgwick's preoccupation in the field with all the structural details of the Lakeland rocks.

If we compare Sedgwick's work with that of Otley and other amateurs, we can recognise significant differences. Otley was born and lived in the Lakes, and knew them intimately. Besides discovering the outcrops and showing them to Sedgwick in a number of important cases, he produced two significant theoretical advances, and moreover taught them to Sedgwick, namely the tripartite division of the Lakeland rocks, and the distinction between stratification and cleavage, the understanding of which was essential to the success of Sedgwick's work, otherwise his 'structural' observations would have been hopelessly confused and in error. But while he knew many of the exposures, Otley did not ascend to any higher theory. Indeed, by virtue of his profession as a part-time guide, he was, I believe, more interested in topography and meteorology than geology. He sometimes sent Sedgwick topographic information or beautifully drawn topographic maps (there are examples preserved at the Sedgwick Museum), but I have no evidence that Otley sent geological information in the form of maps, though he did produce some.

Other amateurs were also at work. There was Sedgwick's friend Joseph Fryer of Keswick, who is thought to have been the anonymous author of the very first geological paper on the Lakes. There was the cobbler from Kendal, John Ruthven. He was employed by Sedgwick as a fossil collector in some of his later Lakeland work, and published his own geological map of the Lakes in 1855. Ruthven had, I am sure, covered the ground over a period of years, though he would not have had time or money to spend months at a time in the field like Sedgwick. Perhaps like another remarkable amateur, John Bolton of Furness in southern Lakeland, he would have had to sleep out on the fells to do his work.

There lay the difference. Sedgwick could approach the task in a professional, full-time manner; and with the advantages of education,

Fig. 8 – The Shap Granite Drinking Fountain, Village Square, Dent.

connections, and libraries, he could ascend to higher levels of geological synthesis. His structural information was put at the disposal of a grand theoretical model, that of Élie de Beaumont. This theory was soon shown to be unsatisfactory; but such efforts towards higher levels of synthesis were what were required of the geological élite. And the élite players had to be unremitting in their efforts towards reading the literature, and constructing and defending their views against all comers. They had to have money or position; and preferably both. By contrast, the 'peripheral' amateurs, whose work was usually confined to a restricted region, had perforce to remain as collectors, and helpers of the 'central' players. If, as sometimes happened, they published grand schemes in local journals, no one took much notice.

Of the English geologists of the day, it was only William Smith who achieved immortality from a position of weakness. And he was given a hard time. But given different circumstances, I dare say Jonathan Otley might have been just as distinguished a professor as Adam Sedgwick. Certainly, he taught him a good deal, and Sedgwick surely appreciated the value of his humble friend, visiting him in Keswick not long before he died at the age of ninety, and being reduced to tears at the sight of his dying former companion in the field. I know of no similar case in the history of geology.

The village of Dent continues to take great pride in being the home of perhaps the greatest of the founding fathers of British geology. Within St. Andrew's Church a century of Sedgwicks is commemorated with an impressive plaque and at the gates of the church in the tiny village square stands a large Shap Granite drinking fountain carved with his name and dates (Fig. 8). In nearby Garsdale, on Longstone Common (SD 695912), a permanent Sedgwick Geological Trail explains the features of the Dent Fault first described by Sedgwick (Leaflet available from the Yorkshire Dales National Park Centres).

BIBLIOGRAPHY.

SEDGWICK, A., 1825, On the origin of Alluvial and Diluvial Formations. *Ann. of Phil.,* Ser. 11, Vol. 9, pp 241 ff., and Vol. 10, pp 18 ff. (Cumberland pp 26-32)

1831, On the General Structure of the Lake Mountains and on the Great Dislocations by which they have been separated from the neighbouring chains. *Proc. Geol. Soc Lond.,* vol. 1. No. 19, pp 247-249.

1831a, Address to the Geological Society, Feb. 18th 1831. *Proc. Geol. Soc Lond.,* Vol. 1, No. 20, pp 281-316 (same material as 1831 paper).

1831b, A Description of Longitudinal and Transverse sections through a portion of the Carboniferous chain between Penighent and Kirkby Stephen. *Proc. Geol. Soc Lond.,* No. 21, pp 318-320.

1832, On the deposits overlying the Carboniferous Series in the valley of the Eden, and on the North-Western coasts of Cumberland and Lancashire. *Proc. Geol. Soc. Lond.,* Vol. 1, No. 24, pp 343-345.

1832a, On the Geological Relations of the Stratified and Unstratified Groups of rocks composing the Cumbrian Mountains. *Proc. Geol. Soc. Lond.,* Vol. 1, No. 27, pp 399-401.

1833, On a band of transition Limestone and on Granite veins, appearing in the Greywacke Slate of Westmorland, near Shap Wells and Wasdale Head. *Proc. Geol. Soc. Lond.,* vol. 2, No. 33, p 1.

1835, Remarks on the structure of large mineral masses and especially on the chemical changes produced in the Aggregation of Stratified Rocks during different periods after their deposition. *Trans. Geol. Soc.,* Vol. 3, ser. 11, pp 461-486, (Lake District, pp 469-479)

1836, Introduction to the General Structure of the Cumbrian Mountains; with a Description of the Great Dislocations by which they have been separated from the neighbouring Carboniferous Chains. *Trans. Geol. Soc.,* Vol. 4, ser. 11, pp 47-68.

1836a, On the New Red Sandstone Series in the Basin of the Eden, and North- Western coasts of Cumberland and Lancashire. *Trans. Geol. Soc.,* Vol.4, ser. 11pp 383-407.

1836b, Extrait d'une letter de M. le professor A. Sedgwick a M. Elie Beaumont. *Bull. Geol. Soc. France,* Vol. 7, pp 152-155, (Succession in Cumberland).

1838, A synopsis of the English Series of Stratified rocks inferior to the Old red Sandstone – with an attempt to determine the successive natural groups and formations. *Proc. Geol. Soc. Lond.,* Vol. 2, pp 675-685, (Lake District, p 678).

1841, Supplement to a Synopsis of the English Series of Stratified rocks inferior to the Old red Sandstone, with additional remarks on the relations of the Carboniferous Series and the Old Red Sandstone of the British Isles. Cumbrian Groups exhibited in ascending order, in a section from Keswick through Kendal to Kirkby Lonsdale. *Proc. Geol. Soc. Lond.,* Vol. 3, pp 541-554, (Lake District, pp 550-552).

1842, Three letters on the Geology of the Lake District in Wordsworth's *Description of the Scenery of the Lakes,* 8vo., Kendal. Subsequent Editions in 1843 and 1846. Further editions in 1853, 1859 and 1864 when Professor Sedgwick's three letters were increased to five.

1845, On the Comparative Classification of the Fossiliferous Strata of North Wales with corresponding deposits of Cumberland, Westmorland and Lancashire. *Quart. Journ. Geol. Soc.,* vol. 1, pp 442-450 and *Proc. Geol. Soc. Lond.,* Vol. 4, pp 576-584.

1846, On the classification of the Fossiliferous Slates of Cumberland, Westmorland and Lancashire. *Quart. Journ. Geol. Soc.,*Vol. 2, pp 106-131.

1847, On the classification of the Fossiliferous Slates of North Wales, Cumberland, Westmorland and Lancashire. *Quart. Journ. Geol. Soc.,* Vol. 3, pp 133-166.

1848, On the Organic Remains found in the Skiddaw Slate with some remarks on the classification of the Older rocks of Cumberland and Westmorland. *Quart. Journ. Geol. Soc.,* Vol. 4, pp 216-225.

1852, On the Lower Palaeozoic Rocks at the base of the Carboniferous Chain between Ravenstonedale and Ribblesdale. *Quart. Journ. Geol. Soc.,* Vol. 8, pp 36-54.

1852a . On the Classification and nomenclature of the Lower Palaeozoic Rocks of England and Wales. *Quart. Journ. Geol. Soc.,* Vol. 8, pp 136-168, (Lake District pp 136-42).

1855, Description of a Series of Dislocations which have moved the Cambrian and Silurian Rocks between Leven Sands and Duddon Sands several miles out of their normal position in the Geological Map of the Lake Mountains. *Proc. Cambridge Phil. Soc.,* No. 13, pp 187-190 and in *Phil. Mag.,* ser. 4, Vol 16, pp 155-158.

1859, Supplementary letter on the Geology of the District in *A complete Guide to the Scenery of the Lakes of England,* by W.Wordsworth. 5 Edition, Keswick.

3. John Bolton (1790-1873)
Pioneer Geologist in the Furness Area
David Kelly

In the villages of Low Furness it is common for garden walls to have an ornamental capping of blocks of Urswick Limestone. However in the case of the former Post Office in Swarthmoor, a variety of rocks is displayed – Borrowdale Volcanics, Brockram, coral limestone and others. The name of the house, Sedgwick Cottage (Fig. 9), is also evidence of the interest of a former inhabitant; this was John Bolton, born at Mountbarrow Farm in 1790 and educated at Urswick Free School. Bolton left the area when a young man and earned his living as a journeyman weaver. He possessed powers of enterprise and intellect, adapting his loom to work on the Jacquard principle and in 1870, his *Personal Narrative of a Twenty-four Year Residence in the Borough of Barnsley* was published.

Bolton's geological interest had been fired as a boy in Urswick by finding fossils in the Carboniferous Limestone of buildings and walls and in the discarded rock from a well sunk behind his school in Urswick. He returned to Furness in 1851 and took up residence in the house in Swarthmoor which he was to name Sedgwick Cottage. At the time only A.

Sedgwick and E. W. Binney had published research into the geology of Furness and the pioneering work of J. D. Kendall was not published until after Bolton's death. The primary survey of the Furness peninsula was carried out in 1865-70 by W. T. Aveline and A. C. G. Cameron. Back on home territory Bolton began his geological investigations in earnest and like others who lacked formal scientific or geological education, he compensated by acquiring a detailed knowledge of field localities. He became a friend and correspondent of many of the leading geological figures of the day, including,

Fig. 9 – John Bolton's House, Swarthmoor, Low Furness.

of course, Adam Sedgwick. This was the time of the Furness iron mining boom and Barrow-in-Furness briefly had more blast furnaces than any other town in the world. However Bolton's geological interests remained firmly focussed on the academic rather than commercial aspects of the subject.

Bolton made a major contribution to our understanding of the geology of Furness through meticulous site investigations and diligent fossil recording. Of particular note are fossil specimens, now housed in national collections, which he discovered in parts of the Windermere Supergroup that today would not considered to be particularly fossiliferous. Although Bolton's contribution to the understanding of the geology of the Furness peninsula is nothing like as great as that of Kendall and others who followed him, he is an interesting character. His published literary output was limited to just two papers: On a deposit with insect, leaves, etc., near Ulverston (1862) and Explorations of a cavern at Stainton, Low Furness (1871). He is best known for his book, published when he was aged 78, *Geological Fragments collected principally from Rambles among the rocks of Furness and Cartmel,* re-published under a similar title by Michael Moon in 1979. This fascinating book provides an insight into the state of geological knowledge and the social and economic history of the time.

Many of Bolton's studies were of the Upper Ordovician and Silurian rocks of south Cumbria now referred to as the Windermere Supergroup but which Bolton called the 'Clay-Slate'. The stratigraphy of these rocks in Furness has continued to prove problematic in more recent times. The lithostratigraphic units identified in the main part of the outcrop in the Windermere area have not been found easy to apply further south west. Norman in an unpublished PhD thesis in 1961 proposed different units for the Blawith area and Rose and Dunham (1977) proposed another set of units for the Furness peninsula. The recently published British Geological Survey Ulverston 1:50,000 sheet 48 uses modern nomenclature. In *Geological Fragments* Bolton described in detail the extent of the outcrop and discussed an apparently upward succession from north west to south east of Coniston Limestone, Coniston Flags, Coniston Grit, Lower Ireleth Slate, Ireleth Limestone and Lower Ludlow Rock. Although he described the outcrop of these units, matching them in detail to modern stratigraphy is not always easy. Bolton examined the fossil content of the Ireleth Limestone in the Mere Beck area and concluded correctly that it was the same age as the Coniston Limestone although he notes that the strike of the two units is different. We now know that these are in fact the same unit - the Dent Group - and the outcrop is displaced laterally some 5km by the Kirkby Fault. Bolton rarely referred to the effects of faulting, even when considering the haematite ore deposits of the district.

Mystery surrounds Bolton's description of finding three or four "characteristic Coniston limestone fossil" species on Todhillbank (now Tottlebank) Fell. This area is now considered to be underlain by the Yewbank and Bannisdale Formations and too high in the succession to be part of the Dent Group. However the limestone outcrop itself (also described by Sedgwick) has also proved elusive. The late Harry Kellett, a noted amateur geologist of a more recent times, failed to find limestone exposures here despite repeated searches.

Bolton spent considerable time searching for 'organic remains' in the relatively unfossiliferous parts of the Silurian. At Knottallow Quarry (SD 270 803) he collected a slab bearing numerous specimens of the crinoid *Scyphocrinites pulcher* (McCoy) and at Rosside (SD 271 788) he collected large, distorted specimens of the bivalve *Cardiola interrupta* (J. de C. Sowerby). Bolton described how, as a seventy year old, he spent two hundred days at the latter locality excavating the crest of a hill on the road in search of fossils, much to the consternation of passers-by.

Bolton's writing on the Carboniferous or 'Mountain limestone' is somewhat disappointing. Although he described the outcrop and fossil localities, detailed studies of the stratigraphy had to wait for Aveline and Kendall and a detailed study of the palaeontology was not carried out until the work of Garwood. Bolton's understanding of the Carboniferous basal unconformity is interesting but at odds with a modern interpretation. The faulted boundary with the Silurian at Castle Head is described as being conformable. In Furness, Bolton noted that the Carboniferous and Silurian are "indented into each other". He imagined an upland, coastal landscape of Silurian rocks with bays into which the Carboniferous carbonate sediments were deposited. The landscape was, however, almost certainly a lowland one and the 'bays' are where the boundary is displaced by north west - south east faulting. Many of these faults carry the commercial haematite deposits yet they are not referred to. In the Lindal Moor - Marton area there are examples of ore bodies occupying faults with Carboniferous rocks on the hanging wall and Silurian rocks on the foot wall. Bolton surmised that this may be a simple sedimentary sequence and, contrary to modern interpretation, used this as evidence against the epigenetic nature of the ore deposits.

Bolton described the 'Magnesian Limestone' in a quarry in the Stank area, quoting the thickness as no more than 20 feet. The rock is not exposed today but is visible in buildings in the area. Bolton commented on its excellent properties as a building stone and considered the decision of the Commission appointed by the Government to choose the Magnesian Limestone from Yorkshire to build the Palace of Westminster a great mistake. The palace built in the 1840's was already weathering badly by the 1860's and Bolton asserted that this would not have happened had what he considered to be the superior 'Magnesian Limestone' of Furness been chosen!

In 1862 Bolton documented what may be an interglacial lake deposit beneath 30m of boulder clay near Lindal. This was found in shafts, including those sunk in the construction of a drainage adit from the Lindal Cote mines to Urswick Tarn. Diatoms, insects, seeds and leaves were identified from a clay or peat that appears to cover an area at least 400m across. In the 1970s the British Geological Survey sank a borehole which failed to find this deposit, possibly because it hit a higher area of Carboniferous Limestone within the hollow.

Typical of Bolton's enterprising nature is the investigation he carried out on Urswick Tarn in the icy winter of 1852-3. Having set up fixed survey stations on the shore, using specially made equipment he drilled 16 holes at regular spacing into the surface of the frozen tarn to take soundings, noting the water depth and the nature of the sediment on the bed. He then measured the discharge and sediment load of the feeder streams and calculated the time required to completely fill the lake basin with sediment. He noted that much of the sediment being deposited at the time was haematite-rich mud from the Lindal mining area and concluded that the rate of sedimentation was much higher than in the past.

Bolton provided a contemporary account of the Rampside earthquake of 1865 and attempted to produce an isoseismal map of the effects. These include fallen chimneys, more than 300 points in the ground from which groundwater rose to the surface of the sands between Concle and Westfield Point and a major crack in the Concle railway embankment. By interviewing people in the area he deduced that the earthquake travelled from south east to north west. He attributes the limited lateral extent of the effects to the shallow depth of the focus.

Geological Fragments contains a contemporary account of haematite mining of interest to the historian. Much of the book is written almost as a "field guide" as a series of localities are described along different routes. In the style of Wordsworth and Coleridge he also indulged in longer distance treks, often sleeping outdoors, and accounts of these journeys are included, written in the literary style of the day. Although by modern standards much of the book could not be considered a scientific work, it is a fascinating account of interest to the geologist and is a fitting memorial to an extraordinary character.

BIBLIOGRAPHY

BOLTON, J., 1862. On a deposit with insect, leaves, etc., near Ulverston. *Quart. Journ. Geol. Soc.,* Vol.18, pp 274-277.

1869. *Geological Fragments collected principally from Rambles among the rocks of Furness and Cartmel* Ulverston, D. Atkinson, King Street, and London, Whittaker & Co. Ave Maria Lane. (A reprint Edition of this was published by Michael Moon, Whitehaven in 1978. 277 pp. This edition contained a new gazetteer prepared especially for this edition by Harry Kellett).

4. John Ruthven (1793-1868)
Geological Map Maker and Fossil Collector
Alan Smith

The inclusion of John Ruthven (Fig. 10) in these accounts of the early geologists is warranted on two grounds. First, he illustrates very well the part the local amateur could play in the early history of geological exploration, and secondly his *Geological Map of the Lake District*, published in 1855 was one of the earliest to be compiled.

Fig. 10 – Watercolour portrait of John Ruthven painted and presented to the Kendal Museum by his son George. (Reproduced by courtesy of Kendal Museum).

According to Cornelius Nicholson, John Ruthven was a "local geologist who, like Hugh Miller, proves how a man may overcome the want of education, and render important services to science, by the bent of natural genius". He was born in Kirkby Stephen in 1793, eight years after Adam Sedgwick had been born in the village of Dent not far away. Ruthven moved to Kendal, where he took up the trade of cobbler, but his real interests came to the fore when he made the acquaintance of three local naturalists and amateur geologists: Cornelius Nicholson, business man and local historian, later Mayor of Kendal; Thomas Gough, surgeon, son of John

Gough, blind mathematician and botanist - said to have been the 'blind philosopher' of Wordsworth's poem *The Excursionist;* and Francis Danby, Curate of St. Thomas's Church, Kendal. These three tutored Ruthven in local geology and he became a keen collector of rocks and fossils, soon becoming so proficient that he was able to sell his specimens at good prices. As well as supplying Gough and Danby he also collected for Sedgwick and slightly later sent a complete collection of Silurian fossils to Sir Roderick Murchison in London. Eventually he began dealing directly with London dealers and established a sound reputation as a person with a detailed knowledge of South Lakeland geology in particular. In 1844 he reported to Sedgwick that he had plotted the course of the Coniston Limestone outcrop across the southern Lake District from Longsleddale to Broughton Fell.

In 1835 Nicholson and Gough founded the Kendal Natural History and Scientific Society. Over the succeeding years it attracted many eminent scientists of the day. In 1838 Sedgwick agreed to become its President, a position he held for thirty-two years. The records of the Society show he frequently lectured to the group on local geology, at which he was assisted by John Ruthven. Sedgwick thought highly of Ruthven, taking him on excursions into Wales in 1846 and 1851, and to Scotland in 1848. In 1845 he described him as a "famous fossil collector, once a cobbler . . . now a geologist whose fame will last longer than the stoutest shoe that ever came of his ancient last"; in 1845 he called him "my old heart-of-oak friend" who, "has Westmorland at his fingertips". Two years later Sedgwick wrote to Harkress, 'I advise you to go to Kendal and call on John Ruthven, the well known collector of northern fossils (Palaeozoic); he knows the country well and as far as I know is the only person to have found fossils in the Skiddaw Slates'. Sedgwick clearly used Ruthven to collect for him, in 1847 he asked Ruthven to go to the Keswick area to search for fossil remains. Ruthven spent over a week in a tent at White Stones on Skiddaw fossil hunting.

John Ruthven's Geological Map of the Lake District was published in 1855 by John Garnett of Windermere. The topographical base map was engraved by W. Banks of Edinburgh. The geological boundaries were drawn in by Ruthven and the strata hand coloured. The scale was approximately three and a half miles to the inch. It was linen mounted and folded into a smart folder made for the pocket. There are geological sections drawn to the same scale as the map along all four of the margin edges.

To accompany the map Ruthven also wrote '*A Description of the Geological Map of the Lake District, to which is added A List of the Fossils and the localities where found".* This description is rarely seen, and never seems to be found together with the map in its folder. It is undated, but we must assume it came out at the same time as the map in 1855. Unfortunately the description is largely geographical rather than geological in content in that "it enables the reader to trace the range of the different series of rocks". Most of it does little more than name the places where the outcrops can be traced.

Given the date of the map, the outcrop patterns shown are surprisingly good. The Skiddaw Slates in the north are accurately delimited, although the Ullswater and Haweswater inliers and the Black Coombe outcrop are less precise. Sedgwick's term 'Green slates and Porphyries' is used for the volcanics for which the map contains no details. Southern Lakeland contains significantly more divisions, although the Coniston Limestone is somewhat diagrammatic in its presentation. Perhaps least accurate of all are the intrusives. Surprisingly he shows Kendal, his home town, on an outlier of Old Red Sandstone, with a further exposure to the north of the town. The key however, which is detailed, reflects his thinking at the time on the classification of strata into systems. He divides the Carboniferous into four – Coal Measures, Millstone Grits, Mountain Limestone and Old Red Sandstone. Below that, in the Silurian, come Kirkbymoor Flags, Ireleth Slates and Coniston Grits. Below these, the Coniston or Brathay Flags, Coniston Limestone and Green Slates and Porphyry, classified as Cambrian, with the Skiddaw Slates beneath being unclassified, by implication Pre-Cambrian.

The *'Description and the List of Fossils'* gives an insight into the areas where Ruthven had made his observations. Being Kendal based, the weight of the records are in South East Lakeland, with a heavy emphasis on the Carboniferous and Silurian areas. His listings of fossils from 'The Mountain Limestone' are relatively extensive as are the Silurian finds from places like Benson Knott, near Kendal, Brigsteer, Tenter Fell and the Underbarrow areas. Several later writers accredit Ruthven as being the first to record fossils from the Skiddaw Slates. He does in fact list finds at Whiteless, near Buttermere, Scawgill, Knockmurton, Blakefell, Undercrag and Lowes Water in his Description.

It has been suggested by some authorities that Ruthven was the author of the section on geology in Harriet Martineau's well known guide book *'A Description of the English Lakes'* published in 1858. In the Publisher's Preface to this, it is recorded that 'a series of papers on the Meteorology, Botany and Geology of the region has been contributed by scientific gentlemen of local experience and long practical observation'. Ruthven would clearly have qualified as one of these. Additionally the publication date (three years after the map) fits conveniently and the fact that the Martineau guide came from the same publisher, J. Garnett of Windermere further supports the contention. To add even more convincing support for this position is the inclusion in the guide of Ruthven's geological map, in full colour, folded and bound into the original editions. Careful reading of the guide book account however, does cast some doubt on Ruthven being the author. First the literary style has few similarities with the Ruthven Description of his map. Secondly it is written in the plural, presumably therefore indicating a combined work from 'the scientific gentlemen'. More directly there is a telling sentence where describing the Skiddaw Slates they say . . . "It has always been held to be destitute of fossil remains, but we understand these have been discovered in it, by Mr. Ruthven, of Kendal, to whose practical knowledge of this branch of local science we are indebted for the geological illustration of our map". The geological account bears heavily on Ruthven's map and material, carrying the same interpretations and descriptions, but it seems most likely other contributors were at work here, even if Ruthven was one of 'the scientific gentlemen'. There is the further factor that Ruthven's educational ability has been questioned in some quarters and whether he was capable of putting such an account together could be in doubt, but the existence of his 'Description' to the map negates this argument somewhat.

Little further remains by way of a record of Ruthven's life. Like Jonathan Otley, his local knowledge and expertise was clearly used by Sedgwick and other professional geologists. His map is the principal tangible document to his work. He died in London at his son's house in 1868.

BIBLIOGRAPHY

RUTHVEN, J. 1855, *Geological Map of the English Lakes and adjoining country, geologically coloured*

1855, *Description of the Geological Map of the Lake District to which is added a list of the fossils and the local ties where found.* 19 pages. London: E. Stanford, 6, Charing Cross, and John Garnett, Windermere.

The Geological Section that may have been written by Ruthven is in Harriet Martineau, July 1858, *A Description of the English Lakes*, London: Simkin, Marshall & Co. and J. Garnett, Windermere. – Geology of the Lake District, pp 167-73. (Note this guide book went to several later editions, 4th Edition 1871 contains an article on Geology and Mineralogy by A.C.G. The original 1858 Edition was reprinted in 1974 by EP Publishing Ltd, East Ardsley, Wakefield, but did not include the section on geology, nor the Ruthven map).

The Early Academics

Sedgwick in many ways could be regarded as the first academic worker to study Lake District geology, but, building on the ground work he laid at the beginning of the Nineteenth Century, there followed increasing numbers of academic workers who began to focus on Lakeland problems. Progressively, geology became established as an academic discipline in the universities, the pace noticeably quickening as the Victorians realised its economic value and the new provincial academic centres of learning opened.

The Lake District afforded a huge range of geological possibilities for the growing number of scientists in the field. Not only were the basics of the stratigraphy and structure of the region still being debated, but also the specialists were beginning to apply the new-found techniques of igneous and metamorphic petrology, palaeontology and biostratigraphy and to ponder the efficacy of glacial events in shaping the landscape. Lakeland provided a wide variety of terrains and geological problems. These ranged from early sedimentary rocks, thick volcanic sequences, igneous intrusions, metamorphosed strata, complex mineralisation, to Mesozoic sediments, all in an intricately sculptured upland environment.

Only five of these early academic workers are included in our review of this period. Robert Harkness picked up the baton left by Sedgwick, befriending the great man in his later life and developing his work on the stratigraphy and structure of the region. Henry Alleyne Nicholson continued the connection, being a student of Harkness. The two collaborated on several papers in the 1860's and 1870's. Alfred Harker, during a very focussed academic career at the end of the Nineteenth Century and into the early years of the Twentieth Century, continued the Cambridge tradition of Lakeland geology established by Sedgwick. He pioneered work on the igneous intrusions of the Lake District and laid the foundations of modern petrological studies.

One man however stands out as the commanding figure of this phase - John Marr. Again from the Cambridge school, he dominated Lakeland academic geology in the early Twentieth Century. Not only was he a prolific writer, producing around 40 papers on the region under his own name as well as collaborating with others, he brought together geological ideas on the area and popularised the district. His book *'The Geology of the Lake District'* published in 1916 became the most authoritative work on the region and the means by which many people were introduced to Lakeland geology for many years. Marr is indeed worthy of the longest section in this book. Lastly, Edmund Garwood, a student of Marr's and yet another Cambridge man, is included for his seminal work on the Carboniferous rocks of Cumbria.

Although these five men, Harkness, Nicholson, Harker, Marr and Garwood illustrate well the path of geological enquiry in the Lake District by academic workers from the Nineteenth into the first part of the Twentieth Century, they are but a small sample of the people who became involved with the geology of the district. Many important personalities are missing. While it is somewhat invidious to list names, a few of the people we have not been able to include must be mentioned. J.D. Kendall between the 1870's and the 1920's wrote profusely on the district and became an authority on the haematite deposits of West Cumbria and the Carboniferous rocks. Earlier both E.W. Binney and W. Brockbank worked and published on the haematite and the Carboniferous rocks too. The work of D. Mackintosh, W.M. Hutchins, J. Phillips and T.V. Holmes must also be acknowledged. The point was made in the Introduction that all the people featured in the book are men. During this late Nineteenth Century period, however, two ladies figured in the pioneering work on the district as well. Gertrude Elles worked tirelessly on the Graptolite fauna in the Skiddaw Group for many years around the turn of the century and published three papers, and in the same period Edith Goodyear worked with E.J. Garwood on the Carboniferous fauna.

5. Robert Harkness (1816-1878)
A Geological Pioneer In Northern England and Southern Scotland
Margaret Fox

If Robert Harkness (Fig. 11) had cared more about immediate glory and less about his future quality of life and the wellbeing of his sister, he might have made less of an impact on Cumbrian geology. For in 1854, five years after Harkness' first visit to Cumbria, Sir Henry de La Beche offered Harkness the appointment of Professor of Geology at the Engineering College of Roorkee, Northern India.

In writing to reluctantly decline this appointment, Harkness expressed concerns about the lack of opportunities to discuss ideas with others; the fact that he could not imagine life without his sister, for whom India would not be a suitable environment; and his fears that, on returning, his health and the social effects of his long absence would mean that he would find little pleasure in life.

Harkness must indeed have been reluctant to turn this offer down, for it would have given him an unrivalled opportunity to extend his knowledge in an area about which little, if anything, had previously been written; but he does not appear to have expressed regret in later life. Instead he used his considerable energies in working out problems in a number of different fields, ready to

Fig. 11 – Robert Harkness

travel widely in the British Isles in search of clues to illuminate aspects of a problem or to link areas together in geological terms.

Robert Harkness' interest in geology seems to have been aroused during his years at Edinburgh University, where he attended lectures by the Wernerian geologist, Professor Jamieson and also those of Professor J. D. Forbes.

Born in Ormskirk in 1816 and educated initially in Ormskirk and later in Dumfries before going to Edinburgh, it was to Ormskirk that he returned when first leaving university. With the prospect of employment in a firm of India Merchants having fallen through, Harkness occupied much of his time in a study of the local rocks. Having read all he could find on the geology of this area he began to use his knowledge on unsolved problems.

This preliminary literature survey was characteristic of Harkness' approach throughout his life. Each time he tackled a new area or a new problem, he first made himself acquainted with any published work and also talked or corresponded with others who had worked in the area. Nor were these discussions one-way. He was always equally willing to make the results of his researches available to others.

In 1843 at the age of 26, Harkness read his first paper, on The Climate of the Coal Epoch, to the Geological Society of Manchester. This was printed the same year in *Annals of Philosophy*. In it he suggested that from the first dawn of animal life to the first terrestrial beings the climate was warmer and more equable than today, due to the greater presence of carbonic acid gas in the atmosphere. This led to absorption of heat when the sun's rays were oblique and prevented dissipation when the rays were vertical, resulting in a more uniform temperature across the earth and supporting luxuriant vegetation. Over 20 years later, similar views were reiterated by Professor T. Sterry.

Later that same year Harkness communicated another paper on climate to the Geological Society of London, this time proposing temperature change as a mechanism for the relative variation of sea level in relation to the land.

In 1848, the Harkness family moved to Dumfries. From then on, Harkness spent much of his time studying occurrences of red rocks, first encountered around Ormskirk, and also the crushed and contorted lower Palaeozoic rocks. Sedgwick had begun a few traverses and collected fossils in the Moffat area, but few other geologists had turned their attention in this direction.

By the time of the British Association (BA) meeting in Edinburgh in 1850, Harkness had a general idea of the structure and characteristics of the area and had collected a range of new graptolites from the anthracitic schists around Moffat. Sedgwick's account at the meeting of his own finds stimulated Harkness into further work. He sent his specimens to the palaeontologist J.W. Salter to be named and shortly afterwards produced the first of his many memoirs on a subject in which he remained enthusiastic throughout his life.

Harkness had been struck by the resemblance between the red rocks of Lancashire and those north of the Solway and had read a paper at the BA on the Position of the Footsteps in the Bunter Sandstone of Dumfriesshire. Sedgwick had been writing about the New Red in Cumberland and Westmorland, with the result that a friendship began between the two men that lasted until Sedgwick's death in 1873.

In 1849, Robert Harkness made his first visit to Cumberland and from then on his name came to be associated with the interpretation of the geology of the north of England. His first paper on the Silurian rocks of the Solway Basin appeared in *The Quarterly Journal of the Geological Society* in 1851. Several other articles on the New Red quickly followed, leading to communications with some of the foremost men of science of his day.

A common interest in graptolites led to a two-way exchange of specimens with Joachim Barrande, who had made a major contribution to knowledge of the older Palaeozoic rocks. Barrande's graptolites of

Bohemia form part of the Harkness collection in Carlisle Museum, along with material Harkness collected himself.

All this activity did not go unrecognised. When in 1853 Harkness applied for the Chair of Geology at Queen's College, Cork, his application was supported by a list of eminent geologists, among them Professor James Nicol, whom he succeeded, J. Beete Jukes and Sir Roderick Murchison. The last named corresponded with and supported Harkness over many years, but relations later cooled over the question of the lower boundary of the Silurian.

Also in 1853, the Geological Society made Harkness a Fellow, a distinction not lightly conferred in those days. This was followed in 1854 by inclusion in the Royal Society of Edinburgh and in 1856 by his election as a Fellow of the Royal Society.

The move to Ireland did not lead Harkness to forsake his interest in the rocks of Cumbria. Rather it allowed him to extend his knowledge of the older rocks in an area different from the Solway, whilst continuing his explorations of Cumbria during the vacations, especially after his sister moved to Penrith.

Initially Harkness' work in Cumbria had been predominantly concerned with the rocks of the Solway Basin, but from about 1856, he turned his attentions increasingly to the rocks of the Lake District. Sedgwick and Otley had laid the foundations, but much more detailed work was needed to fill out their general ideas of the structure. As usual, Harkness studied all the available literature and Sedgwick, now too infirm for fieldwork, placed the results of his own experience at Harkness' disposal. Sedgwick suggested useful contacts and possible fossil localities, and urged him to examine rocks in south west Cumberland, raising questions over the pressure-only theory of cleavage development.

At an early stage, Harkness had assumed an axis matching south Scotland with north Cumberland. Having found graptolites in the older Palaeozoic of South Scotland he expected to find their equivalents in Cumberland. The results of his early investigations were read before the British Association in 1857, in a paper on the geology of the Caldbeck Fells and the lowest sedimentary rocks of Cumberland. This area remained a source of particular interest throughout Harkness' life. He collected a fine suite of minerals as well as fossils, and his knowledge of the area probably remained unsurpassed until the work of J. Clifton Ward.

During his increasingly frequent visits to Cumbria, Harkness came to recognise the full extent of the unconformity between the lower Palaeozoic of the Lake District and the flanking Carboniferous, realising that nearly five miles thickness of rock had been eroded. In an attempt to shed some light on this, he visited other areas where a time lapse had been implied. He communicated his intention of visiting the area of Hugh Miller's Old Red Sandstone to others. Back came letters from Sir Charles Lyell, lending him a copy of part of Sir Charles' field map and asking him to check some details for a student handbook; and from Murchison, entreating him to conduct a detailed examination of some rocks around Achintoul. The results of his investigations were communicated in several papers in 1862

Harkness next turned his attentions to the red rocks of the Eden Valley. At that time there were few records of the best exposures. It was necessary to traverse in every likely direction, record details and then attempt to collate the observations to discover agreements and differences. The findings then needed to be related to sections elsewhere, both in Britain and Europe. Harkness recorded his observations on a large map, which was probably the earliest large-scale geological map of this district. J. G. Goodchild, who later mapped the same area for the Geological Survey, commented of the map: 'Although here and there I have been led to put a slightly different construction upon some of the facts he has recorded, I can bear the fullest testimony to its accuracy as a whole'.

The results of his Edenside researches appeared in *The Quarterly Journal of the Geological Society,* followed the next year by a paper on the Skiddaw Group with notes on the fossils by Salter. The fruits of Harkness' careful searching are now in Carlisle Museum.

Not long after came a paper that Goodchild considered to be one of the most important contributions to the geological history of Edenside, marking a great advance beyond the contributions of previous writers. It concerned the older Palaeozoic rocks associated with the Pennine faults between Warcop and Gamblesby. Later Survey mapping differed in minor detail, but there were numerous points of agreement.

In 1865, Harkness took Murchison to the main locations of his paper on the New Red of the Basin of the Solway. As a result Harkness seems to have been induced to make important modifications to his scheme of classification concerning the dividing line between the Palaeozoic and the Secondary rocks. Red-stained Carboniferous fossils had been assigned to the New Red, but the higher New Red had affinities with the Secondary rocks, especially around Carlisle. This suggested that the dividing line should be drawn through the New Red but in the joint paper that was published in the *QJGS*, it was Murchison's views that prevailed. Harkness never again wrote on the stratigraphical relations of the New Red rocks.

At the same time, Harkness was working on the older Palaeozoic with Dr H.A. Nicholson, later to become Professor of Natural History at Aberdeen. They had succeeded in discovering fossils below the Coniston

Limestone, in rocks previously considered barren. Together they produced four joint memoirs bearing on the older rocks of Cumbria.

Alarm over the possible exhaustion of coal resources was at that time occupying the concerns of a large part of the scientific world. Harkness was asked by the Government Coal Commission for his opinion on the possibility of Coal Measures beneath the New Red of Cumberland and Westmorland.

Always a regular attendee and contributor to the meetings of the British Association for the Advancement of Science, Harkness was elected President of the Geological Section in 1869. In his Presidential Address on the relations between the Devonian and its adjacent strata, he summarised all his observations on those strata missing from Cumbria, giving rise to the unconformity between the older and newer Palaeozoic.

Harkness had been busy collecting evidence of the distribution beyond outcrop of boulders of Shap Granite, publishing the results in an 1870 paper. He was also puzzled as to how boulders of Brockram and other low lying Eden rocks could have crossed Stainmore to the North Sea, corresponding with Professor John Phillips on the subject.

At around this time, the question of the base of the Silurian was being argued over. The Ordovician had not yet been proposed, and the base of the Silurian had been taken as the lowest level at which fossils had been found, the underlying Cambrian being considered lifeless. As fossils were found at lower and lower levels, Murchison simply moved the base of the Silurian lower; but not all scientists agreed, because of the existence of a stratigraphic break above the lowest fossils. With Dr Hicks, Harkness had collected fossils below the *Lower Lingula* Flags and their conclusions were read before the Geological Society in 1870. Murchison is unlikely to have been pleased.

We must not forget that during all this time, Professor Harkness had been diligently carrying out his duties in Cork. Somewhere around the mid 1870s, he was required to teach not only geology but also physical geography, mineralogy, palaeontology, zoology and botany. Since his interests had been widespread, there is little doubt that he was capable of fulfilling this duty, but to do so as well as he wished put a great burden on him. When the prospect of a Chair of Geology at Edinburgh seemed likely, Harkness had hopes of winning the appointment with the support of Sir Roderick Murchison; but Murchison had already thrown his support behind Archibald Geikie – and in any event, the Chair never materialised.

This left Harkness with retirement as the only option of escaping the burden of his duties at Cork. In October 1878 he made the necessary arrangements and said goodbye to his students and colleagues. In Dublin, on his way back to Penrith to join his sister, he died of the heart disease that had been troubling him for a few years.

It is perhaps difficult for today's geologists to really appreciate the problems faced by those early men. Transport was considerably poorer and Harkness must have walked many miles and climbed many thousands of feet over rough ground in the course of his investigations. Useful exposures had to be sought, necessitating many traverses and scrambling into every likely ravine. Only a limited amount of previous work was available to direct researchers to key localities. Moreover, fossils were rare and cleavage, metamorphism and dislocations obscured the stratigraphic relations. The physical effort involved, together with the intellectual burden of his duties at Cork had taken their toll on Harkness, and his retirement came too late to give him the rest he had hoped for.

Robert Harkness was laid to rest in Penrith Cemetery (Fig. 12). At Queen's College a window was erected in his memory. Some of Harkness' Scottish material had already been given to the British Museum (Natural History) and to the Geological Society, but the remainder of his collection was presented by his sister to Carlisle Museum.

His last published paper, on the Borrowdale Series and Coniston Flags, was written with Prof Nicholson and appeared in *The Quarterly Journal of the Geological Society* in 1877. In July of the year he died, he read a paper on Cotterite, a new form of quartz, to the Mineralogical Society.

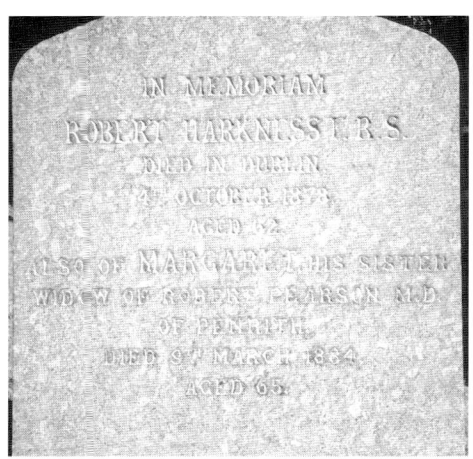

Fig. 12 – Headstone of Shap Granite on the Harkness grave at Penrith Cemetary, Beacon Edge, where he was laid to rest along with his beloved sister, Margaret.

Professor Robert Harkness wrote over 83 papers, for the most part appearing in *The Quarterly Journal of the Geological Society* and the *Reports of the British Association*. His original memoirs on the Solway Basin rank among some of the most important contributions to the geological literature of the time. His knowledge extended not only to the geological structure of an area but also fossils, minerals and natural features. He had an extensive knowledge, too, of the early history of mankind. But those who were fortunate enough to meet him remembered him as much for his personal qualities as for his contribution to geological knowledge.

Goodchild, who first met Harkness in 1887, considered that the professor was gifted 'with the power of rapidly taking in structural details . . . and . . . the facile pen of a practised writer.' He commented on the fact that Harkness was always ready to discuss, in perfect good temper, any point that was made to him contradicting his own published ideas. Goodchild also felt that Harkness relied to a large extent on his memory, for his field notebooks have sketches and data but only very condensed notes.

But perhaps the strongest tribute to his personal qualities came in that oft-quoted note written by Sir Archibald Geikie and published in Nature the week after Harkness' death:

'Who that has been privileged with his friendship will not cherish the memory of his earnestness over even the driest of details, his quiet enthusiasm, his genuine admiration for the work of others, his unfailing cheerfulness? Who will forget that beaming ruddy face, never absent from the platform of Section C at the British Association meetings, always ready to rise among the speakers there and to reappear at the festive gatherings in the evening? There have been men who have graven their names more deeply on the registers of scientific thought and progress, but there have been few whose sunny nature has more endeared them in the recollection of their friends than Robert Harkness.'

BIBLIOGRAPHY.

HARKNESS, R., 1857. On the Geology of the Caldbeck Fells and the lower sedimentary rocks of Cumberland. *Rep. Brit. Assoc. Trans. Sects.*, pp 67-8.

1861, On the sandstones and their associated deposits of the valley of the Eden and the Cumberland Plain. *Rep. Brit. Assoc. Trans. Sects.*, p. 115.

1862, On the sandstones and their associated deposits in the Vale of Eden, the Cumberland Plain and the South-East of Dumfries-shire. *Quart. Journ. Geol. Soc.*, Vol.18, 205-218.

1863, On the fossils of the Skiddaw Slates. *Rep. Brit. Assoc.Trans Sects*, p. 69.

1863a, On the Skiddaw Slate Series. *Quart. Journ. Geol. Soc.*, Vol.19, pp 113-140.

1865, On the lower Silurian rocks of the South-East of Cumberland and the North-East of Westmorland. *Quart. Journ. Geol. Soc.*, Vol.21, pp 235-249.

1870, On the distribution of the Wasdale Crag blocks, "Shap Fell Granite Boulders", in Westmorland. *Quart. Journ. Geol. Soc.*, Vol.26, pp 517-528.

1873, On the occurrence of faults in the Permian rocks of the

Lower portion of the Vale of Eden, Cumberland. *Rep. Brit. Assoc. Trans. Sects.*, pp 81-82.

HARKNESS, R. and NICHOLSON, H. A., 1866, Additional observations on the Geology of the Lake Country. (With a note on two new species of Trilobites by J W. Salter). *Quart. Journ. Geol. Soc.*, Vol.22, pp 480-486.

1868, On the Coniston Group. *Quart. Journ. Geol. Soc.*, Vol.24, 29-303. Abstract of this paper in *Rep. Brit. Assoc.*, 1867, p.61.

1870 On the Green Slates and Porphyries of the Lake District. *Rep. Brit. Assoc. Trans. Sects.,* p.74.

1877 On the strata and their fossil contents between the Borrowdale Series of the North of England and the Coniston Flags. *Quart. Journ. Geol. Soc.,* Vol. 33, 461-484. Abstract of this paper in *Rep. Brit. Assoc.* 1876, p 90.

6. Henry Alleyne Nicholson (1844-1899)
A Reknowned Cumbrian Polymath
Dennis Dickins

Henry Alleyne Nicholson is regarded as one of the greatest Cumbrian pioneers of geology from the Victorian era (Fig.13). He was born at Penrith, Cumberland, where his father, Dr. John Nicholson, was a well-known biblical and oriental scholar. He received his early education under Francis Newman and at Appleby Grammar School and although little is known of his boyhood it is assumed that his interest in natural history was stimulated by his childhood surroundings. His ambles into the Lake District in his youth initiated his subsequent interest in geology, especially palaeontology and

Fig. 13 – Henry Alleyne Nicholson.

stratigraphy, and led to his future research publications on the various aspects of the geology of the area.

His higher education commenced at the University of Gottingen, where he worked under Professor Keferstein, the distinguished zoologist. He then studied medicine at the University of Edinburgh from 1862 to 1867 and graduated as a Bachelor of Medicine and Master of Surgery, taking first-class honours in all subjects and in 1869 he received the degree of Doctor of Medicine. He was additionally awarded the Ettles Medical Scholarship of the University as the most distinguished student of his year in medicine. Simultaneously, whilst studying medicine, he found the time to get involved in the study of the natural sciences and was taught by Goodsir, Ailman and Balfour. He graduated as a Bachelor of Science in 1866, receiving the Baxter Scholarship in the Natural Sciences. In the following year he took the degree of Doctor of Science and received the University Gold Medal for his graduation thesis, 'On the Geology of Cumberland and Westmorland'. This was subsequently published, with a dedication to his friend and teacher, Professor Harkness of Queen's College, Cork, with whom he had undertaken the fieldwork.

His enormous appetite for assimilating knowledge as a student set the tone for the hard work of research which he continued throughout his life, in addition to the variety of posts which he subsequently held. His first position was that of Lecturer in Natural History at the Extra-Academical School of Medicine at Edinburgh where, initially, he also practiced medicine. In 1871 he accepted the Chair of Natural History at the University of Toronto, which he held for three years. During his time in North America he collected geological material, particularly the varied forms of corals and monticuliporoids, which he used for further research after his return to Britain. He also undertook, at the request of the Provincial Government of Ontario, an investigation into the fauna dredged from Lake Ontario, as well as an examination of the fossils of the Silurian and Devonian rocks of the Province. The collection was described and featured in two reports which were published by the Government of Ontario. He was also commissioned by Dr. Newberry, the State Geologist of Ohio, with the description of the fossil corals and polyzoa of that State. This appeared in the Second Volume of the Palaeontology of Ohio and was illustrated by Nicholson. Here he displayed yet another talent with his ability to provide precise illustrations of his fossil subjects. In addition to his post and the above works, he found time to produce his Manual of Palaeontology and the first part of a detailed treatise of British Graptolites, both of which were published in 1872.

The isolated nature of Toronto, in comparison to Britain, which was at that time the hub of research in geology, resulted in Nicholson accepting the position of Professor of Comparative Anatomy and Zoology at the Royal College of Science, Dublin, in 1874. However, before taking up this post he was offered the position of Professor of Biology at the Durham College of Physical Science and Medicine, which he accepted. Additionally, for two sessions he lectured at the University of Newcastle-upon-Tyne and then, in 1875, he took the offer of the Chair of Natural History at the University of St. Andrew's, where he remained for seven years.

He was largely responsible for establishing the study of Natural History and, likewise, he also took a very active part in the extension of

University teaching to Dundee. He also undertook an immense amount of research, mainly into fossil corals, producing numerous minor papers, two major Monographs, one in 1879, *On the Structure of and Affinities of the 'Tabulate Corals' of the Palaeozoic Period* and, in 1881, *On the Structure of and Affinities of the Genus Monticulipora and its Sub-genera*. Another important Monograph of this period was a joint production with Mr. R. Etheridge, Jun., on the Silurian Fossils of the Girvan District in Ayrshire. Additionally he wrote a popular volume entitled *The Ancient Life-History of the Earth*, new editions of the manual and textbooks of zoology and in 1879, a second edition of the *Manual of Palaeontology.*

In 1878 he was invited to deliver the natural history lectures at his former University in Edinburgh for three sessions, but was disappointed at not being recommended for the appointment of Chair of Natural History at the University when it became vacant. In 1882 he accepted the appointment of Regius Professor of Natural History at the University of Aberdeen, which he held for the remainder of his life. His output of research papers continued and apart from his official work he maintained his interest in research into fossil corals and Monticuliporoids. His most important publication in this period was his Monograph of the *British Stromatoporoids*, which was published by the Palaeontological Society between 1886 and 1892. He also introduced courses on systematic and practical geology and such was his enthusiasm, ability as a teacher and a lecturer that his classes increased fourfold. He was also invited to deliver the Swiney lectures at the British Museum in South Kensington between 1878-82 and 1890-94.

Professor Nicholson's greatest academic strengths lay in field geology and invertebrate palaeontology and he chose to conduct his field researches in his boyhood Lake District. In addition to his thesis he produced, in association with Professor Harkness, a paper on Additional observations on the Geology of the Lake Country and also On the Coniston Group [he discovered the rich graptolite fauna of the Coniston Flags of Sedgwick]. Other papers included those on the Green Slates and Porphyries of the Borrowdale Series and on the Coniston Flags which were published in 1871 and 1877. Additionally he produced a memoir on the Lower Palaeozoic Stockdale Shales and their division based on lithological characteristics and their contained fossils, mainly graptolites, which could be correlated with similar sequences in other areas. He produced this in conjunction with his friend Professor J. E. Marr in 1888, and they subsequently produced a paper on the age and the fossils of the various formations within the Cross Fell Inlier. He was the first to recognise the similarities of the graptolites from the Skiddaw Slates with those of the Quebec Group of Canada.

The Monograph of the *British Stromatoporoids* will probably be regarded as Nicholson's most important contribution to palaeontology. Also, he further developed the making of thin sections because he recognised the advantages of using this method to describe in detail the interior structure of fossils and personally made more than a thousand to use in compiling the above treatise.

Professor Nicholson drew excellent illustrations, including those of microscopic structures from thin sections and produced 138 single papers and 27 joint papers. He was elected a Fellow of the Geological Society in 1867, of the Linnaean Society in 1876 and of the Royal Society in 1897, whilst, in 1879 he received an award from the Lyell Fund and in 1888 was awarded the Lyell Medal. His intellectual ability, teaching and fieldwork skills were supplemented by a genial and sympathetic personality which won him many admirers, because he was always approachable and willing to give advice and assistance to fellow workers. Professor Nicholson had a high capacity for work, which could have resulted in his sudden death, since he was at his post until the week before he died.

BIBLIOGRAPHY

NICHOLSON, H.A.,1866, On the Occurrence of Fossils in the Old Red Sandstone of Westmorland. *Trans. Edinburgh Geol. Soc..*,Vol. 1.

1868, The Graptolities of the Skiddaw Series. *Quart. Journ. Geol. Soc.*, Vol.24, pp 125-245.

1868a, On the Graptolites of the Coniston Flags; with notes on the British Species of the Genus Graptolites. *Quart. Journ. Geol. Soc.*, Vol. 24,pp 521-546.

1868b, On the Granite of Shap. *Trans. Edinburgh Geol. Soc.*, Vol.1, p.133.

1868c, *Essay on the Geology of Cumberland and Westmorland.*

Robert Hardwicke; London. Alex. Ireland & Co. : Manchester., 93 pp.

1869, On the relation between the Skiddaw Slates and the Green Slates and Porphyries of the Lake District. *Geol. Mag.*,dec. 1, Vol.6, pp 105-108, pp 167-173.

1869a, Notes on the Green Slates and Porphyries of the neighbourhood of Ingleton. *Geol. Mag.*, dec. 1, Vol. 6, pp 213-215. (Lake District, pp. 214-215).

1869b, Notes on certain of the intrusive Igneous rocks of the Lake District. *Geol. Mag.*, dec. 1, Vol.6, pp 435-441.

1869c, On the Occurrence of Plants in the Skiddaw Slates. *Geol. Mag.*, dec. 1, Vol. 6, pp 494-498.

1869d, Notes on the Geology of Derwentwater, Cumberland. *Trans. Edinburgh Geol. Soc.*, Vol.1, pp 274-278.

1869e, On some new species of Graptolites. *Ann. Mag. Nat. Hist.*, ser. 4, Vol.4. pp 231-242.

1870, Notes on the lower portion of the Green Slates and Porphyries of the Lake District between Ullswater and Keswick. *Quart. Journ. Geol. Soc.*, Vol.26, pp 599-610.

1870a, On the Coniston Limestone Series of Cumberland and Westmorland and its associated rocks. *Trans. Edinburgh Geol. Soc*, Vol.2, pp 84-94.

1870b, On the correlation of the Silurian Deposits of the North of England with those of the South of Scotland. *Trans. Edinburgh Geol. Soc.*, Vol.2, pp 105-113.

1872, On the Occurrence of the Genus Endoceras in Britain. *Geol. Mag.*, dec. 1, Vol.9, pp 102-104 (Coniston Series).

1873, On the Silurian Rocks of the English Lake District. *Proc. Geol. Assoc.*, Vol. 3, pp 105-114.

1875, On a new genus of some new species of graptolites from the Skiddaw Slates. *Ann. Mag. Nat. Hist.*, ser. 4, Vol. 16, pp 269-273.

1875, NICHOLSON, H.A. and LAPWORTH, C., On the Central Group of the Silurian Series of Northern England. *Rep. Brit. Assoc.*, p 78.

1887, NICHOLSON, H.A., and MARR, J.E., On the occurrence of a new fossiliferous horizon in the Ordovician Series in the Lake District. *Geol. Mag.*, dec. 111, Vol. 4, pp 339-344.

1891, The Cross Fell Inlier. *Quart. Journ. Geol. Soc.* Vol. 47, pp 500-529.

7. John Edward Marr (1857-1933)
The Foremost Lake District Geologist of His Era
David Oldroyd

Johnny Marr, as he was known to his acquaintances, was born in Morecambe, Lancashire, on 14 June 1857, youngest of the nine children of John and Mary Marr (née Simpson) (Figs. 14, 15 and 16). His father, who retired in 1850, had been a Lancaster merchant trader and partner in a silk mill at Wray.

Following his family's removal to Caernarvon in 1863, Marr became interested in geology, and an Arenig fossil he discovered was subsequently named after him by Henry Hicks (the shrimp-like *Caryocaris marrii* (Hicks) [1876]). Marr's interest in geology was also stimulated during his studies at Lancaster

Fig. 14 – J.E. Marr.

▲ Fig. 15– The house
on the Promenade
(Marine Road Central),
Morecambe where
Marr was born in
1857.

◄ Fig. 15 – Detail of the
plaque

43

Grammar School, when he met Richard Tiddeman of the Geological Survey, who was working in the area at that time, and accompanied him on field excursions in north Lancashire. In 1875, Marr went up to St John's, Cambridge, as an Exhibitioner. Three years later – and already with a paper on his Caernarfon fossils read for him at the Geological Society by his professor, Thomas McKenny Hughes (Marr, 1876) – he gained a First in the natural science tripos, with geology as his main subject. At St John's, he was tutored by the petrologist Thomas Bonney, who was at Marr's college.

After graduating, Marr worked as a university extension lecturer for four years, during which time he developed an interest in the relationship between geology and scenery. He worked briefly at Leeds University and in 1881 was elected to a fellowship at St John's. In 1886 he was appointed university lecturer in geology and in 1917 he succeeded McKenny Hughes as professor, a position he held until 1930 when he retired due to ill health.

Marr was elected Fellow of the Geological Society in 1879 and served as Secretary (1888-98), Vice-President (for several periods), and President (1904-6). He was a member of Council for thirty-four years and was awarded the Lyell Medal (1900) and the Wollaston Medal (1914). Marr was President of Section C (Geology) of the British Association (1896), was elected Fellow of the Royal Society (1891), and served on its Council from 1904 to 1906. He was awarded a Cambridge ScD (1904), an honorary doctorate from Prague (1908), and a Royal Medal (1930). In his prime, then, Marr was one of Britain's leading geologists, and – until he began to go blind in the latter years of his professorship, when he concentrated on Pleistocene geology and stone implements in East Anglia, and sought to evaluate the claims for the occurrence of Pliocene man – his chief area of research was Lakeland geology, for which topic his *Geology of the Lake District* (1916) was for long the standard text. The complete set of Marr's field notebooks is held at the Sedgwick Museum Cambridge, forming an invaluable source for students of the history of Lakeland geology.

Marr must have been a good lecturer, if the following newspaper report (of uncertain provenance) on a field excursion he ran near Keswick as an accompaniment to a series of lectures in Penrith (1881) is anything to go by:

'The learned but youthful lecturer (only a few years out of his teens) . . . has won golden opinions from his numerous hearers, not only by his giving indisputable proofs of the perfect mastery of his subject, lucid arrangement, clear and distinct enunciation, but also by his striking modesty, total absence of pretension, pedantry, or dogmatism, as well as by his engaging affability and anxious desire to give full information to every one desirous of having any difficulty or obscurity elucidated; so that it may be safely asserted that if his hearers had not profited by his lectures it was not the lecturer's fault'.

The clarity of Marr's speech may, however, have been less evident in Cambridge, where a student who later became one of his colleagues, Tressilian Nicholas, recalled that Marr had a "burring Lake District voice which I found extremely difficult to understand. [Indeed, for] the first few lectures I really couldn't understand what he was talking about" (John Thackray, record of interview with T.C. Nicholas, 4 November 1975). His voice was also described as being rather high-pitched.

As said, Marr's early work was carried out in Caernarfonshire (1876). He also geologised in the Dee Valley (1880a), near Haverfordwest (1885), and did fieldwork in the Lake District for the greater part of his career. In his early years he also determined to examine the controversial work of Continental geologists in Bohemia and Scandinavia, to which regions he journeyed in 1879 and 1880 respectively, with the assistance of the Cambridge University Worts Travelling Fund.

In Bohemia, Joachim Barrande had proposed the notion of "precursoral forms" or "colonies", in cases where certain fossils appeared to be "out of order", according to the usual stratigraphic sequence (Horny and Turek, 1999). They had supposedly accomplished this by migration into a localised basin area, later dying out there when that basin subsequently filled with sediment. The same fossils might, however, reappear if and when appropriate conditions recurred in that area. This idea had regarded with some favour amongst British Survey geologists such as Roderick Murchison (1872)[1]. It could help solve stratigraphic problems that sometimes arose in tectonically disturbed areas such as the Southern Uplands. But Marr showed that Barrande's "colonies" were in fact the result of younger rocks having been faulted into older strata. So there was no Bohemian contradiction of orthodox stratigraphic principles. (Like criticisms of Barrande's hypothesis had earlier been made by Charles Lapworth in connection with his work on the Southern Uplands of Scotland. See Oldroyd [1990].)

It is hard to know just how Marr knew how to reinterpret the Bohemian observations as he did. He was first shown around by Barrande's assistant, and later he was able to meet the eminent French/Bohemian palaeontologist and stratigrapher himself. Initially, the young Marr seemed persuaded of the ideas of his Bohemian hosts (Notebook IV, June 29), but already by July 3 he was drawing sections (see, e.g., Fig.17), which showed how the unexpected stratigraphic order might be explained by faulting.

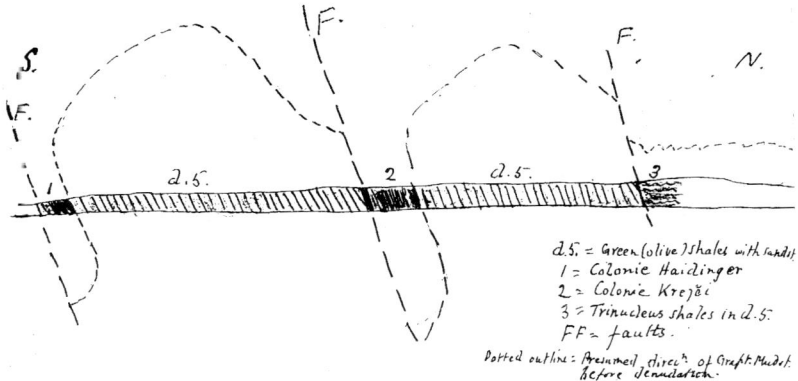

Fig. 17 – Structures for Strata near Prague, as interpreted by Marr (Field Notebook 1V, 1879, July 3)

It is significant that Marr used the stratigraphic succession known to him from the work of the Survey officers in the Lakes (Graptolitic [Skelgill] Mudstones/Pale Shales/Brathay Flags/Middle Coldwell Beds/Upper Coldwell Beds) as a guide to what he thought should be the correct sequence in Bohemia. Marr's ideas on Bohemian geology were published in 1880 (Marr, 1880b), and largely brought about the demise of the colonies theory at least in Britain.

As a Lancastrian and Cambridge man, and a protégé of the Sedgwickian McKenny Hughes (who had worked for the Survey in the southern Lakes before gaining the Cambridge chair in 1873 and took members of the Sedgwick Club there, including Marr, in 1882), it is hardly surprising that Marr should have been sympathetic to the Sedgwick side of the Sedgwick–Murchison controversy concerning the placement of the boundary between the Cambrian and Silurian[2]. Marr's Sedgwickian views were particularly manifest in his prize-winning Sedgwick Essay on the classification of Cambrian and Silurian strata (Marr, 1883), in which he divided the stratigraphic column as follows:

Downtonian
Salopian (Wenlock and Lower Ludlow) } Silurian
May Hill (Valentian)

Upper Bala
Middle Bala
Lower Bala (Llandeilo)
Llanvirn } Cambrian
Arenig
Tremadoc

It will be noticed that Charles Lapworth's (1879) proposal for an Ordovician System to occupy the contested ground in the middle of the foregoing sequence was not adopted. The Cambridge Sedgwickians had their own turf to protect, as did the Murchisonians in the Survey.

But things were not to stay thus. The Upper Bala were to become the Ashgillian, at the top of the Ordovician; and Marr was to play an important part in this change. The first hint of the Ashgillian appeared in the Catalogue . . . of Cambrian and Silurian Fossils . . . of the University of Cambridge by Sedgwick and his assistant John Salter (Sedgwick and Salter, 1873), where Salter had proposed dividing the Upper Bala into: 1. Hirnant Limestone of Merionethshire (supposedly above the Bala Limestone) and 'Ash Gill Slates, &c., above the Coniston Limestone'; and 2. Llandovery Rocks. The fossils at Cambridge on which he made this suggestion had come chiefly from the area of AshGill, near Torver, to the west of Coniston Water. They were evidently at a lower horizon than the Brathay Flags, recognised near Ambleside, and the two units were placed in the Upper Cambrian and Lower Silurian respectively.

Marr visited Ash Gill and the nearby Ashgill Quarry in 1877 (Notebook II) and in 1878 published a paper suggesting characteristic *phacopid* trilobites for strata (excluding the "Green Slates" or Borrowdales) all the way from the Kirkby Moor Flags right down to the Skiddaw Slates. He had been told by Hughes in 1876 that there were beds near Sedbergh that resembled those at Ash Gill, suggesting that the unit might be of more than local importance. It was suggested that there was an unconformity above the Ash Gill beds, and so it was (for the Cambridge Sedgwickians) at this horizon that the boundary between the Cambrian and the Silurian was to be drawn.

In 1887, Marr began collaborative work with Henry Alleyne Nicholson, Professor at Aberdeen, who had published the first book on Lakeland geology in 1868, and was an expert zoologist, palaeontologist and stratigrapher. The two were introduced by Lapworth and soon became great friends – to the extent that Marr later named his son Alleyne. In 1887, they reported the discovery of fossils in brown shales – the Drygill Shales – to the northwest of Carrock Fell in northern Lakeland (Nicholson and Marr, 1887) and placed them in the Ordovician. (Perhaps Nicholson, who was a friend of Lapworth, urged Marr in the direction of accepting the Ordovician.) They were thought to be intercalated with the lavas and ashes of what are now called the Eycott Volcanics, which were at that time not distinguished from the Borrowdale Volcanics. So this appeared to provide the first palaeontological evidence for the age of the Lakeland volcanics.

How first of all it came about
    I do not care a fico [fig];
But something turned without a doubt
    To octobrachiate *Dicho*.

[*Dichograptus*: Arenig]

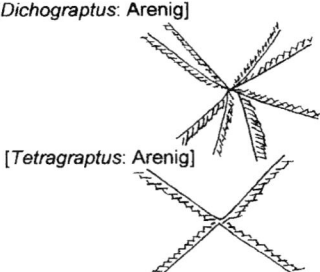

Then 'Evolution once again
    Came into play', &c.
And thus we find our old sea-pen
    Is posing as a *Tetra*.

[*Tetragraptus*: Arenig]

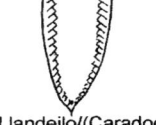

Another pair of branches drops
    As Mother Nature bid em, oh!
And in the sea are many crops
    Of double-branching *Didymo*.

[*Didymograptus*: Arenig/Llandeilo]

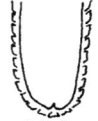

Through nearly half a circle sweeps
    Each stipe from off its fellow
And from each hydrotheca peeps
    The flesh of a *Dicello*.

[*Dicellograptus*: Llandeilo/(Caradoc)]

Now trouble comes about and s[d]wells
    In corpore non sano
So back to back the early cells
    Unite to form *Dicrano*.

[*Dicranograptus*: Llandeilo]

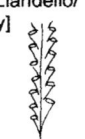

The distal thecae follow suit
    Unto the very tip. So!
The first Diprionidian brute
    Emerges as a *Diplo*.

[*Diplograptus*: Arenig/Llandeilo/
  (Caradoc)/ Llandovery]

Each theca finds opposing cell
    Is to itself a sore foe;
So some are dropped, and all is well
    At first with the *Dimorpho*.

[*Dimorphograptus*: Llandovery]

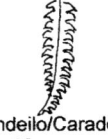

But not for long, and so at last
    One row of cells is gone oh!
Our beast (through many stages passed)
    Becomes the perfect *Mono*.

[*Monograptus*: Llandeilo/Caradoc
/Llandovery/ Wenlock]

Fig. 18 – Sketches and Lines of Verse from Marr (Notebook XXIII 1892).

Today the Drygill Shales are regarded as having been emplaced by faulting rather than having been originally intercalated with the volcanics.

In conjunction with Nicholson, Marr carried out further exemplary studies of the Cumbrian Palaeozoics, working out successions at other key sites such as Skelgill near Ambleside (Marr and Nicholson, 1888), Stockdale in Longsleddale (ibid.), and in the Cross Fell area (Nicholson and Marr, 1891). Graptolites were used as zone fossils according to the techniques developed by Lapworth in the Southern Uplands (Oldroyd, 1990: 226–234), and the evolutionary history of these organisms was investigated. Attention was given to the conditions under which the ancient rocks were deposited. In his Presidential Address to the Geological Society, Marr (1905) introduced the concept of the Ashgill Series as the top of the Ordovician, and subsequently published his definitive account of the strata at Ash Gill, with the boundary there between the Ashgill Shales and the overlying Skelgill Beds (Lower Silurian, Llandovery) visible in Ashgill Quarry (Marr, 1915)[3]. In 1892, he published three papers (Marr, 1892, b, c) in which the stratigraphic work was extended into the Silurian. All was accomplished with fine palaeontological control.

Marr (1894) also published on the Skiddaw Slates, where Nicholson and other geologists such as Robert Harkness had earlier spent much time on the tedious task of collecting graptolites and trying to establish the stratigraphy. It is interesting to remark that Marr was by then familiar with the whole range of Palaeozoic graptolites and was evidently trying to discern some kind of evolutionary pattern in the ever-growing collections. As a broad generalization, it seemed that there was a gradual reduction in the number of stipes, so that one had eight-branched *Dichograptus* low in the Skiddaws (Ordovician) gradually giving way to the single-stiped *Monograptus* towards the top of the Silurian[4]. Marr mused on the problem in some interesting doggerel verses and accompanying sketches in his Notebook XX111 (30th July 1892) which are reproduced as Fig. 18.

Such musings can sometimes tell us more about a geologist's ideas than many pages of technical writing; and I think they do so in this case. They are also interesting because they hint at what Marr was very likely teaching in his classes at Cambridge. The idealized evolutionary model seems to have been picked up by Marr's student Gertrude Elles, who was to become one of the aficionados of graptolite studies in the first half of the twentieth century. Moreover, according to a later authority on Lakeland graptolites, Dennis Jackson (record of interview, 4 July, 1998), some of Elles's work, based on museum studies as much as her own field investigations, took a wrong turn because of undue adherence to such an evolutionary model. But I do not seek to pursue this question here.

Another of Marr's co-workers in the Lake District was his St John's colleague, the petrologist Alfred Harker. They worked on the igneous rocks at Shap, Marr being chiefly responsible for the map work and stratigraphy, while Harker concentrated on the petrology (Harker and Marr 1891). Marr was much more at home with palaeontology, stratigraphy, and geomorphology than with igneous petrology. Indeed, he did not find the latter field particularly congenial, as the following rhymes from his notes (Book XXII, 24 September, 1890), when he was visiting Mardale with Harker, reveal:

A plague upon lavas and ashes,
    Agglomerates also be banned,
Away with contortions and smashes;
    Such games I don't understand

Let thrusts be consigned to the devil,
    May 'tears' go along with them too;
Let imps of Beelzebub revel
    In rocks which are twisted askew.

Accurst be the lavas of Stanah;
    The rocks of Galleny be blowed;
Whilst as for the Eycotts, how can a
    Man tell where the mischief they're stowed?

The White Stones agglomerates, drat 'em,
    As also the tuffs of Bowfell:
I dedicate every atom
    To innermost recesses of h[ell].

The rocks which occur on Torpenhow
    Make any geologist swear:
Oh! send the whole lot to Gahenna,
    To fuse and solidify there.

In Hades there may be a Johnny
    Would venture such rocks to descry
For instance, our underground B[onney]
    Might work his experienced eye.

For my part I hold the volcanic
    Deposits are rather too much;
Beds furnishing relics organic
    Alone, in the future I'll touch.

Yet needless to say, Marr could not avoid igneous petrology and problems of structure in Lakeland geology. Let us consider a couple of examples where he got into a little difficulty in this area.

As mentioned, Marr and Harker produced a paper on the geology of the Shap area in 1891; and a supplement to this was published in 1893. The first paper included a map that was particularly detailed in the immediate vicinity of the Shap Wells Hotel (on which see below), but as I have argued elsewhere (Oldroyd, 1999a) the map was somewhat schematic, making considerable extrapolations beyond what could actually be seen in the field. Marr also exhibited some of his Shap specimens at the Geological Society in 1902. The paper of 1893 involved some significant modifications to the statements made two years earlier. By 1893, the rocks to the north of the pink granite of Shap had become more basic – even basaltic – having earlier been represented as intermediate andesites. This change was said to have been made in response to the examination of more basic rocks in the interim. These would clearly be the exposures of the Eycotts that Harker and Marr worked on in the years 1890–93, sometimes together and sometimes separately. But it should be emphasized that what they had as Eycotts were not necessarily the rocks mapped as such today[5].

Harker (Notebook 17, 1890, Sedgwick Museum) was looking round the northeastern side of the Lakes, and so too was Marr (Notebook XXII) when he scribbled his verses above. They were trying to make sense of the structure of the area between Ullswater and Haweswater, supposing that the Eycotts were appearing in this region; and they were invoking various tear and thrust-faults to make sense of it all. Harker prudently never published the complicated structural ideas that the two friends were trying to develop, but in the 1893 paper just talked about the metamorphism in the Shap aureole, claiming that chemical and mineralogical evidence suggested that it did not involve changes in the bulk chemical compositions of the rocks in the aureole. Marr said something about the fossils recently found by Nicholson near Shap Wells, but kept quiet in the discussions following the presentation of the paper at the Geological Society about petrological questions. Subsequently (1902), he did offer the suggestion that the certain vein-like structures near the Shap granite represented pre-existing metalliferous veins that had been altered when the granite was intruded – an idea that found no favour with later workers such as Ronald Firman

(1954), who did his PhD on the problem of the metasomatism and metamorphism associated with the Shap (and Eskdale) granites. (He regarded Marr's suggestion as "untenable".)

As said, Harker never made public any ideas he may have had about thrust-faulting in the Lakes, but Marr certainly did (claiming that his speculative theory had Harker's support). Marr, as we have seen, first made a name for himself by showing that Barrande's ideas could be explained more satisfactorily by invoking faulting rather than colonization, and perhaps this was why he was willing to offer the bold hypothesis, outlined below. In his paper with Nicholson on the Stockdale Shales (1888), Marr suggested – quite reasonably – that rocks of different competence might move differentially in response to lateral forces. The idea was developed further in a speculative paper on the overall structure of the Lake District, designed to account for the presence of the Drygill Shales (Caradoc) in the northern Lakes, near Carrock Fell, well away from the also fossiliferous, but younger, rocks of southern Lakeland; and in addition the problem – one that is, even now, not fully settled – of the relationship between the Borrowdale Volcanics and the Skiddaw Slates (Marr. 1900).

The relationship between the Skiddaws and the Borrowdales was already causing trouble in the nineteenth century, long before it became a really hotly debated issue in the 1970s (Mitchell *et al.*, 1972). The early investigators such as Nicholson (1868) thought that the relationship was one of conformity. The surveyor John Dakyns (1869) claimed, however, that there was a marked unconformity between the two. His colleague Clifton Ward (1876) thought the contact was faulted, and his Survey maps (e.g., the Keswick Sheet, Sheet 101 S.E., 1875) showed a string of interconnected high-angle faults along the line of contact between the two units.

By the end of the nineteenth century, as a result of the work of Lapworth, Peach and Horne, and others in northwest Scotland, the idea of thrust-faults was well established in Britain, and was quite frequently invoked. Marr's view was that there had been a pushing of the Lakeland rocks from the south; but because of the different natures of the three principal units the underlying Skiddaws had been pushed furthest; then came the Borrowdales; and then the Upper Slates (Windermere Supergroup in modern parlance). Put another way, the Borrowdales had lagged behind the Skiddaws; and the Windermeres had lagged behind the Borrowdales. Thus (so far as I am aware) Marr introduced a new kind of fault into the geological literature: "lag-faults". These, like thrust-faults, were low-angled; but there was no inversion of the strata during their formation, as was the case with thrust-faults as envisaged by Lapworth and others for the Northwest

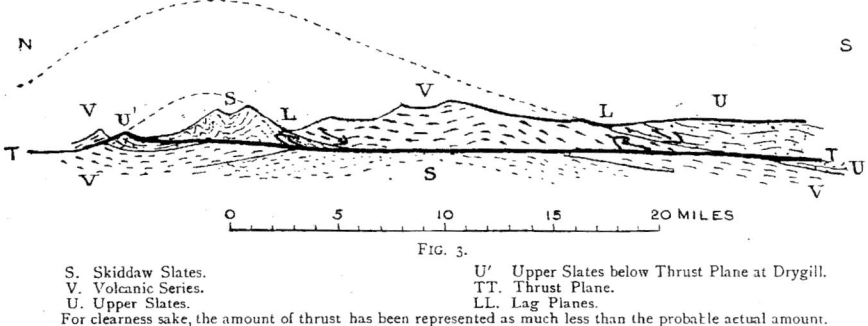

FIG. 3.

S. Skiddaw Slates.
V. Volcanic Series.
U. Upper Slates.

U'   Upper Slates below Thrust Plane at Drygill.
TT. Thrust Plane.
LL. Lag Planes.

For clearness sake, the amount of thrust has been represented as much less than the probable actual amount.

Fig. 19 – Marr (1900a, page 468)

Highlands of Scotland. Because of the supposed differential south-to-north movement in the Lakes – unequal at different points from east to west – there were also high-angle faults, striking approximately north–south and producing erodible shatter belts – fracturing the outcrop of the Coniston Limestone, for example – as had long been known.

But to make such a differential lagging movement geometrically possible, there had to be compensating thrust-faulting. Marr had no direct evidence for such a fault (though he drew some in his field notebooks), but the occurrence of the Drygill Shales seemingly allowed a "way out" of his problem. His students Gertrude Elles and Ethel Wood had suggested on palaeontological evidence – especially that of *graptolites* – that these Shales were of the same age as the Coniston Limestone in the southern Lake District. With these factors in mind, Marr developed the model shown in Fig.19. It repays close study.

What we have here is the idea that Ward's zig-zag chain of high-angle normal faults between the Skiddaw Slates and the Borrowdale Volcanics was representable by a low-angle "lag" fault (L); and there was a similar one between the Volcanics and the Upper (= Windermere) Slates. But at the same time this differential movement was compensated by the movement along the large (hypothetical) thrust fault (T–T), which supposedly underlay the whole of the mountain range (but being beneath the exposed outcrop of the Skiddaws it was invisible, except, one must suppose, near Drygill). Put another way, above the thrust plane there had supposedly been a general northward movement of the main sequence (Skiddaws, Borrowdales, and Upper Slates), but of these the Skiddaws had travelled further than the Borrowdales, which in turn had travelled further than the Upper Slates. The Drygill Shales were to be seen further north than the Skiddaws, as a small exposure of the youngest of the three main units. They had not been pushed forward by the thrusting but had been there all the time, and were now visible "peeping through" where erosion had cut down to below the level of the hypothetical thrust. It will be noted that Marr had the northernmost volcanics (the Eycotts) as belonging to the same unit as the Borrowdale Volcanics; but, as said, that was usual at that time.

It is, I think, virtually impossible to envisage a system of forces that would give rise to such a state of affairs[6], but by the early years of the Twentieth Century Marr's reputation and position were such that he could command assent—or at least he could get his ideas published by Cambridge University Press! He took members of the Geologists' Association with him to the Lakes in August 1900, and proposed the idea of the major thrust-fault (Marr, 1900b: 530). Whether it was received positively by the excursionists I do not know, but I would say that the sketch map produced for their benefit (Marr, 1900b: Plate XIII) is almost impossible to reconcile with the section of Figure 19. However, Marr's ideas remained in the public domain for some twenty years, being re-affirmed in his *Geology of the Lake District* (1916). It will be noted that his structure (Figure 19) rightly allowed for a syncline in the high fells around Scafell. His idea was that the main body of these fells was produced by a kind of "tectonic accumulation". The ashes and lava flows had, so to speak, been gathered together where they now stood by means of tectonic activity (not by the accumulation of volcanic debris from a volcano in the locality of the highest mountains). This idea was odd too, even for its time.

As for the thickness of the Borrowdales, Marr (1916: 7 and 17) estimated that they were of the order of 10,000–20,000 feet, the higher figure being more likely. For while the rocks were supposedly thrown into broad folds, they were not held to be repeated by faulting (the supposed "tectonic accumulation" notwithstanding) so the apparent thickness was approximately the real one, so to speak.

Marr's structural ideas were challenged by the amateur geologist J.F.N. Green in one of the great brouhahas in the history of Lakeland geology. In 1908, Green had successfully sorted out some major geological problems in Pembrokeshire (Oldroyd, 1990), and he then turned his attention to the Lake District, starting work in the area of the Duddon Valley. Green read a paper on his Duddon work to the Geological Society on November 15, 1911, proposing a new classification for rocks of that area. He claimed that the Skiddaws passed conformably into the Volcanic Group. Further, he maintained that the succession of rocks was thrown into folds striking northeast–southwest. Green also suggested that there was an unconformity below the Coniston Limestone, not a lag-fault.

In the event, the Geological Society only published Green's paper in summary and the full version was rejected. According to the Society's archives (COM/P3/2), the referees were Harker, Marr, and William Watts of Birmingham University – a reasonable choice, given that potential Survey referees such as Bernard Smith, who had been re-surveying in southwest Lakeland, had a kind of vested interest in the issue. But so too did Marr, given his published views on Lakeland structure, with his system of lag-faults, with one at the base of the Coniston Limestone. Whether Green was offered the chance to revise his paper is not known, but in the event he withdrew his contribution and published privately (Green, 1912). The paper contained a sketch map, which is almost impossible to reconcile with any other map known to me, ancient or modern, and his hypothesis of low-angle folds with repetition of beds may have arisen from the fact that he did not achieve a precise characterisation and differentiation of the various units in the volcanic sequence. On the other hand, Green did recognise the occurrence of different lenticular sheets of andesites within the sequence; and his idea that there was a kind of transition of conditions from the Skiddaws to the Volcanics was worthwhile and has attracted later support.

Undeterred by his rebuff by the Geological Society, Green turned to the more difficult area of the eastern Lakes around Haweswater (Green, 1915). Lakeland andesites, he pointed out, frequently had a brecciated structure, attributable to the shattering of a cooling and solidifying crust on a flowing lava. So the brecciation would be expected to occur on the upper surface; but he also envisaged the possibility that it might occur more rarely in the emplacement of sills. Here he was on the right track, perhaps groping his way towards the notion of what today are called peperites, but his application of his Duddon Valley stratigraphic sequence to the eastern Lake District led to problems and errors. With broad-brush mapping, he summarily dismissed Marr's theory of lag-faults, saying that it was a "task of great difficulty to conceive the peculiar system of mixed pressures and tensions apparently required to produce lag-faults in association with a great thrust in rocks that are not behaving as viscous fluids". Rather, drawing on early ideas of Robert Harkness (1863), he supposed that the region had been thrown into a series of isoclinal folds. This meant that the overall thickness of the Borrowdales would be much less than that estimated by Marr.

The effect of all this on the history of Lakeland geology was curious. Geologists did not take up Marr's structural suggestions, and seemingly began to wonder whether Green might have been right after all about the geology of the Duddon area, even if his mapping was crude. So it was that

Green's anticlinoria theory held the field for many years, being deployed by G.H. Mitchell in the 1920's and 30's for example and only relinquished by him in the 1950's.

In his Lakeland work, Marr also gave particular attention to the effects of earth movements and glaciation on topography and scenery, considering their roles in the formation of lakes and drainage patterns. In his earlier work, he ascribed much of the topography to erosion along "shatter belts", but after visiting the Lakes with the American geologist W.M. Davis in 1907 Marr placed greater emphasis on the erosive powers of glaciers.

In the late nineteenth and early twentieth centuries British geologists such as James Geikie were endeavouring to apply the idea of multiple glaciations to British geology, according to the Continental observations of the likes of Albrecht Penck and Eduard Brückner (of Günz, Mindel, Riss, and Würm fame), and the astronomical theory of the ice ages of Geikie's Survey colleague, James Croll. From such a perspective, one might have hoped to find a series of tills and various deposits representing interglacials (Oldroyd, 1999b). But Marr could find little evidence for such sequences in the Lakeland deposits. He rightly pointed out that in the Lakeland mountains the deposits left by earlier glaciations would be likely to be obliterated by later ones. He did mention a section near Elterwater Bridge where red boulder-clay underlay a grey variety, with stratified gravels between (Marr, 1916: 194). But such a sequence cannot be seen today, as the left bank of the river near the bridge is disturbed by human habitation while the right bank is covered with slate quarry waste[7].

On the whole, then, Marr (1916: p.147) doubted the idea of multiple Lakeland glaciations. However, in a late paper (1924), he did offer some interesting evidence for at least two glacial epochs. In Church Beck, running down from Coniston Old Man to Coniston Water there is a gorge near the Miners' Bridge; and there are (according to Marr – but I have not been able to locate them) glacial striae on some of the rocks within the gorge. The beck runs down from what is evidently a hanging valley, produced in some earlier glaciation. The gorge could plausibly have been cut during an interglacial epoch; and then a later cold period had ice working within the pre-formed gorge. Interestingly, though Marr was somewhat out of step with his fellow geologists on the question of multiple glaciations in northern England, he would appear to be vindicated by recent thinking, which allows "firm and extensive evidence for only two glacial events: the Anglian and the Devensian" in the British Isles (United Kingdom Nirex Limited, 1997: 11).

Marr's other special interest was sedimentology, which he treated in a textbook of his old age: *Deposition of Sedimentary Rocks* (1929). This work gives a good idea of the stratigraphic principles being taught at Cambridge in the 1920s, under the influence of the likes of Johannes Walther and William Henry Twenhofel. Marr was at once a uniformitarian (using knowledge of present modes of deposition to understand stratigraphic problems) and a progressionist (being a Darwinian evolutionist). Different kinds of deposits, with different organic remains, were formed simultaneously in "belts", at different distances from the shore-line. So a horizontal cut through a series of sediments did not necessarily mark a time horizon. By the same token, fossils of the same kind, found at some considerable distance from one another, might well be separated in time as sedimentation proceeded oceanwards. Harking back to his old thoughts about Barrande, Marr gave special attention to the formation of deposits in isolated ocean basins. In general, he displayed a sophisticated understanding of the principles of sedimentology and stratigraphy, which he had come to understand so well after years of practical experience, much of it in the Lakes. The topic, though not one that was then specially popular, required as clear a head as that needed for studies in tectonics or petrology, which, by his own admission, Marr had found perplexing.

Marr wrote a considerable number of popular essays, lectured regularly to amateurs, and conducted excursions for them, but there is little record of his doing much other than working single-mindedly at his science. Apart from the books previously mentioned, he wrote volumes on the geography and natural history of *Westmorland* (Marr, 1909), *Cumberland* (Marr, 1910) and *North Lancashire* (Marr 1912); and textbooks on *The Scientific Study of Scenery* (Marr, 1900) and *Agricultural Geology* (Marr, 1903), the former being essentially a volume on physical geography and the latter on general geology and British stratigraphy. In his later years, as blindness came upon him, and he could no longer work up in the Lakes, he turned his attention towards prehistoric archaeology, studying the Pleistocene deposits in the neighbourhood of Cambridge; but this work lies beyond the scope of the present paper.

Marr married Amy, daughter of the late John Stubbs of Shap Wells, Westmorland, early in 1893, which explains why – according to the evidence of his field notebooks – he seemed to find it necessary to spend so much time in the Shap area in the years 1890–1892. Curiously, having proposed to Amy, he seemed to have had serious regrets about his action (Notebook XXII, July 15–20, 1891). The first night of their marriage was spent at the unromantic Midland Grand Hotel, St Pancras.

However, to the best of my knowledge the marriage was successful and Mrs Marr is recorded as acting regularly as hostess to her husband's appreciative students in Cambridge. But I would not be surprised if she found the move from the remote locality of Shap Wells to the garden parties of Cambridge quite a strain. Their son, Alleyne, who as a lad used to help his father in his Lakeland fieldwork, fought in World War I and was killed in the World War 2. Marr died of a stroke at Cambridge on 2 October, 1933.

BIBLIOGRAPHY.

MARR, J.E., 1878, On some well-defined life-zones in the lower part of the Silurian (Sedgwick) of the Lake District. *Quart. Journ. Geol. Soc.*, Vol. 34, pp 871-875.

1880, On the Cambrian (Sedgwick) and Silurian Beds of the Dee Valley as compared with those of the Lake District. *Quart. Journ. Geol. Soc.*,Vol. 5, pp 277-284.

1889, On the Superimposed Drainage of the English Lake District. *Geol. Mag.*, dec. 11, Vol 6, pp 150-155.

1890, *The Geology of the Appleby District*. In Mathews Guide Book to Appleby. 1st Edition, pp 70-72, 2nd. Edition 1891, pp 71-75.

1892, The Coniston Limestone Series. *Geol. Mag.*, dec. 111, Vol. 9, pp 97-110.

1892a, Further Remarks on the Coniston Limestone. *Geol. Mag.*, dec. 111, Vol. 9, pp 443-447.

1892b, On the Wenlock and Ludlow Strata of the Lake District. *Geol. Mag.*, dec 111, Vol. 9, pp 534-541.

1894, Notes on the Skiddaw Slates. *Geol. Mag.*, dec. 1V, Vol. 1, pp 122-130.

1894a, Physiographic Studies in Lakeland: 1 Church Beck, Coniston.*Geol. Mag.*, dec. 1V, Vol. 1, pp 489-492.

1894b, Physiographic Studies in Lakeland: Swindale. *Geol. Mag.*, dec 1V, Vol. 1, pp 539-545.

1895, Physiographic Studies in Lakeland: 111 The Rivers Caldew and Glenderamackin. *Geol. Mag.*, dec. 1V, Vol. 2, pp 299-303.

1895a, Forms of Mountains. *Natural Science*, Vol. 6, April, pp 240-243.

1895b, The Tarns of Lakeland, *Quart. Journ. Geol. Soc.*, Vol. 51, pp 35-48.

1895c, On the Lake Basins of Lakeland. *Proc. Geol. Assoc.*, Vol. 14, pp 273-286.

1896, Additional notes on the Tarns of Lakeland. *Quart. Journ. Geol. Soc.*, Vol. 52, pp 12-16.

1896a, The Waterways of E. Lakeland., *Geogr. J.*, Vol. 7, pp 602-625.

1900, Notes on the Geology of the English Lake District. *Proc. Geol. Assoc.*, Vol. 16, pp 449-483.

1900a, Long Excursion to Keswick, Monday 20th. August to Saturday 25th August, 1900. *Proc. Geol. Assoc.*, Vol. 16, pp 526-531.

1902, Exhibit of Specimens from a metamorphosed metalliferous vein in basic andesite near the Shap Granite. *Quart. Journ. Geol. Soc.* Vol. 58, pp lxxx-lxxxii.

1906, The influence of the Geological Structure of English Lakeland upon its present features. A study in Physiography. Address Anniv. Meeting Geol. Soc. *Quart. Journ. Geol. Soc.*, Vol. 62, pp lxvi-cxxviii.

1906a, On the stratigraphical relations of the Dufton Shales and the Keisley Limestone of the Cross Fell Inlier. *Geol. Mag.,* dec. V, Vol. 3, pp 481-487.

1907, On the Ashgillian Series. *Geol. Mag.,* dec. V, Vol. 4, pp 59-69.

1907 to 1908, The Geology of the Appleby District. *Proc. Geol. Assoc.,* Vol. 20, pp 129-149, 193-200.

1908, Geology and Palaeontology. *Victoria County History ; Westmorland,* 24 pp.

1909, *Westmorland,* Cambridge County Geographies, Cantab UP, 151 pp.

1910, *The Lake District and Neighbourhood; - Lower Palaeozoic Times.* Geology in the Field, Jubilee Volume of the Geologists' Association, (1858-1908), Ed. Stamford: London. Chapter XXVI, pp 624-641 – Upper Palaeozoic and Neozoic Times, Chapter XXVIII, pp 642-660.

1910a, *Cumberland,* Cambridge County Geographies, CantabUP, 169 pp.

1912, *North Lancashire,* Cambridge County Geographies, Cantab UP, 180 pp.

1913, The Lower Palaeozoic Rocks of the Cautley District. *Quart. Journ. Geol Soc.,* Vol. 69, pp 1-18.

1915, The Ashgillian Succession in the tract to the West of Coniston Lake. *Quart. Journ. Geol. Soc.,*Vol. 71, pp 189-204.

1916, *The Geology of the Lake District.* Cantab. UP, xii + 220 pp.

Reprinted by Cedric Chivers Ltd. Bath, 1968.

1924, Notes on the Glaciation of the Coniston Fells. *Geol. Mag.,* Vol. 61, pp 264-269.

1925, Conditions of deposition of the Stockdale Shales. *Quart. Journ. Geol. Soc.,* Vol. 81, pp 113-133.

1926, The Kailpot, Ullswater. *Geol. Mag.,* Vol. 63, pp 338-341.

1927, The deposition of the later Silurian rocks of the English Lake District. *Geol. Mag.,* Vol. 64, pp 494-500.

MARR, J.E., and FEARNSIDES, W.G., 1909, The Howgill Fells and their Topography. *Quart. Journ. Geol. Soc.,* Vol. 65, pp 587-610.

1910, Notes on the Lower Palaeozoic rocks of the Cautley District, Sedbergh, Yorkshire. *Rep. Brit. Assoc.,* p 603.

1910a, The Graptolite Zones of the Salopian rocks of the Cautley area, near Sedbergh, Yorkshire. *Geol. Mag.,* dec. V, Vol. 7, p 374.

MARR, J.E., and NICHOLSON, H.A., 1888, The Stockdale Shales. *Quart. Journ. Geol. Soc.,* Vol. 44, pp 654-732.

8. Alfred Harker (1859-1939)
The 'Founding Father' of
Modern Petrology
Mervyn Dodd

Fig. 20 – Alfred Harker.

Alfred Harker (Fig. 20) spent almost all his long adult life (61 years) at St John's College, Cambridge, where he arrived as an undergraduate in 1878. His first degree was in Mathematics in 1882 as the 8th Wrangler, the 8th in order of merit in the First Class Honours in Mathematics in the University, He then read for the Natural Science Tripos, specialising in Physics with Geology, which he first read as a subsidiary subject in his final year. His 'Double First' in both parts of the Tripos in 1882 and 1883 was followed by his unexpected appointment as University Demonstrator in Geology in 1884. This involved him teaching Mineralogy and Lithology, supplementing his miserable pay by coaching undergraduates, probably in Mathematics and Physics. He was elected to a Fellowship at St John's College in 1885, which position he retained until retirement in 1931. In 1904 he became a University Lecturer and in 1919 the University created for him the special post of Reader in Petrology. His interests were academic, being particularly interested in research. Thus he preferred to remain a Lecturer to give his time to scholarship rather than become an administrator or get involved in University politics. He was much more effective in lecturing to the knowledgeable and committed than in giving elementary lectures to beginners. After retirement he became Honorary Curator of the Cambridge Petrological Museum (now part of the Sedgwick Museum) much of the collection being rock slices he had provided. He was the guest of honour at a dinner organized for his 80th birthday by a group of eminent geologists. A few months later he died in Cambridge.

Harker's initial researches (1886-9) were into the volcanic rocks of Snowdonia, where his approach was mathematical with an accompanying insistence on crustal processes and relating these rocks to the regional cleavage. This was unusual then. He worked with Marr around Shap and Carrock Fell between 1889 and 1894. His study of the Shap contact aureole was an early excursion into thermal metamorphism, where he analysed the sequence of mineralogical changes (which he found to be much less than was generally thought), and drew attention to the survival of quite small scale sedimentary structures. I recently read the paper written by Harker and Marr about the Shap Granite and its metamorphic aureole, and found it to be very lucid, clearly and convincingly argued, with relevant detail, reflecting thorough fieldwork and laboratory analyses. They had written without unnecessary jargon and with an easy flow of language. It is a classic paper that remains usable today, over 100 years after publication, with its map of the Shap Granite and the rocks around still being reproduced for at least one field course. Other workers at the time found his work on the Carrock Fell gabbros and granophyre contentious. He attributed marginal variations in the gabbros to localized concentrations of the early crystallizing minerals, and thoroughly investigated mutual reactions between the gabbro and granophyre

Harker's main area of research was in the volcanic districts of Western Scotland, particularly in Skye, Rhum, Eigg and Muck. Between 1895 and 1905 he worked on a part-time basis for the Geological Survey, something previously unheard of. His skills as an expert petrologist and field geologist mapping on the 6-Inch scale, combined with his exceptional stamina, allowed him to make an outstanding contribution to the understanding of these complicated rocks. His work was published in parts of at least three of the Survey memoirs that appeared between 1900 and 1910. Some of his interpretations did not find favour with the autocratic Director of the Survey, Geikie, leading to an acrimonious and pungent correspondence. In a then unfashionable way he recognised and emphasised the erosive action of ice in the Cuillins. The Western Highlands of Scotland were his favourite region, which he visited two or three times a year, leading study parties and continuing his researches.

His output of research papers was considerable, appearing in a very wide range of learned journals and spanning the years 1886 to 1939. Harker's elementary textbook *Petrology for Students* appeared first in 1895 and its final edition was in 1935, such was its very considerable impact. More advanced texts were *The Natural History of Igneous Rocks* (1909) and *Metamorphism* (1935). These works established the claim for him to be regarded as the founding father of modern Petrology.

The world of Science recognised Harker's eminence early, electing him as a Fellow of the Royal Society in 1902. The award of a Royal Medal in 1935 was the honour he most treasured. The Geological Society of

London, of which he was President between 1916 and 1918, awarded him the Murchison Medal in 1907 and the Wollaston Medal, their highest award, in 1922. The University of Edinburgh and McGill University both gave him honorary doctorates. He was an honorary or corresponding member of many foreign scientific societies and academies but rarely attended international scientific conferences or foreign study tours. The most significant of these was his visit in 1906 to Oslo Fjord, a particularly fine source of unusual petrological specimens and a great fillip to his developing ideas on igneous petrology. He maintained a considerable interest in his native Yorkshire, serving as President of both the Yorkshire Geological Society and the Yorkshire Naturalists' Union, writing many papers for both societies.

Harker was a rather a retiring individual, often shy and diffident in company, remaining a bachelor. He had an exceptional capacity for enjoying his own company, but after retirement came out of his shell, expressing trenchantly and unexpectedly strongly held views. While he was not a man inclined to enjoy a wide circle of acquaintances he had several close friends to whom he remained loyal.

BIBLIOGRAPHY

HARKER, A., 1888, The igneous dykes of the North of England. *Naturalist,* pp 349-353.

1889, Notes on North of England rocks. *Naturalist,* p 207 and Ibid., 1890, p. 237.

1891, Cambrian and Silurian Rocks at Ewcross, Dufton and Shap. *Naturalist,* pp 63-64 (Discussion of Balderston R.R. 1890)

1891a, The ancient lavas of the Lake District. *Naturalist,* pp 145-147

1891 (with Marr, J.E.), The Shap Granite and Associated rocks. *Quart. Journ. Geol. Soc.,* Vol. 47, pp 266-328.

1892, Some North Country Quartzites. *Naturalist,* pp 73-75.

1892, The lamprophyre dykes of the North of England. *Geol Mag.,*dec. 111, Vol. 9, pp 199-206

1894, Carrock Fell. A study in the variation of igneous rock masses: Part 1. The Gabbro. *Quart. Journ. Geol. Soc.,* Vol. 50, pp 311-317.

1894a, On some variolitic rocks on Carrock Fell. *Geol. Mag.,* dec. IV, Vol 1, pp 551-553.

1895, Carrock Fell: Part II. The Carrock Fell Granophyre. Part III, The Grainsgill Greisen. *Quart. Journ. Geol. Soc.,* Vol. 51, pp 125-148.

1895a, The English Lake District. *Trans. Hull Geol. Soc.,* Vol. 2, pp 18-19.

1899, Chemical notes on the Lake District rocks. Part I, The Ordovician Volcanic Series. Part II. Intrusive and Sedimentary rocks. *Naturalist,* pp 53-58, 149-154, 156.

1902, Notes on the Igneous rocks of the English Lake District. *Proc. Yorks. Geol. Soc.,* Vol 14, pp 487-493.

1902a, List of the principal publications dealing with the petrology of the English Lake

District. *Proc. Yorks. Geol. Soc.* Vol. 14, pp 494-496.

1903, Chemical data for the rocks of the English Lake District. . *Proc. Yorks. Geol. Soc.,* Vol. 15, pp 59-69.

1906, A cordierite-bearing lava from the Lake District. *Geol. Mag.,* dec. V, Vol.3. pp 176-177.

1912, Lamprophyre Dykes of Long Sleddale, Westmorland, *Naturalist,*
pp 266-267.

HARKER, A. and MARR, J.E., 1891, The Shap Granite and Associated Rocks. *Quart. Journ. Geol. Soc.,* Vol. 47, pp 266-328.

1903, Supplementary notes on the metamorphic rocks around the Shap Granite. *Quart. Journ. Geol. Soc.,* Vol. 49, pp. 359-371.

9. Edmund Johnston Garwood (1864-1949)
Carboniferous Biostratigrapher
Murray Mitchell

Born at Bridlington, schooled at Eton and educated at Trinity College, Garwood studied geology at Cambridge as an extra subject to supplement courses in chemistry and physics. To his professor T. McKenny Hughes, he owed his introduction to fieldwork in the Ingleborough area; and with his lecturer, J.E. Marr, he formed a life-long valued friendship. It was Marr, with his vast local knowledge and scientific enthusiasm, who initiated Garwood into the geomorphology and stratigraphy of the Pennines and Lake District

After leaving Cambridge in

Fig. 21 – A pencil sketch of Garwood by Miss de Biden Footner when he was President of the Geological Society in 1931, the year of his retirement from University College London. To W.B.R. King" it was an extremely good likeness for it caught the expression with one eyebrow raised, an expression often seen when he was telling some anecdote or making a play upon words in his conversation. It also shows him as extremely neat and tidy in his dress, which was characteristic of him whether he was in London or in the country, and with this went the easy, perfect manners of a natural gentleman."

1887, Garwood followed family interests and for a few years was engaged with the Jarrow Chemical Company before becoming a Cambridge University Extension Lecturer in 1892. While resident in Northumberland, he had begun studies of the local Carboniferous. He then extended work to the collecting of fossils from the Lower Carboniferous of the Ingleborough area. This work initiated the zonal stratigraphy of the Lower Carboniferous (Dinantian). In 1895, he communicated his preliminary results before the British Association and published them in a joint paper with Marr. Following this paper, a B.A. Committee was formed to investigate Lower Carboniferous zoning, with Marr as chairman and Garwood, for a few years, as secretary. During these years, he met other workers on the Lower Carboniferous, and developed his interests in glaciation and exploration. In 1901, Garwood was appointed to the Chair of Geology at University College London, and devoted himself to the building of the department, almost from its foundation. His success in this task is a lasting memorial to his energy and commitment. From 1903, Miss Edith Goodyear became his assistant, and was to be co-author of some of his important zonal contributions.

During the short period when Garwood's interest in Carboniferous faunas was in abeyance, Vaughan (1905) published his work on Lower Carboniferous zones, which was based on the Avon Gorge section at Bristol. There were serious problems particularly with the middle ($C_1 C_2$; Chadian & Arundian) part of the Avon sequence where there is much oolitic and dolomitic rock with few, mostly non-diagnostic, fossils. This led to confusion and criticism when attempts were made to use the Avon-based zones to classify sections as close to Bristol as the Mendips. It is now known that these problems arose because the Avon section is incomplete, with important faunas not present, and was an unfortunate choice as typical section. However, Vaughan continued with his work, and with the help of many fellow workers studied sections away from Bristol. Frequent revisions and modifications were made to his zonal scheme to accommodate faunas not found at Bristol, but the principle of zoning by means of faunal assemblages was established for the Lower Carboniferous.

Garwood and Miss Goodyear, together with other students, began work again in the north and chose the Ravenstondale-Shap succession as their standard. Thousands of fossils were meticulously collected, registered and named, and many of these are now housed in the British Geological Survey Collection at Keyworth, Nottingham. Garwood was able to describe a succession of zonal assemblages within a framework of well-defined faunal bands. Provisional correlations were published in 1907, followed by full details in his classic N.W. England paper (1913) which established Garwood's geological eminence. In 1913 he was President of Section C of the British Association, and 1914 was elected to fellowship of the Royal Society.

Garwood's 1913 paper set the standard for all subsequent work on the Lower Carboniferous rocks round the Lake District, and his 1924 paper with Miss Goodyear equally became the standard for Pennine areas. Although Garwood attempted to correlate his N.W. England zonal sequence with Vaughan's (1905) Avon Gorge sequence, there were problems with detailed correlation, particularly with the middle part of the sequence. The analysis by Hudson and Dunnington (1945) was of major importance to the understanding of this confusion, with C_1 and C_2 having different meanings in the south and north of England, and they contributed greatly to our knowledge.

Four important Lower Carboniferous faunas have not been recorded from the Avon Gorge. They were described in detail by Garwood (1913) and precisely recorded in the sequence. Perhaps the most important of these faunas are those of the *Michelinia grandis* Zone from the Kendal - Arnside – Grange-over-Sands area, the descriptions of which are essential to the understanding of the Bristol sequence. The range of the distinctive brachiopod *Delepinea carinata* (Garwood) proved to be of particular significance. The details of the faunas and lithologies in the *M. grandis* Zone part of the succession are also critical to the present understanding of the stratigraphy and structure of the Carboniferous Limestone of South Cumbria.

The recognition that these northern England faunas were missing at Bristol, together with the new synthesis of regressions and transgressions in the British Dinantian by Ramsbottom (1973) were important steps leading to the erection by George and others (1976) of Regional Stages, for the correlation of British Dinantian successions. It was no coincidence that three of the six stages are based on localities in N.W. England where more complete sequences are known.

In addition, Garwood and Goodyear's 1924 (Settle) paper showed that the upper part of the Lower Carboniferous (D2 of Vaughan) is thicker, more fossiliferous and more complete in the Yoredale facies rocks of the north Pennines. This led to later work by Hill (1938) who proposed three coral zones for this part of the sequence.

After the Settle paper, his role became something of an 'elder statesman'. He was President of the Yorkshire Geological Society for 1924 and 1925, and of the Geological Society of London for 1930 and 1931. In 1931, he retired from the Chair of Geology at University College, London, and retired from active fieldwork. He then spent many happy hours arranging his collection of fossils which numbered some 85,000 specimens and reviving old memories. In 1938, the Yorkshire Geological Society celebrated its Centenary and chose Professor Garwood, their most honoured and respected member, as Centenary President.

In summary, Garwood published two major contributions on the faunal zones of the Lower Carboniferous of northern England, the N.W. England paper (1913) and the Settle paper with Miss Goodyear (1924). The value of these is two fold. Firstly, they established standards for all subsequent research into the stratigraphy of Lower Carboniferous rocks in the Lake District and N.W. England. Secondly, and perhaps of more lasting significance, the detailed descriptions of precisely located faunas were of vital importance to our present understanding of the biostratigraphy of the Lower Carboniferous (Dinantian) rocks of Britain.

The Student's Garwood

Eric Robinson

Until quite recently, on the wall of the finest small lecture theatre in the South Wing of University College London in Gower Street, hung a framed copy of a map of the Himalayan peak of Kangchenjunga and the valleys and glaciers which make the approaches a feat in itself. This map was the work of Garwood, the keen mountaineer, the photographer and a geologist seeking a satisfaction not coming from teaching the Army Class at Harrow. Quite rightly, the lecture theatre is known as the Garwood Theatre. Garwood had become the mountaineer through his frequent holidays at Cadenabbia on Lake Como where his uncle had a villa within easy reach of the challenging alpine peaks and glaciers which invited the testing of the ideas of Agassiz and Tyndall and Forbes. He naturally was a member of the Alpine Club and the National Clubs of France and Italy. In 1896, he made an epic crossing of Spitzbergen, again surveying glaciers and geology to a result that won him a Wollaston Fund from the Geological Society. In 1899, in the Himalayas, he was official photographer to the expedition to Kangchenjunga before his map-making achievement already mentioned. Torrential rainfall during that work gave him first-hand experience of the eroding powers of flood waters and an awareness of the combined roles of glaciers and rivers in shaping of the Himalayan landscape, views he presented to the Geological and Geographical Societies at the turn of the century.

It was at this point that he was invited to take the Yates-Goldsmid Chair at University College, a chair vacant on the retirement of Professor

T.G. Bonney. When he left Cambridge in 1887, Garwood had hoped to join the Geological Survey, then Directed by Sir Archibald Geikie. At that time, the call of the family business, The Jarrow Chemical Company, had taken priority over what might have been a very successful pathway in geology. In 1901, however, Garwood was backed for the post at UCL by one of the shortest testimonials ever from Geikie. He wrote quite simply 'Garwood's your man" and the appointment was made. The department he inherited was poorly equipped and run down. His predecessor Bonney had always had his eye on retirement to St John's College, Cambridge and latterly spent less and less time in London. Garwood set about fund raising by lecture tours and writing, all the money used to have museum cabinets and show cases of finest mahogany made at his own expense.

Predictably, Garwood's teaching involved a strong element of field-work, setting precedent which is still maintained, and this was how the mapping of the Carboniferous of the North West Province was undertaken. It was Garwood-led but student powered. Easter and Summer Mapping Classes were based at Arnside, Kendal and Coniston, and faced with the familiar successions, punctuated by distinct fossil 'bands' and lithological markers, students were sent out to trace their continuity in much the same way that archaeological parties complete field walking in search of human debris. The definitive fossils were collected in quantity, given a preliminary trimming, and then taken back to Gower Street to be housed in those specially made cabinets organised as the *Michelinia grandis* collection from Grange, Arnside, Meathop and all the separate geographical subregions of the 'Province'. As has been mentioned by Murray Mitchell, Garwood saw shortcomings in the zonation set up by Vaughan in the Bristol region and without a direct refutation, preferred to amass the evidence of fossil assemblage which was easy to acquire in the country of the south Lake District. This took him closer to the sound appreciation of faunal facies shown by Dixon and Sibly in South Wales than the use of the familiar KZCSD zones of Vaughan. In this field work the student participation was a voluntary effort, actually figuring in the aims and objectives of the student Geological Society, The Greenough Club, whose motto was 'Fun, Fieldwork and Fitness' with the rider 'to help Professor Garwood with the mapping of the Carboniferous of Northern England' (Fig. 21).

Garwood's lectures were popular even if long (one hour often became two), probably helped by his extensive use of his own photographs converted into plate-sized slides. Right up to the 1960's the bank of wooden drawers housing these large glass slides formed a central core and meeting place to the Department in the South Wing. In 1903 he recruited Miss Edith Goodyear to be his main assistant in teaching and administration, joined by her friend Miss Longstaff, both ladies being active in Carboniferous palaeontology. With Miss Goodyear he (and the student classes) completed the mapping of Ingleborough after the first world war and using Burlap and Plaster of Paris, constructed the three-dimensional model of the Craven Fells which was copied in many departments including the Survey Museum in Exhibition Road. The fruitful years for Garwood have to be the Edwardian years when he was prominent in links with world geology for the Geological Society and The British Association. He was also involved in an early attempt to set up a National Photographic Record for British Geology on the strength of his own work which was on a par with that of Godfrey Bingley and Welsh. In the Italian Campaign of 1917, his advice as an Alpine climber and geologist were invaluable in plotting the strategy for the fighting against Austrian positions in the Tirol, just as the work of his eventual successor at UCL, W.B.R. King, were proving on the Western Front.

His teaching and research in the late 1920's and early 1930's took him back to the Lake District, often through the work of research assistants who he drew to him by his personality and the prospect of that new Degree, the PhD borrowed from the German Universities. One, Kenneth Earle, mapped most of the limestone outcrop round the northern Lake District. Others worked on the igneous rocks, or fossils. The team included MacGregor, Helen Muir-Wood, Kirkaldy and Doris Reynolds, but when the work extended to the Bewcastle area, apart from the new status for calcareous algae, the model that had worked so well for the North West Province (including the Lake District) began to break down in the unruly conditions of the Northumberland Trough.

At that point in time, 1931, he retired to be succeeded by W.B.R. King, very much a Cambridge don with extensive First World War experience as a Western Front geologist advising upon the water supply problems faced in the trenches. With Miss Goodyear now accustomed to running the Department, he maintained the Garwood tradition of fieldwork parties in the Lake District, only moving downwards into the Lower Palaeozoic of Ashgill and the Cross Fell Inlier and substitution of trilobites for brachiopods and corals. The Greenough Club celebrated with 'Trilobite Teas', musical evenings and pantomimes, all of which were Garwood habits responding to a very close-knit staff-student life which the cello-playing Old Prof sustained right through to the Second World war when King was called back into military service. After all, Miss Goodyear was still influencing things from retirement and Leonard Chubb was running fieldwork in the north. When Garwood died in 1949, it was only a short break before the appointment of Sidney Hollingworth with his Lake

District background. At that point I joined the Gower Street Department, still built around those mahogany cabinets housing the wealth of North west Province fossils even after most of the designated types and several representative collections had been presented to the Geological Survey and the Natural History Museum. I didn't need that framed map of Kangchenjunga to remind me of the Garwood Tradition, but that was strangely sustained in the Hollingworth years.

BIBLIOGRAPHY.

GARWOOD, E.J. 1907, Notes on the faunal succession in the Carboniferous Limestone of Westmorland and the neighbouring portions of Lancashire and Yorkshire. Geol. Mag., dec. 1, Vol. 4, pp 70-74 and in *Rept. Brit. Assoc.Trans. Sects.,* 1906 p 564.

1910, On the horizon of Lower Carboniferous Beds containing *Archaeosigillaria Vanuxemi (Goppart)* at Meathop Fell. *Geol. Mag.,* dec. V, Vol. 7, pp 117-119.

1912, The Lower Carboniferous Succession in the North-West of England. *Quart. Journ. Geol. Soc.* Vol. 68, pp 449-586.

1914, Some new rock-building organisms from the Lower Carboniferous Beds of Westmorland. *Geol. Mag.,* dec. VI, Vol 1, pp 265-271.

1916, The faunal succession of the Lower Carboniferous rocks of Westmorland and North Lancashire. *Proc. Geol. Assoc.* Vol. 27. pp 1-43.

The Survey Geologists

Without doubt 'The Survey' can rightly claim to be one of the oldest national geological organisations anywhere in the world. The existence of the Geological Survey of Great Britain can be traced back to at least 1835 when the first appointment of a geologist was made. Even before that date the geological branch of its better-known parent, the Ordnance Survey was active. Today , BGS, BRITISH GEOLOG-ICAL SURVEY, is the official National organization responsible for all geological matters under the wing of the National Environment Research Council.

The Survey only started to turn its attention to the Lake District towards the end of the 1860's. Changes in the organization around that time led in particular to great increases in the number of staff available, the number of 'surveyors' for example virtually doubling between 1867 and 1868. Apart from the need to move towards a complete geological survey of the country, a particular spur to activity was the completion of the new six-inch to one-mile scale topographical survey maps of the Lake District by the Ordnance Survey. As a result, field geologists were dispatched to the Lakes to complete the task of systematically mapping the ground and producing complete geological surveys of the district. Initially W.T. Aveline, T. McKenny Hughes and R.H. Tiddeman were sent to look at the eastern and southern parts of the area and the Furness peninsula. In 1869 James Clifton Ward was sent to Keswick to examine the Northern Lakes District. Ward is the first of the Survey men to be described in this volume. Much remains of Ward's legacy. Here was one of the first professional geologists to devote time to the district, to examine the rocks and landscape in a systematic way and, most importantly for Keswick and the Northern Lakes, to popularize the subject in the local community. Ward proved to be an indefatigable exponent of the science of geology in the district.

Following those early days, Survey geologists have continued to work on the area, constantly re-examining the rocks and geological resources, producing new maps and new interpretations of the geology. The work of four other 'Survey Men' – J.G. Goodchild, F.M.Trotter, Bernard Smith, and Tom Eastwood working in the first part of the Twentieth Century feature next in our review. They are but a sample of the many people who have contributed to the Survey's work over what is approaching 150 years in

Fig. 22 – Oddfellows Hall, Queen Street, Whitehaven (taken at the time of its demolition). The location of the Regional Office of the Geological Survey 1921-26.

the area. All, however, were very significant figures as the accounts reveal. An extremely important landmark in Survey activity in Cumbria was the decision after the First World War to establish a Regional Office in Whitehaven in November 1920. Along with Manchester, Newcastle and York, Whitehaven was chosen as one of four new regional centres with particular responsibility to speed up the revision of the maps of the English coalfields. Within the Survey this was not a universally popular decision, many staff did not relish such a transfer to the provinces – at the time it is clear Whitehaven was not high on many peoples list of desirable postings. Fortunately, as the accounts reveal, Bernard Smith was the man chosen to head up the Cumberland Unit in Whitehaven, an outstanding man and a person who did regard Lakeland and West Cumbria as 'desirable'. The Whitehaven Office was established first in the Oddfellows Hall, in Queen Street (now demolished) (Fig. 22), but was moved to St Nicholas Chambers in Church Street in 1926 (Fig. 23). The importance of this Office for Cumbrian geology was extremely significant. Not only did it focus a deal of professional attention on to the geology of the Coalfield and to the

Fig. 23 – St. Nicholas Chambers, Church Street, Whitehaven – location of the Regional Offices 1926-27.

haematite and other economic resources, it raised the profile of geology in the whole area and community. The office became a focal point for local people with geological interests, inspiring several people to take up the subject and become involved – notably Charles Edmonds – one of the amateur pioneers featured in the last section of this book. The profession-al staff lived locally and several became involved with local groups, giving

Fig. 24 – Staff of the regional Office of the Survey in Whitehaven in 1927.
Back row (from left to right) Tom Eastwood, Kidd, S.E. Hollingworth.
Front row (seated left to right) F.M. Trotter, Bernard Smith, E.E.L. Dixon.
(Photograph courtesy of the British Geological Survey)

talks and leading excursions. Fig. 24 is a studio portrait of the six staff at the Whitehaven Office in 1927.

The Whitehaven Office closed late in 1927. Bernard Smith continued to supervise the unit from the London Headquarters of the Survey, but most of the staff stayed in the district continuing to work on the mapping of the north of the County. Tom Eastwood took charge of the group in 1930. Since those days Survey geologists have continued to work in the County right up to the present day, but they have had no permanent base here. All Survey work in Cumbria is now controlled from the BGS base in Edinburgh.

Finally in this section on the Survey geologists, we come to more recent times with a review of the work of G.H. Mitchell. He worked on the Lake District from the mid 1920's up until 1970, during which time he became an acknowledged authority on the Borrowdale Volcanic Group in particular. His contribution to Cumbrian geology was extremely significant; even more remarkable, knowing the unique way it was achieved.

10. James Clifton Ward (1843-1880)
An Early 'Populariser' of Geology
Alan Smith

Clifton Ward's association with geology in Cumbria was rather like his life as a whole; short but active and influential. In barely ten years he had completed the first mapping of the Keswick area for the Geological Survey, written the accompanying Memoir, published 22 papers on the district, become a pillar of the scientific community in the County, changed profession and moved (Fig. 25).

He was born on the 13th April 1843 at Clapham in South London, the son of James Ward, a schoolmaster. It appears his health was always delicate and, as a result, he was sent to school at Hastings. The bracing air of the Sussex coast did not improve his health and for a

Fig. 25 – James Clifton Ward (Photograph courtesy of the British Geological Survey)

long time he was taken out of school and given free rein for an outdoor life on the Sussex Downs. He learnt very early in life the joys of observing natural history. He came back to London in 1861 and entered the Royal School of Mines, gaining the Edward Forbes Medal in 1864. Ill health continued to trouble him and consequently he never graduated, but was granted the Associateship of the Royal School of Mines. In 1865, at the age of 22 he was appointed to the Geological Survey and was sent to the West Riding of Yorkshire where he worked on the Millstone Grit and the Lower Carboniferous. In 1868 he was transferred to the Lake District and was based in Keswick. It was there that his life as a professional geologist blossomed.

His task for the Survey in Keswick was to carry out the first professional mapping of the area (Quarter Sheet 101 SE), covering over 200 square miles of the northern Lake District. It stretched from Ennerdale in the west, to Ullswater in the east and included the high fells from Great

Gable and Helvellyn to Skiddaw and Blencathra. It seems clear Ward did this single-handedly. Although he was 'under the superintendence' of the District Surveyor W.T. Aveline, examination of the field slips still in the BGS archives reveal the work was Ward's alone. (D. Oldroyd : Personal Communication). His map published at one inch to one mile scale in December 1875, and the Memoir *The Geology of the Northern part of the English Lake District* published in June 1876 remained the only official Survey work on the area for 123 years.

Ward's map bears comparison with the new re-surveyed map which BGS published late in 1999 (Keswick Sheet 29 at 1:50,000 scale). In very few areas is the pattern of outcrops at odds. Ward's interpretation of the Castle Head intrusion south of Keswick, the eastern margins of the Threlkeld microgranite, the size of the Skiddaw Granite exposure in Sinen Gill and some of the minor dykes in the Skiddaw Group outcrop are very slightly different from the modern sheet. Modern work on the Crummock Water Metamorphic Aureole at the southern end of Mellbreak has led to a different interpretation of the outcrop pattern there. Nevertheless the broad outlines of the surface outcrops, the complex junction line between the Skiddaw Group and the Borrowdale Volcanic Group, and the Devonian and Carboniferous margins remain as Ward drew them a century and a quarter ago.

However, Ward's interpretation of the major rock groups and the structural geology did differ considerably from present day thinking. Given the level of geological knowledge at the time, for a man still in his late 20's and with relatively little geological experience his descriptions of what he saw were very accurate and the questions he posed highly perceptive. Interpreting the Skiddaw Group posed problems for him, as in fact it has done for geologists ever since. He saw they were structurally very complex, but the series of sketch sections drawn in the Memoir paint a simpler picture than we now know is the case. He did not subdivide them, but went into considerable detail on their alteration by lateral pressure, action of igneous rocks beneath, alteration close to quartz veins and the numerous exposed igneous intrusions. He estimated their thickness as between 10,000 and 12,000 feet, and suggested they originated in marine conditions ("in a more or less shallow sea") with a probable proximity to land. He appeared uncomfortable with the palaeontology, only fleetingly referring to the "scant remains of life forms". The final chapter of the Memoir produces a list of known fossils and locations (largely based on the work of Nicholson) and there is an appendix by R. Etheridge describing the new finds.

Ward paid more attention to the volcanic rocks. It was he who first described them as "the Volcanic Series of Borrowdale". His training in petrology and the influence of H. C. Sorby is very evident in the Memoir, which is one of the first to use thin section slides in the text. He subdivides the Series into nine units, which are difficult to equate precisely with modern views. However, his descriptions of many of the lavas and pyroclastics remain clear today. His travels to Vesuvius and other volcanic sites in Italy had clearly been a seminal experience with which he drew parallels with the Lakeland rocks. He was convinced that Castle Head just south of Keswick was an important vent - relating many of the sequences (including the Eycotts) to eruptions from this source. He interpreted the sequences as possibly of sub-marine origin in the very early stages but obviously sub-aerial for most of the period.

On the relationship between the Skiddaw Group and the overlying volcanics, he was convinced that everywhere the junction was a faulted one. In terms of dating he placed the Skiddaw Group in the Cambrian and equated them with the Manx Slates. The volcanics he suggested were Tremadoc and Arenig in age.

Of equal interest to Ward was the glacial history and the relationships between the scenery and the geology. Almost a quarter of the Memoir is devoted to these topics. Much of the material is primarily descriptive, but he clearly appreciated the great differences between the various rock types and their response to the forces of weathering and erosion. He was intrigued with what he calls 'transported and perched blocks', and with the location of glacial striae. The Memoir is still the most detailed catalogue of erratics and striae alignments in the district. Ward did not, however, subscribe to the new theories of land-based ice that were being propounded at the time to explain glacial phenomena. Instead he retained the view of glacial-submergence theory, invoking subsidence beneath the sea after a period of intense cold, the district gradually being converted into an archipelago with powerful currents circulating among the islands. When depression had gone on to the amount of 1000 feet or less, the cold returned and ice rafts bore blocks from one part to another. These were very much the views propounded by A. C. Ramsay at the time and perhaps significantly the line taken by all the Survey geologists at this period.

Ward's field note books in the Survey archives at Keyworth give a fascinating insight into the man, his approach to fieldwork and of the way he conducted his work. It is clear he conversed with local people a great deal. This is particularly seen in his very detailed notes on the non ferrous mines of the district; he records detailed information from a Mr. Crosthwaite and a Captain Francis. The books contain large numbers of field sketches – some merely aide memoirs in pencil, others very neat, precise pen and ink sketches. He seems to have liked to put his thoughts on paper – laying out his analysis of problems, giving the theoretical background and field evidence for his opinions. Most interesting of all is his propensity to write in poetry, often expressing a deep religious outlook on things and an almost mythical philosophy. A classic example is three pages of verse running to 19 stanzas which are recorded simply as 'after-noon walk – 9/8/71 '. Quoting just one typical stanza of this-

The flowers that by the wayside grow
The insect, bird and creeping things,
Wood, rock and everlasting hills
All glory to their God do bring.

– it is clear that underpinning all his thoughts were deep religious convictions.

Apart from his work for the Survey, Ward was also a prolific writer and lecturer, not just on geological topics. During his short stay in Yorkshire before coming to Keswick he produced an elementary school book on Physics. During his Keswick years he repeated a similar exercise for Geology, the text being essentially nine talks he first delivered to school-children and as public lectures in Keswick. Between 1870 and 1879 he published 22 papers in a variety of scientific and geological journals, all essentially stemming from his Survey work and developing his ideas on Lakeland rocks and landscape. Around half of these papers related to glacial phenomena (see bibliography).

The character and dynamism of the man is best exemplified by his contributions to popularise science, and geology in particular, in Keswick and Lakeland society of the day. Close to his time of arrival in the north-ern Lake District the Keswick Literary Society had been founded. His name was not on the original list of members in 1869 but in the second session in 1870 he gave a lecture on 'The Geological History of Italy'. From that point on his name appears frequently in the Society Minutes. By 1872 he had proposed the Society should become 'The Keswick Literary and Scientific Society' which it eventually did in 1874, with James Clifton Ward its President in 1874, 1875 and 1876. The Society still exists as 'The Keswick Lecture Society' and has currently just completed its 131st Season. Ward's name appeared frequently in the list of speakers and it is remarkable the range of topics he was able to speak upon, apart from the geological ones. In 1874 he spoke on 'The Ear, its structure and Development', in 1876 on 'Electrochemical Decomposition' and 'Some Analogies between Sound and Light – experimentally illustrated', and then in 1877 on 'The Life of Faraday '.

In 1873 Ward was instrumental in forming a Committee to set up a local Museum in Keswick, which came to fruition with Ward naturally being responsible for the rock and mineral collections. This too still exists and contains many of Ward's original specimens, as well as some of the physical models of the district made by Ward to illustrate his Survey work.

In June 1873 he instigated geological field trips into the local area and the press reports in the West Cumberland Times of the day make fascinating reading of Ward's irrepressible leadership in the field. They paint evocative pictures of Victorian life – 170 people to Borrowdale in 1873 where 'the grass fields of the Howe at Rosthwaite provided a convenient auditorium for Mr Ward to describe The Geological History of Borrowdale'. In 1874 on a trip to Greenside Mine, Glenridding, he led a large section of the party first over Sticks Pass on foot where 'the inquisitive hammer was in constant requisition to enquire within'. Or, in 1875 'Mr J.C. Ward took twenty men and nine women in three waggonettes to Seathwaite and on foot "by easy stages" to the summit of Sca Fell Pike. There were still large patches of snow and ice in Piers Ghyll and, needless to say, Mr Ward took the opportunity of making remarks at suitable places upon the geological features of the district'.

One of Ward's most valuable contributions to scientific life was the setting up of 'The Cumberland and Westmorland Association for the Advancement of Literature and Science' in 1875. This was done at Ward's instigation. He became its first Secretary and Editor in 1875 and continued to hold both offices until 1879 when the Editorship was taken over by another geologist, J. G. Goodchild. The published Transactions of the Society became a significant record of local scientific research for many years. Unfortunately it has not survived.

Ward's work with the Survey in Keswick was completed in 1876 with the publication of the Memoir. For a short time he was transferred to the Carlisle area and worked around the Bewcastle district. There is some indication that his health was not good in 1876-7 and that he was seeking a less physically exhausting job than a field geologist. Throughout his life he had held deep religious beliefs. The next biographical record of him was his ordination into the Church of England at Carlisle Cathedral in 1878. He gave up his position with the Survey in 1877 and became assistant curate at St John's in Keswick. In 1880 he was appointed Perpetual Curate at Rydal in south Lakeland. Within a few weeks of taking up the post he caught a chill and died on the 16th April at the age of 37.

Tributes to him were lavish. The Cumberland and Westmorland Association raised money to mount a tablet to his memory, with £300 surplus money going to assist with the education of his two young daughters. Fittingly he is buried at St John's, Keswick where the memorial plaque in the church reveals his contribution to geology and life in Keswick.

Canon Rawnsley, an eminent Keswick figure and later to be one of the founders of The National Trust wrote a sonnet to his honour for his funeral. This was a fitting tribute to an indefatigable man.

'The Geologist's Funeral'

Bury him here, and let his body's dust
Be ash to ash in this volcanic land
Whose fiery secrets he could understand
Right well may we his dissolution trust
To that same Will that through the lava crust
Spouted the granite fountains God ! whose hand
Of this earth's waste new continents hath planned,
Into thy potter's clay a gem we thrust.
No more his feet we follow up the cleft,
Or hear his questioning hammer tap and ring,
And learn which way the primal bergs were rolled;
But, till the Greta ceases sorrowing,
We leave him here, contented to be left,
Schooled in a lore whose days are aeons old.

BIBLIOGRAPHY

WARD, J.C., 1870, On the Denudation of the Lake District. *Geol. Mag.*, dec. 1, Vol. 7, pp 14-17.

1870a, Ice: a lecture delivered before the *Keswick Literary Society*, 8vo Trubner & Co. 27pp

1871, The Development of Land. *Geol. Mag*, dec. 1, Vol. 8, pp 11-15.

1873, Scenery of the Lake District Geologically considered. *Science Gossip*, Vol, 9, 121-128 and in 2oth *Annual Rep. Brighton & Sussex Nat. Hist.* Soc. p. 39.

1873a, On Rock Fissuring. *Geol. Mag.*, dec. 1, Vol. 10, pp 245-248.

1873b, Glaciation of the Northern part of the Lake District. *Quart. Journ. Geol. Soc.*, Vol. 29, pp 422-441.

1873c, On Block Rock Surfaces. *Geol. Mag.*, dec. 1, Vol. 10, p. 384. (Correspondence).

1874, On the Old Glaciers of Cumberland. 21st. *Annual Rep. Brighton & Sussex Nat. Hist. Soc.* p. 37.

1874a, On the Origin of some of the Lake Basins of Cumberland. *Quart. Journ. Geol. Soc.*, Vol. 30, pp 96-104.

1875, Modern Vulcanicity. *Geol. Mag.*, dec. 11, Vol. 2, pp 38-41.

1875a, A Voice from the Past. (Correspondence). *Geol. Mag.*, dec. 11, Vol. 2, pp 285-286.

1875b, Ice Phenomena in the Lake District. *Nature*, Vol. 11 No. 271, pp 309-310.

1875c, The Glaciation of the Southern Part of the Lake District and the Glacial origin of the Lakes of Cumberland and Westmorland. *Quart. Journ. Geol. Soc.*, Vol. 31, pp 152-166.

1875d, Notes on the Comparative Microscopic Rock Structure of some ancient and modern volcanic rocks. *Quart. Journ. Geol. Soc.*, Vol. 31 pp 388-422 (Lake District, pp 405-418).

1875e, On the Granite, Granitoid and associated metamorphic rocks of the Lake District, Parts 1-11, *Quart. Journ. Geol. Soc.*, Vol. 31, pp 568-602, Parts 111-V, *Quart. Journ. Geol. Soc.*, Vol. 32, pp 1-34.

1875-76, Sketch of the Geological History of the Lake District. *Trans. Cumb. & West. Assoc. Adv. Sci. & Lit.*, Pt. 1, pp 59-64.

1876, *The Geology of the Northern Part of the English Lake District.* Mem. Geol. Surv., 12 + 132 pp.

1876a, Absence of Llandovery Rocks in the Lake District. *Geol. Mag.*, Vol. 3. p. 383.

1876-77, Remarkable Boulders of the Keswick District. *Trans. Cumb. & West. Assoc. Adv. Sci. & Lit.* Pt 11, pp 71-75.

1877, On the Lower Silurian Lavas of Eycott Hill, Cumberland. *Monthly Micro. Journ.*, Vol. 17, pp 239-246.

1877a, Jonathon Otley, the geologist and guide. *Trans. Cumb. & West. Assoc. Adv. Sci & Lit.*, Pt 11, pp 125-169.

1877-78, Quartz, as it occurs in the Lake District, its Structure and its History. *Trans. Cumb. & West. Assoc. Adv. Sci. & Lit.*, Pt 11, pp 77-90.

1879, On the Physical History of the English Lake District, with Notes on the possible subdivisions of the Skiddaw Slates. *Geol. Mag.*, dec 11 , Vol. 6. pp 49-61, and pp 110-125.

DAKYNS, J.R. and WARD, J.C., 1875, Volcanic Rocks of the Lake Country. (Letter). *Geol. Mag.* Dec. 11. Vol. 2, p 95.

11. John Goodchild (1844-1906) and Frederick Trotter (1897-1968)
Pioneering Workers on the Glaciation of Cumbria
Angus Lunn

The lives of John Goodchild (1844-1906) and Frederick Trotter (1897-1968) together spanned more than a century. Each produced a major classic paper on the glaciation of respectively the southeastern and northeastern parts of Cumbria, with Trotter building upon and extending geographically the work of Goodchild. Between them – exploiting their good luck in the number of distinctive lithologies incorporated in glacial deposits – they established broad ice-flow patterns for the last glaciation. Inevitably, however, in a region such as this of great topographical complexity, and receiving ice flows of temporally varying strength from several adjacent

Fig. 26 – J. G. Goodchild , March 1875.
(Photograph courtesy of the British Geological Survey)

upland areas, there remain even now many unanswered questions in this regard. Goodchild was himself extending the glaciation work of Tiddeman (1872) in north Lancashire. While some of Goodchild's and Trotter's interpretations of Quaternary events and processes would not now be accepted, including the latter's account of deglaciation in northeast Cumbria, the two men were responsible for an enormous body of original observations on glacial features. Both, also, had diverse interests in other fields of geology, Trotter particularly in economic geology. Their careers followed similar paths, as career-long officers of the Geological Survey.

John George Goodchild (Fig. 26) was born in east London, and although apprenticed as an engineer was attracted to geology partly by being present at the discovery of Quaternary mammals in Kent brickyards. Following private study, he was appointed to the Geological Survey in 1867. His first posting was to Westmorland as an assistant to Professor McKenny Hughes in mapping work, but unfortunately his enthusiasm for hill-climbing had an adverse and enduring effect on his health. such that his field career lasted only sixteen years. During his time in Cumbria he became involved with the Cumberland and Westmorland Association for the Advancement of Literature and Science, whose Transactions he edited, and with Carlisle Museum, for which he obtained its main geological collection (the Harkness Collection). Such extra-mural professional activity was a feature of his life.

In 1883 he was transferred to the London headquarters to help with the production of maps and memoirs. In London he became deeply involved in adult education for disadvantaged members of society, through the new Toynbee Hall Universities' Settlement in Whitechapel. Here he was also able to develop an earlier interest in (non-geological) natural history. In 1889 he was appointed as Curator with the Scottish Geological Survey

Fig. 27 – The small country church yard of St. Cuthbert's, Milburn in the Eden Valley where Goodchild is buried.

Fig. 28 – Row of the Goodchild family graves at Milburn. John's headstone (at the extreme left) is a simple boulder of Shap Granite inscribed only with his initials and dates.

based in the Edinburgh Museum of Science and Art, where he specialised in mineralogy. From Edinburgh too, he continued lecturing to the public and leading excursions widely through southern Scotland. He was buried at Milburn in Westmorland (Figs. 27 and 28).

Goodchild's extensive publication list (some 200 papers) includes contributions not only on glacial geology but also on the New Red

Sandstone, igneous rocks and mineralogy (he discovered wulfenite at Caldbeck and wrote a three-part description of Cumbrian minerals) and geological time. His best known publication, however, is his 1875 paper on the Glacial phenomena of the Eden valley and the western part of the Yorkshire-dale district, based both upon official survey work and what he described as "holiday rambles". Later he published a summary (Ice work in Edenside, etc.) of his Cumbrian glacial work (Goodchild, 1887).

In the 1875 paper he presented evidence confirming the flow of land-ice from the Vale of Eden through the Tyne Gap and over Stainmore. The latter ice-stream had originally been suggested by Buckland (1840) on the basis of the distribution of Shap granite erratics, but since then submergence and iceberg drift had become fashionable as explanations of glacial phenomena. Then Croll (1871) and Tiddeman (1872) published evidence for the existence of land-ice in the region, and Goodchild in turn was able to demonstrate that the transport of Permian Brockram uphill towards Stainmore could not be explained other than by the flow of land-ice.

He mapped striae, and boulder and drift limits, over a wide area and drew in, on the coloured map accompanying his paper, an inferred main ice divide. He showed that, at some stage, southwest Scottish ice (as well as local ice) had flowed up the Eden valley and over Stainmore. Apparent anomalies in flow patterns in the Vale of Eden led him to advance the idea of "cross glaciation" or "undercurrents" (layers of ice within the same sheet flowing in different directions), and later (1887) "circulatory flow". Nowadays such ideas are glaciologically unacceptable, and shifting divides are called in aid. He accepted the existence of local ice caps in the Pennines, but considered glaciation of the highest ground unlikely.

Goodchild advanced an entirely original theory on the origin of much of the drifts and was one of the first to recognise their complexity. The theory was based largely on numerous figured sections, some through drumlins, along the line of the Settle & Carlisle Railway that was then under construction. He suggested that the drifts were emplaced by what would now be called melt-out – the rapid release of abundant englacial debris from a stagnant ice sheet. In this way complexly interstratified tills and water-laid sediments were deposited, the latter by powerful subglacial streams. Otherwise puzzling steeply inclined or contorted laminated clays were also deposited subglacially. Debris had become englacial as a result of layering within the ice sheet, with tributary ice streams flowing over trunk streams, so presaging Carruthers' (1953) controversial ideas, and also through the thrusting up of basal debris. The lowest tills, however, were moraine profonde (now lodgement till). He also identified ice-contact meltwater deposits in the Vale of Eden. His interpretation of the drifts was based partly on clast shape and clast fabric, and it is remarkable how many modern techniques and interpretations feature in Goodchild's work, and how many of his conclusions are either accepted today (for example final ice stagnation in some circumstances), or remain actively debated.

Goodchild also tackled glacial erosion, and advocated a glacial erosional origin for cirques and also, with close argument in his 1887 paper, for the characteristic benching of dale-sides in the Pennines. He argued that not only could glacier ice deepen valleys, it could also make them shallower by "grinding down" intervening ridges. He was an early advocate of glacio-isostasy, and presciently suggested that switches in ocean currents were involved in climate change. He recognised from local evidence a final limited phase of glaciation (our Loch Lomond Advance).

Away from glaciation, Goodchild advanced radical ideas on the origin of dykes by replacement, related to alkaline solutions soaking downwards from the sea, and he also considered that volcanic action was related to seawater penetration. He recognised that the New Red Sandstone, with its evaporites, was deposited in a desert environment, as were other red sandstones. A notable insight was that the local haematite ores in the Carboniferous were due to the leaching (he thought by meteoric waters) of iron from the overlying red rocks followed by metasomatic precipitation. And Goodchild particularly addressed himself to the age of the earth. Noting how little topographic change had occurred in the Lake District since the end of glaciation, he placed deglaciation at 12,000 to 20,000 years ago, a pretty good estimate for his time. He also estimated 42 million years for the duration of the Cambrian period, based on calculated sedimentation rates; this is remarkably close to the duration based on radiometric dates.

Virtually all of Goodchild's official mapping work was in Cumbria and adjacent parts of Yorkshire, and he co-authored the Appleby, Ullswater and Haweswater memoir (1897). He received the Wollaston Fund in 1874.

Outside of geology he published papers on feather structure in bird classification (with his own meticulous illustrations), on the relationship between ants and flowers, on the depth-distribution of corals, on museum methods, on the Helm Wind, on Japanese clocks (an interest from his early engineering days) and on dialect, place-names and archaeology.

As an obituarist fairly put it (Gregory, 1909), "he was a walking note of interrogation". Goodchild was shrewd, original almost to the point of heresy, somewhat dogmatic, had an extraordinarily wide range of interests, and a keen desire to share his knowledge and enthusiasms with a wider audience. While some of his ideas on glaciation have proved very wide of the mark, others were spot on.

Frederick Murray Trotter (Fig 29) was born in Gateshead and was a graduate (interrupted by war service) of Armstrong College, Newcastle (later the University of Newcastle). He joined the Royal Engineers, and, as a dispatch rider, lost an eye from shrapnel at Vimy. (So ended a promising footballing career). After a short spell of teaching, Trotter joined the Geological Survey in 1921, later becoming District Geologist, north-west England and, in 1955, Assistant Director. He retired in 1963. His early field career was spent in Cumbria under Bernard Smith, where he worked in the east (the Vale of Eden and the North Pennines), the north (the Carlisle plain)

Fig. 29 – Frederick Trotter.
(Photograph courtesy of the British Geological Survey)

and the west (the Gosforth district), being co-responsible for the Carlisle, Longtown and Silloth, Brampton (1932a), Gosforth and Cockermouth and Caldbeck memoirs and 1" maps; he also contributed to the 3rd edition of the Northern England Regional Memoir (1953). Much of his work was in collaboration with Professor S.E. Hollingworth, who was a life-long friend. After 1933 Trotter worked in the Forest of Dean (near to which he retired) and South Wales before returning to the north-west.

He published his classic paper on The Glaciation of Eastern Edenside, the Alston Block and the Carlisle Plain in 1929 (1929a). This deliberately complemented Hollingworth's (1931) paper on western Edenside. Apart from his work on glaciation, Trotter was interested in denudation history and contributed a then influential paper on the denudation chronology of the Alston block (1929b). He argued that the radial pattern of the North Pennine dales was the result of late-Tertiary doming of a peneplain. Such interpretations, once popular, are now considered to be based upon rather little evidence.

His detailed account and interpretations of the glacial phenomena of eastern Edenside, etc. were, like those of Goodchild, based both upon his official survey work and unofficial work during vacations in the 1920s. The results were published in the 1929 paper and in the Brampton memoir. He established drift and boulder limits, based on hundreds of clast lithological analyses, and on drumlin (including rock drumlin) orientations – thus extending northwards Goodchild's equivalent observations. He recognised a "Cross Fell escarpment drift", and considered that it was emplaced by short glaciers occupying escarpment valleys and also, at the glacial maximum, by ice draining through these valleys from higher ground above. Although some escarpment valleys were shaped by these glaciers, others, without their own glaciers, retained a preglacial V-shape. Cold Fell, at the northern end of the escarpment, must have nourished its own ice cap judging by the erratic 'shadow' on it and to its east. Like Goodchild, Trotter considered that the ice flowed in different directions at different levels within the ice sheet. Also like Goodchild, he thought that small nunataks may have existed in the North Pennines at the glacial maximum – a possibility even now not ruled out for the last glaciation.

Trotter gave particular attention to deglaciation, where the model he used was that of Kendall (1902), invoking lakes dammed against a continuously retreating ice front and draining largely through overflow channels. Eskers, kames, ice-contact deltas and fans, fed by englacial streams and retaining essentially their original form, were deposited at the ice margin and provided evidence of its successive positions. Land streams also constructed deltas in the glacial lakes. A map depicts no less than 24 detailed ice-front retreat positions ("halt-stages"), based on supposed ice-frontal deposits, glacier lakes and their overflow channels (he mapped about 200 of the latter), as the ice sheet withdrew from the Pennines to source areas in the Lake District and south-west Scotland. This model of deglaciation is now largely superseded; most channels are now regarded as having formed subglacially and many of the Lakes were inferred on flimsy evidence. Rather, somewhat as Goodchild had suggested, the ice sheet may finally have stagnated in situ over a wide marginal zone (Huddart, 1991; Huddart, Tooley & Carter, 1977). The spectacular moundy deposits mapped by Trotter are now regarded as having formed in a variety of subglacial, ice-marginal fluvial and lacustrine environments amidst and against this stagnant ice. However, Trotter's observations, particularly in his "Brampton kame-belt", are an invaluable body of data, and some lakes undoubtedly did exist, both in proglacial and ice-walled environments (Huddart, Tooley & Carter, 1977).

Trotter recognised that on the basis of the extent of meltwater deposits in the Tyne Gap, a huge volume of meltwater must have drained from a vast glacial catchment area eastwards through this lowest col on the main

British watershed between Derbyshire and central Scotland. He considered that after the ice had withdrawn west of the col at Gilsland, a Lake Eden was impounded between the ice and the watershed, although the evidence for this is not convincing.

Detailed mapping also led Trotter to the view that there had been a "Scottish Readvance" glaciation after the main ice sheet had retreated, across the Solway and advancing as far inland as Brampton (although later reconstructions are more restrictive: Huddart, 1991). The evidence took the form of an upper till, which overlay both "Middle Sands" and glacio-lacustrine deposits associated with the main retreat. He also mapped Scottish Readvance retreat stages. The existence, and status, of such a readvance remains a live issue.

Trotter (1929a) and Trotter & Hollingworth (1932b), suggested tele-correlations of the glacial events recognised in Cumbria, always a fraught business.

Much of Trotter's work was in economic geology. As regards the haematite ores he considered magmatic, not Goodchild's meteoric, waters to be responsible for ore genesis. Later, Rose & Dunham (1977) suggested that hypersaline fluids driven up from the Irish Sea basin leached the New Red Sandstone to produce the ores, so combining elements of both Goodchild's and Trotter's ideas. Trotter also worked on coal rank, including on the genesis of the low-volatile semi-anthracites of the Alston block, and on the relationship between mine gases and pneumoconiosis.

He was awarded the Geological Society of London's Murchison Medal in 1956, and his glacial work gained him his DSc.

Trotter – The Economic Geologist

Mervyn Dodd

Angus Lunn in the preceding section has written about Trotter's work in deciphering the sequence of glacial events in the Vale of Eden and the Alston Block. This short additional contribution looks at other aspects of Trotter's career complementing Angus Lunn's appreciation.

Trotter's first posting in his Survey career was to the Cumberland Unit based in Whitehaven, beginning his fieldwork in the Carlisle area. Bernard Smith, then in charge of the Unit thought highly of Trotter who satisfied his demanding standards of accuracy of detail. S.E. Hollingworth and Trotter were the gifted junior members of the Survey team in Cumberland, beginning their long and fruitful academic partnership then. While working in Cumberland Trotter became interested in glacial geology and in the iron ore deposits, but above all, in coalfield geology, which eventually became the centerpiece of his geological career. He produced an interpretation of the coalfield geology of the Cumberland field then regarded as most unlikely, but as Bernard Smith pointed out in correspondence, borehole data proved him to be correct. Even then he was happy to work with those who needed to use geological information, as with the management of the Workington Iron & Steel Company and the Bekermet Mining Company, discussing borehole data on site on the concealed ore field south of Egremont.

In the 1937 Gosforth District Memoir Trotter described the distribution of iron ores in the region, showing clearly they were absent where St Bees Shales lay between the surface and the underlying Dinantian Limestones (host rocks for the ore bodies). This observation is still regarded as very important. His 1945 paper, researched in his leave time, not as part of his official work, showed several changes in his ideas. He regarded the ore as magmatic in origin, coming from Lower Palaeozoic rocks directly underlying the New Red Sandstones, a view held , in part at least, by some more recent workers. The brockrams were regarded as the conduit whereby the ore reached the limestones, not generally accepted now. Thus there were no ore bodies where brockrams were absent. The age of the ores he thought was post-Triassic, still a generally held opinion.

In the mid 1930's Trotter was responsible for the primary mapping of the coal and iron ore deposits in the Forest of Dean. This was followed in the Second World War by work in the Ammanford area of the South Wales coalfield – essentially revision mapping, with the help of a local enthusiast of the calibre of Charles Edmonds. This became the basis for his ideas of how coal ranks developed. His earlier paper (1948) arguing the devolatization of the coals in that area was due to an underlying thrust plane was particularly controversial at the time. His 1950 paper established the general theory how ascending coal ranks were generated, initially by dewatering the peat with volatiles being driven off later by increasing heat and tectonic activity. He also wrote about the relationship between pneumoconiosis and the escape of mine gases.

As Area geologist (NW), 1947-55, based on Manchester, he was responsible for four coalfields, continuing to research their stratigraphy. He insisted that economic geology was almost as important as pure geology and that a balance between the two must be struck, thus making economic geology accepted and respectable part of the subject. Relevant data was readily made available to mining, quarrying and engineering groups as a matter of course. During that period he published an important paper distinguishing between primary and secondary reddening of

Carboniferous rocks in North West England, a continuation of some of his earlier field work in Cumbria. While President of the Manchester Geological Society he delivered a remarkably lucid and convincing paper on Namurian stratigraphy of Northern England. One of his great strengths was his ability to present an argument clearly in easily readable prose containing only as many technical terms as absolutely essential to support his ideas.

His last position with the Geological Survey was as Assistant Director (England and Wales) between 1955 and 1962. Day to day administrative matters increasingly occupied his time, but he was regarded as a safe pair of hands, who consolidated and enhanced the reputation of the Survey at home and abroad. One particular task of his was to oversee the United Kingdom contribution to the Tectonic Map of Europe and to the provision of accurate maps of coal and iron resources as part of the same general remit.

Like so many Survey geologists he was active in the academic geological societies. He was awarded the Lyell Fund and Murchison Medal of the Geological Society of London. When the Liverpool and Manchester Geological Societies were combining their publications as the Geological Journal, he was the Manchester Society's President, making certain they had a Presidential Address of real academic quality in the midst of the turmoil of administrative change. Twice President of the Yorkshire Geological Society, he was awarded the Sorby Medal but was too ill to travel from his retirement home in The Forest of Dean to receive it in person. Only a few months before he died he sent a long written contribution to a Yorkshire Geological Society discussion on the influence of the Archaean basement on the stratigraphy of Northern England.

Trotter had lost an eye in the First World War in a life threatening wound and thereafter wore an eye patch. His first marriage was rather difficult as his wife suffered many long illnesses which put much pressure on him. He seems to have had a very happy second marriage, especially after his retirement to the Forest Of Dean. However, Trotter was not regarded as an easy person with whom to work. His own ideas and theories were presented enthusiastically and forcefully, but he was often scathing in his criticisms of individuals with whom he disagreed. Apparently this was, in part at least, a façade, a means of assessing the evidence and fieldwork of those who held different opinions. He was extremely good at training young recruits to the Geological Survey, some of whom spoke with appreciation of his loyal support. If he accepted a person's worth nothing was too much to do for them. His loyalty to the Geological Survey was wholehearted and unswerving.

BIBLIOGRAPHIES.

GOODCHILD, J.G., 1874, Note on the Carboniferous Conglomerates of the eastern part of the basin of the Eden. *Quart. Journ. Geol. Soc.* Vol. 30, pp 394-400.

1874a, On Drift (Wasdale striation, p 502), *Geol. Mag.*, dec. 11, Vol. 1, pp 496-520.

1875, Glacial Erosion, *Geol. Mag.*, dec. 11, Vol. 2, pp 323-328, 356-362.

1875a, On the origin of Coums. *Geol. Mag.*, dec. 11, Vol. 2, pp 486- 497.

1875b, Wulfenite at Caldbeck Fell (Correspondence).*Geol. Mag.*, dec. 11, Vol. 2, pp 565-566.

1875c, The Glacial phenomena of the Eden valley and the western part of the Yorkshire Dales District.*Quart. Journ. Geol. Soc.*, Vol. 31, pp 55-99.

1881, The physical history of Greystoke Park and the valley of the Petteril. *Trans. Cumb. & West. Assoc. Adv. Lit & Sci.*, No. 13, (1887-1888), pp 89-104. (Reprinted from the Penrith Observer, 9th August, 1881).

1882, Contributions towards a list of minerals occurring in Cumberland and Westmorland. *Trans. Cumb. & West. Assoc. Adv. Lit. & Sci.*, No. 7, pp 101-126. Addenda p. 178. Pt 11, Ibid, No. 8, pp 189-204. Concluding part, Ibid, No. 9, pp 175-199.

1882a, On the Geological evidence of the former extension of coal measures over Edenside. *Trans. Cumb. & West. Assoc. Adv. Lit. & Sci.*, No. 7, pp 163-177.

1883, Professor Robert Harkness. *Trans. Cumb. & West. Assoc. Adv. Lit & Sci.*, No. 8, pp 145-188.

1883a, Pyrrhotite. *Trans. Cumb. & West. Assoc. Adv. Lot. & Sci.*, No. 8, pp 214-215.

1884, The Penrith Sandstone. *Trans. Cumb. & West. Assoc. Adv. Lit. & Sci.*, No. 9, pp 31-51.

1884a, *Geology of the Kirkby Stephen District.* In J.W. Braithwaite, 'Guide to Kirkby Stephen, Appleby, Brough, Warcop, Ravenstonedale, Mallerstang, etc ', pp 100-116.

1885, Observations on the stratigraphical relations of the Skiddaw Slates. *Proc. Geol. Assoc.* Vol. 9. pp 469-481.

1887, Ice work in Edenside and some adjoining parts of North west England. *Trans. Cumb. & West. Assoc. Adv. Lit. & Sci.*, No. 12, pp 111-167.

1888, The Old Lakes of Edenside. *Trans. Cumb. & West. Assoc. Adv. Lit. & Sci.*, No. 13, pp 105-113.

1889, The History of the Eden and some rivers adjacent. *Trans. Cumb. & West. Assoc. Adv. Lit. & Sci.*, No. 14, pp 73-93. (Based on original address, 'An Outline of the history of the River Eden' given to the Carlisle Society, August 1880).

1889a, An outline of the geological history of the Eden Valley or Edenside. *Proc. Geol. Assoc.*, Vol. 11, pp 258-284.

1901, Notes on some of the limestones of Cumberland and Westmorland. *Trans. Cumb. & West. Assoc. Adv. Lit. & Sci.*, No. 16, pp 125-138.

1892, Observations on the New red Series of Cumberland and Westmorland with especial reference to classification. *Trans. Cumb. & West. Assoc. Adv. Lit. & Sci.*, No. 17, pp 1-24.

1892a, Notes on the Coniston Limestone Series. *Geol. Mag.* Dec. 111, Vol. 9, pp 295-299.

1892b, The Coniston Limestone Series (letter). *Geol. Mag.*, dec. 111, Vol. 9, pp 526-527.

1892c, The St Bees Sandstone and its Associated Rocks. *Rep. Brit. Assoc.* Sect. C, pp 722-723.

1892d, The St Bees Sandstone and its Associated Rocks (Note). *Geol. Mag.*, dec.111, Vol. 9, pp 564-565.

TROTTER, F.M., 1929, The glaciation of Eastern Edenside, the Alston Block and the Carlisle Plain. *Quart. Journ. Geol. Soc.*, Vol. 85, pp 549-612.

1929a, The Tertiary uplift and resultant drainage pattern of the Alston Block and adjacent areas. *Proc. Yorks. Geol. Soc.*, Vol. 21, pp 161-180.

1939, Reddened Carboniferous Beds in the Carlisle Basin and Edendale. *Geol. Mag.*, Vol. 76, pp 408-416.

1944, The age of the ore deposits of the Lake District and the Alston Block. *Geol. Mag.*, Vol. 81, pp 223-229.

1945, The origin of the West Cumberland Haematites. *Geol. Mag.*, Vol. 82, pp 67-80.

1952, Sedimentation of the Namurian of North-West England and adjoining areas. *Liverpool & Manchester Geol. Journ.* Vol. 1, pp 77-112.

1952a, The West Cumberland Haematites. *Congress Geol. Int. Symposium sur le fer.*, Chapter V, pp 427-431.

1953, The Cumberland Coalfield, in Trueman, A.E., *The Coalfields of Great Britain*. Ed. Arnold, London. P 314.

TROTTER, F.M. and K.C. DUNHAM, 1952, Genesis of the West Coast Haematite Deposits. *Congress Geol. Int. Symposium sur le fer,* Chapter V11, pp 435-438.

TROTTER, F.M., and S.E. HOLLINGWORTH, 1927 On the Upper Limestone Group and 'Millstone Grit' of North-East Cumberland. *Summary of Progress Geol. Surv.,* (for 1926), pp 98-107.

1928, The Alston Block. *Geol. Mag.*, Vol. 65, pp 433-448.

1932, *The Geology of the Brampton District*. Mem. Geol. Surv., xviii + 223 pp.

1932a, The glacial sequence in the North of England. *Geol. Mag.*, Vol. 69, pp 374-380.

12. Bernard Smith (1881-1936)
An Accomplished Man
Alan Smith

Fig. 30 – Bernard Smith

Bernard Smith was both an outstanding geologist and an extremely effective and influential officer of the Geological Survey. His research record alone is impressive. His work spanned many geological fields with major contributions not only to Cumbria, but also to the Midlands and North Wales. He worked for the Survey for 30 years, progressively working his way to the very top, becoming its Director in 1935. It seems without doubt that his premature death in 1936 cut short a career that would have gone on to even greater heights and achievements (Fig. 30).

Smith was born on 13th February 1881 in Grantham, Lincolnshire. He was educated at King Henry V1's School in Grantham from where he gained a Scholarship to Sidney Sussex College, Cambridge in 1900. His academic record at Cambridge was exemplary, gaining First Class Honours in both parts of the Natural Science Tripos, He was a prominent member of the Sedgwick Club, the activities of which for many years played an important part in the early training of geologists of the Cambridge School. He spent much of his leisure time rowing, his diminutive stature making him the ideal candidate for cox in the Sydney boat. After graduating, he stayed on in Cambridge for two years, researching, demonstrating in the Sedgwick Museum and lecturing to University Extension Courses in East Anglia and London. In 1906 he was awarded the much prized Harkness Scholarship.

His first published geological papers stem from these early Cambridge days. In 1905 the *Geological Magazine* published his paper 'On a Lepidodendroid Stem from the Coal Measures'. Its interest lies in the fact that it contained one of his magnificently detailed fossil drawings. He had developed this skill producing exhibits for class demonstrations. This particular drawing of a specimen from the British Museum had proved to

The Nettle-Crags Channel, looking northwards.

The Damkirk Channel, Damkirk Bottom, looking northwards, with the delta of Old Close Gill in the right foreground.

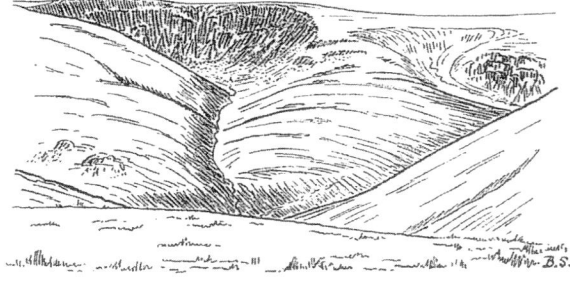

The Black Combe hanging valley and corrie, looking westwards.

Fig. 31 – A group of Bernard Smith's field sketches, all neatly initialed at bottom right hand corner.

be a hitherto unrecorded type. His ability to draw specimens and to produce beautiful field sketches and detailed maps was a feature of many of his later papers (Fig. 31 illustrates some Cumbrian examples of his work). His second paper published in 1906 resulted from a summer field trip to the Lake District with R.H. Rastall, a fellow Cambridge geologist. Again this paper is illustrated with original field sketches and maps and records the beginning of his lifelong interest in the physiography of the Lake District. It examined 'The Tarns on the Haystacks Mountain, Buttermere' and is very much in the mould of J.E. Marr – one of his tutors at Cambridge. It explored the problem of whether these mountain top tarns lay in glacially excavated rock basins.

Smith joined the Geological Survey in 1906 and spent the first four years mapping the drift deposits and Triassic sequences in Nottinghamshire. He produced original work on the sedimentation of the Triassic and made some precise records of underground water supplies in the area. In 1910 he was transferred to Denbighshire and tackled some complex geology and tectonics in the Ordovician of the area. Interestingly, it was while he was still in Denbighshire that his first Cumbrian physio-graphical paper – 'The Glaciation of the Black Combe District' was published. He spent most of his vacations in the Lake District and this long and detailed paper was the result of his own leisure time observations, when he invariably resorted to his abiding passion for Lake District physiography. It records the glacial features of the area, focusing in partic-ular on the then fairly new ideas of elaborate sequences of meltwater channels and deglaciation features. It is profusely illustrated with 12 of his own field sketches, 4 of his own photographs and 4 very detailed maps. While in today's terms his interpretations can be challenged, at the time it represented the first study of its kind in Cumbria and is a landmark paper in the study of Lakeland physiography.

It was during this period of his life that he suffered from his first spell of ill health. He had nervous problems which took him away from field work. He married in 1912 to Miss May Ferguson, a nurse who had helped him through his illness. Following his marriage, he resumed his mapping in the Wrexham and Oswestry areas of Denbighshire. During the years of the First World War however, he was diverted towards work on securing reliable information on mineral resources. This resulted in important publi-cations on gypsum and anhydrite, ganister, silica rock and fire clays and significantly for Cumbrian geology, work on the haematite deposits. He had access to mining records and developed strong links with mineral owners, mining engineers and ironmasters, in which he showed his admin-istrative abilities and his skill of dealing with people tactfully. His work on the haematite convinced him that the mode of emplacement of these ores was by descending surface waters from the overlying Triassic, a view that was by no means popular and one he had to defend very strongly.

The Survey was reorganized after the First World War and a priority was the intensive revision of the geology of the country's coalfields. Smith was promoted to District Geologist and was appointed head of the new Cumberland Coalfield District Unit. Reputedly, much to his great delight, he was dispatched with Tom Eastwood, to set up the new local office in Whitehaven in November 1920. Initially, contact had to be established with local coal, iron and other mining interests and a systematic collection of borehole data and mining records started. The mass of information to be examined proved to be voluminous and the lateral variation of the Cumbrian Coal Measures so unpredictable that mapping progress was slower than expected. With a district team of five or six geologists, including, T. Eastwood. E.E.L. Dixon, L.H. Tonks, S.E. Hollingworth and F.M. Trotter, Smith was responsible for a group that re-mapped the coalfield area and extended mapping eastwards on to the Silloth, Cockermouth, Carlisle, Brampton and Longtown areas. Under Smith's strong and effective supervision the Cumberland team produced an impressive amount of map, memoir and published data on the west and north of Cumbria. He clearly adopted a 'hands on' approach, frequently accompanying his officers on their fieldwork. 13 of his own field books still exist in the Survey archives and they reveal his own meticulous field-work standards, his drawing ability in his maps and sections, and his precision over detailed observations. Interestingly his early field books were particularly verbose and very wide ranging in their recording of detail. The material included data on settlement locations, churches, landforms, pre history and history, as well as the geological information. He was a hard taskmaster, being prepared to be critical of his officers; correspondence remains for example of his dissatisfaction with E.E.L. Dixon in particular, who caused him irritation because of his indecisiveness, poor organisation and his failure to meet deadlines. Smith was also politically very astute. He realized that he needed to be acceptable to both miners and the mine owners. He carefully avoided becoming embroiled in the long running disputes between the Whitehaven Colliery Co. and the Harbour Commissioners over problems in Whitehaven Harbour in the 1920's. The Whitehaven Harbour bar was of disputed origin. The Harbour Commissioners claimed it was predominantly colliery waste, whereas the Colliery Company insisted it was a natural feature produced by longshore drifting. He also was very aware of the local gloom that followed the Wellington Pit Disaster in 1922 and later of the problems with the 1926 coal strike in the district. In all of this he came out well and demonstrated his outstanding managerial and organisational abilities.

Smith lived in west Cumbria for seven years during which, apart from his official duties, he continued to pursue his personal geological interests. A series of papers on the Cumberland haematite and on borings for coal in the district were published. In the spring of 1923, during a field meeting of the Sedgwick Club, along with T.C. Nicholas, he rediscovered the welded junction demonstrating the unconformable base of the Coniston Limestone near Torver. In July 1924, along with his Survey colleagues he conducted the Long Excursion for the Geologists' Association for which 'A Sketch of the Geology of Whitehaven' was written. Work was also published on the stratigraphy of the Permian and Triassic rocks of the area. All the time his interests in physiography and Quaternary deposits had been maturing. Much of his work and ideas appear in the official Survey memoirs and publications – notably his work on 'The origin of the St Bees – Whitehaven Gap 'and his paper' On borings through the Glacial Drifts of the Northern Plain of the Isle of Man'. His major paper on 'The Glacial Lakes of Eskdale, Miterdale and Wasdale, Cumberland, and the Retreat of the ice during the Main Glaciation', however was very much the crystallization of many years of personal observations. It followed on from his 1912 work on the Black Combe area, but extended the ideas of ice sheet oscillation, containment of pro-glacial lakes and the cutting of sequences of channels by overflowing meltwaters into a wider area of western Lakeland.

In the same year he contributed an essay on 'The Building of the Lake District' to W.G. Collingwood's very popular book 'The Lake Counties'. Even during this busy period Smith also continued to publish material on Denbighshire and N.E. Wales, work going back to his earlier Survey days.

The Survey took the decision to close the Whitehaven Office in November 1927. Compilation of mining records was complete, but work on the mapping of the Maryport, Brampton and Cockermouth areas had to continue and be supervised from the Jermyn Street Headquarters of the Survey in London. Smith moved his family to Hove on the Sussex coast and thereafter commuted daily into the Survey Headquarters in London. He continued in charge of the Cumberland district for two more years until in 1930 he was moved to be in charge of the West Midlands District. Tom Eastwood was then promoted to be in charge of the Cumberland operation.

In 1931 Smith's talents as an administrator and manager were recognized when he was appointed Assistant Director of the Survey on the retirement of J.A. Hume. This was a demanding time for the senior officers of the

Survey. A move to new headquarters in Exhibition Road was in process. Smith was left to supervise all the field activities, and the production of maps and memoirs for the whole of England and Wales. It was Smith, who during this period was also responsible for the new series of 'Regional Guides', prepared to present authoritative popular regional accounts. These were to accompany the new displays in the new museum in Exhibition Road. Interestingly he was not able to shed his Cumberland responsibilities, correspondence still exists of the continual political pressure he was under from West Cumberland politicians to instigate a re-survey of the haematite reserves of the County to help economic regeneration.

At the same time Smith spent much time on new work and publications on water supply in Britain – a critical problem for the country after several years of low rainfall in the early 1930's. He acted as an advisor to various Government Departments, spoke to the British Association on the problem, delivered lectures to the Royal Society of Arts and wrote some of his last papers on the topic. The new Headquarters of the Survey were duly opened by HRH The Duke of York in July 1935 and marked the culmination of the work of Sir John Fleck, Director of the Survey. He retired in September 1935 and was succeeded by Bernard Smith.

Unfortunately Smith had only 8 months in this high office. He was on a tour of Scotland examining the work of his field officers when a dormant inoperable growth developed. He died from a stroke shortly afterwards in a Hove nursing home on 19th August 1936. Smith's time as Director of the Survey was too short lived to have made great changes. L.J. Wills writing in 1936 wrote " those who new him well, predicted a brilliant Directorship as an outcome of a thorough scientific outlook, deep knowledge and proven organizing capacity". The legacy he left to Cumbrian geology alone was very substantial, but a mere fragment of his total contribution.

Above and beyond all his official duties as a Survey geologist and his interest in Lake District physiography, Smith must also be remembered as an educationalist. From his early days in Cambridge and throughout his career, wherever he was based – the Midlands, West Cumbria, North Wales, London and Hove, he was active in giving well illustrated lectures to local audiences and leading local field excursions. He wrote 'Physical Geography for Schools' in 1910, second and third editions following in 1916 and 1931. In this he brought together English examples of landforms and geological features and he used the book with school and adult classes. For more than 25 years he was an Examiner in Physical Geography for the Cambridge Local Examinations Syndicate, through which he had a profound influence on the scope of physical geography teaching in schools Smith also examined for the Civil Service Examinations, acted as an external examiner in various universities from 1920 to 1936 and an examiner for the Natural Science Tripos in Cambridge. In a relatively short life he accomplished a great deal.

BIBLIOGRAPHY.

SMITH, B., 1912, Glaciation of the Black Combe District, Cumberland. *Quart. Journ. Geol. Soc.* Vol. 68, pp 402-448.

1919, *Iron-ores: Haematites of West Cumberland, Lancashire and the Lake District.* Special Reports on the Mineral resources of Great Britain. Mem. Geol. Surv. Vol.8, iv + 182 pp.

1920, On a boring for coal at Brayton Domain Colliery, Cumberland. *Summary cf Progress Geol. Surv.* (for 1919) pp 50-56.

1921, On borings for coal near Maryport, Cumberland.*Summary of Progress Geol. Surv.,* (for 1920), pp 85-91.

1924, The Unconformable Base of the Coniston Limestone Series in the Lake District. *Geol. Mag.,* vol. 61, pp 163-167.

1924a, On the West Cumberland Brockram and its Associated Rocks. *Geol. Mag.,* vol. 61. pp 289-308.

1924b, *The Haematites of West Cumberland, Lancashire and the Lake District.* Mem. Geol. Surv., 2nd Edit., vi + 236 pp.

1925, Cumberland District. (Whitehaven and Brampton Sheets), *Summary of Progress Geol. Surv.* (for 1924), pp 70-80.

1926, Cumberland District (Whitehaven, Maryport and Brampton Sheets), *Summary of Progress Geol. Surv.* (for 1925), pp 72-85.

1927, Cumberland District (Whitehaven Sheet), *Summary of Progress Geol. Surv.* (for 1926), pp 51-54.

1929, Cumbrian District (Maryport Sheet 18, Brampton Sheet 23 and Cockermouth area), *Summary of Progress Geol. Surv.* (for 1928), pt. 1, pp 68-71.

1930, Cumbrian District (Cockermouth Sheet 23), *Summary of Progress Geol. Surv.,* pp 63-66.

1930a, On the origin of the St Bees-Whitehaven Gap. *Summary of Progress Geol. Surv.* (for 1929), pt 111, pp 37-41.

1932, Glacier lakes of Eskdale, Miterdale and Wasdale, Cumberland : and the retreat of the ice during the Main Glaciation. *Quart. Journ. Geol. Soc.* Vol. 88, pp 57-83.

1932a, The Building of the Lake District. In *The Lake Counties* by W.G. Collingwood. Frederick Warne: London. Pp 228-241.

RASTALL, R.H., and SMITH, B., 1906, Tarns on the Haystacks Mountain, Buttermere. *Geol. Mag.* Vol. 42, pp 406-412.

SMITH, B., DIXON, E.E.L., EASTWOOD, T., EDMONDS, C., and HOLLINGWORTH, S.E., 1925, A sketch of the Geology of the Whitehaven District. *Proc. Geol. Assoc.,* vol. 36, pp 37-62. Excursion to the Whitehaven District, pp 62-75.

13. Tom Eastwood (1888-1970)
An Eminent Survey Geologist in Cumberland
Mervyn Dodd

Tom Eastwood's career as a geologist spanned the two World Wars
and was interrupted by 3 years'
service in the Royal Army Medical
Corps in France, 1915-1918. He was
one of a group of eminent members
of the Geological Survey who spent
over 20 years working in Cumbria
before promotion to more senior
roles. His colleagues working in
Cumberland included Bernard
Smith, E.E.L. Dixon, 'Syd' Hollingworth and F.M.Trotter. Eastwood
was posted to what was the temporary Whitehaven office in 1920,
becoming Senior Geologist in 1922.
After the closure of the Whitehaven
office in 1927 he became District
Geologist in 1930, succeeding
Bernard Smith as leader of the
Cumberland Unit. In 1937 he became
Assistant Director (England and
Wales) of the Survey, a position he
held until his retirement in 1949
(Fig. 32).

Fig. 32 – Tom Eastwood
(Photograph courtesy of the British Geological Survey)

Eastwood, a bluff Lancastrian, was very much at ease socially and a
good raconteur. He began his service in the Geological Survey mapping
the Warwickshire and Staffordshire Coalfields, experience very helpful to
so much of his work in Cumberland. His particular strength was in
coalfield geology. Just after the end of the First World War he was involved
in the logging of exploratory boreholes searching for oil reserves in the
Staffordshire coalfields. It was then he developed his skill in drawing up
stratigraphic sequences and annotating sections, so characteristic of his
Cumberland fieldbooks.

Bernard Smith regarded him as the best of his officers working on the
geology of Cumberland. Eastwood was the officer he could spare least for
other assignments, yet the one he normally recommended when tactful,

sensitive and cautious contact with the public was essential. A particularly good example of this was his investigation of the nature and provenance of the Whitehaven Harbour bar. This was the subject of a financial disagreement between the Whitehaven Harbour Commissioners and the then Whitehaven Colliery Company. His report was very precisely written, eschewing opinions and theories, thus very carefully politically neutral. Eastwood was regularly involved on behalf of the Geological Survey in cooperation with the Ministry of Agriculture and Fisheries to produce combined Drift Geology and Soil maps. This project was eventually abandoned, but not before Eastwood produced in 1925 a Geology and Soils 6-inch map of the St John Beckermet area of West Cumbria, currently in the British Geological Survey archives at Keyworth. He attended annual Soil Survey conferences between 1925 and 1928 to represent the Geological Survey.

Eastwood's fieldbooks for the survey of Cumberland in the 1920's are amazing. A brief reconnaissance of the Borders is the only section that is not neat, meticulously drawn and remarkably precise. This must have been due to rigorous self discipline on his part as his handwriting was rather large, flowing and far from neat. The field books show his particular expertise in coalfield geology and his abiding interest in the non-ferrous mines of the Lake District. Where he was less expert he consulted with experts, for example with Charles Edmonds and Kitchen on the Carboniferous Limestone and Coal Measure fossils. Similarly he sought Carruthers' advice on interglacial and fluvioglacial deposits.

Correspondence in the British Geological Survey archives reveals very little about his life in West Cumbria or his time as leader of the Cumberland Unit. He seems to have kept quite separate his professional and private lives, throughout his career in the Geological Survey. His marriage, which took place in 1915, seems to have been very happy. His wife, who survived him, seems to have been very supportive. I am told he was quite diminutive in stature, but quite strong in character. Interestingly he was well aware of the cost/time limitations involved in mapping of the Whitehaven 1 inch sheet. We know he lived at Bellevue, Common End, Distington, near Whitehaven, at least between 1925 and 1927. This remains today rather a gracious house with finely proportioned rooms, quite a contrast to the usual indifferent accommodation officers working in the field often suffered (Fig. 33).

Eastwood was author or co-author of the Geological Survey Memoirs for the Maryport District, Whitehaven and Workington, Cockermouth and Caldbeck (delayed printing taking place in 1968), produced with the appropriate maps, largely in the 1930s and based on field work in the

Fig. 33 – Bellevue, Common Lane, Distington, the home of Tom Eastwood.

1920s. He was co-author of the British Regional Geology volume on *Northern England*. There are several papers written by him in the Summary of Progress of the Geological Survey, including discussions of the South Cumberland, Furness and Cartmel areas. He read a paper about the Lake District at the Blackpool meeting of the British Association for the Advancement of Science in 1936. While working in Cumberland he was one of the joint leaders of a weeklong excursion to West Cumberland, reported in Vol. 36, Part 1, (1925) of the *Proceedings of the Geologists Association*. In the 1930s he led a similar excursion to South Cumberland and Furness for the Yorkshire Geological Society. In 1928 his paper about the Cockermouth Lavas was the first recognition of this Carboniferous episode, rather unusual in Cumbria.

Economic Geology in general played an increasingly large part in his work, writing in 1921 *'The Lead and Zinc Ores of the Lake District'*. During the Second World War, while he was Assistant Director in charge of the economic mineral investigation of England and Wales, he initially concentrated half the available manpower of the Geological Survey on basic mapping and surveys of groundwater resources, previously a very neglected topic. This was followed by investigation by specially equipped units of the reserves of Jurassic iron ore in the Midlands, to replace the Dutch bog ore previously regarded as essential by Midland steelmasters. Assessment of non-ferrous and other strategically important mineral deposits was the next task needed to reduce wartime shortages. 1943 saw the assessment of coal resources with publication of 1 inch to 1 mile maps of the major coal seams. In the immediate post-war years he obtained funds, from the powers that be, for then almost unheard of sinking of deep exploratory boreholes for 'purely' scientific purposes. In the last few years before retirement he dealt with a wide variety of queries and problems, coastal erosion, isostatic adjustment and subsidence being some.

His skills in man management were considerable. He knew how to encourage and support, as shown in particular by Charles Edmonds' involvement with the Survey in West Cumberland and frequent visits to the Whitehaven office. Youngsters like Charles Edmonds' son (who later became an officer of the Survey) were equally welcome. He got the best out of his colleagues, on field trips to solve specific problems and in the office discussions subsequently. Wartime surveyors of Midland iron ore resources felt able to write to him about their considerable difficulties in finding accommodation realising they would get sympathy, even if he could not give practical help. He was both a good organiser and farsight-ed, able to take an overview of likely future requirements.

As Assistant Director of the Survey he followed the traditional 'carrot and stick' approach happily. He chivvied former members of the Survey to hand over to the Survey archives their field notebooks. He demanded and obtained from his officers a standard format for the text of memoirs and precision in section drawing, stratigraphic sequences etc. We read of him encouraging Frederick Trotter, who was working on the Ammanford Memoir, an area of notoriously complex coalfield geology, to make use of a local amateur with similar encyclopaedic knowledge to Charles Edmonds. He corresponded with Rose and Dunham and was keenly inter-ested in the Alston Block mining field.

Eastwood's involvement with matters geological continued after his retirement, as illustrated by his 1965 revision of *Stanford's Geological Atlas* and his work as a consulting geologist with Messrs Craelius. His interest in mining almost took on a new lease of life. We read of him giving a paper in 1958 about Lake District mines at an Institute of Mining and Metallurgy symposium, after having a furious disagreement with Frederick Trotter about access to supposedly confidential wartime reports on the Carrock mines. To the delight of many geologists of the day Eastwood prevailed. Similarly he successfully sought the right to inspect the cores and documentation of a borehole reaching the concealed coalfield below the Cotswolds. He regularly attended meetings of the Geological Society of London which awarded him their Murchison Medal. As expected he was Vice-President of the Institute of Mining and Metallurgy and served as President of the Geologists' Association.

The Cumberland Geological Society came into being long after his retirement, but his generous gift of books and maps in 1964 formed the nucleus of the Society Library. This was recognised by his election as an Honorary Life Member of the Society in that year, rather belatedly, local recognition of his services to the geology of Cumbria.

BIBLIOGRAPHY

EASTWOOD, T.,1921, *The Lead and Zinc ores of the Lake District*. Mem. Geol. Surv., Mineral Resources, No.22, iv plus 56 pp.

1928, The Cockermouth Lavas, Cumberland. A Carboniferous episode. *Summary of Progress Geol. Surv.,* (for 1927), pt. 11, pp.15-22.

1929, 'Nips' and 'rock-riders' in the West Cumberland Coalfield. *Summary of Progress Geol. Surv,* (for 1928), pt. 11, pp.115-119.

1930, *The Geology of the Maryport District*. Mem.Geol. Surv., xiii + 137 pp.

1931, Cumbria District. (Cockermouth Sheet 23). *Summary of Progress Geol. Surv.,* (for 1930), pt. 1, pp. 52-55.

1931 with DIXON, E. E. L. and HOLLINGWORTH, S. E. and SMITH, B., *The Geology of the Whitehaven and Workington District*. Mem. Geol. Surv., xvii + 304 pp.

1932, Cumbria District. (Cockermouth Sheet 23). *Summary of Progress Geol. Surv.,* (for 1931), pt. 1, pp.52-54.

1933, Cumbria District. (Cockermouth Sheet 23 and Gosforth Sheet 37). *Summary of Progress Geol. Surv.,*(for 1932), pt. 1, pp.59-64.

1935, *British Regional Geology: Northern England*. Geol. Surv., 2nd Edit., 1936, 3rd Edit., 1953, vi plus 71 pp. (with some additions by TROTTER, F.M., and ANDERSON, W.).

1936. The Lake District: Geology. Brit. Assoc Scientific Surv., for the Blackpool Meeting, 1936, pp. 130-134.

1938, South Cumberland and Furness. (Bootle, Ulverston and Barrow Sheets, 47, 48 and 58). *Summary of Progress Geol. Surv.,* (for 1937), pt. 1, pp.48-50.

1939, South Cumberland, Furness and Cartmel area. *Summary of Progress Geol. Surv.,* (for 1938), pt. 1, pp.43-47.

1959, The Lake District Mining Field in *"The Future of Non-Ferrous Mining in Great Britain and Ireland, a symposium"*. London Inst. Mining & Metallurgy, Sect. 3, Northern England and the Midlands, pp.149-174.

1968 with HOLLINGWORTH, S. E., ROSE, W.C.C. and TROTTER, F. M., *Geology of the Country around Cockermouth and Caldbeck*. Mem. Geol. Surv., x + 298 pp.

14. George Hoole Mitchell (1902-1976)
Pioneer Mapper of the Borrowdale Volcanic Group
David Millward and Jack Soper

Known affectionately to friends, colleagues and family alike as 'Mick', Dr George Hoole Mitchell (Fig 34) is best known for his contributions on the Borrowdale Volcanic Group, arguably one of the most exquisitely preserved subaerial volcanic successions in the geological record. In the year that remapping of the entire outcrop of these rocks has been completed by the British Geological Survey, it is fitting to remember Mitchell's contribution to our understanding of these complex and difficult rocks. Though he spent his working life with the Geological Survey, none of his research in the Lake District was officially for that organisa-

Fig. 34 – G.H. Mitchell
(Photograph courtesy of the British Geological Survey)

tion. Thus, his immense contribution is all the more impressive because much of it was achieved through fieldwork carried out during his annual leave.

Born in 1902, the son of a Liverpool teacher with an avid interest in landscape and geology, Mick's own interest in the Lake District developed during his childhood, when from the age of about 6 or 7 he spent most summers with the family in Little Langdale. During this time the young Mitchell developed an affection for the Lake District and its people, and also an interest in the geology that was to become a lifetime's enjoyment. Inevitably, it seems, he read geology at Liverpool University, and then embarked on a study of the Coniston Limestone in the Kentmere area (published in 1925), for which he was awarded his MSc. However, this line of research went no further, because it strayed into the influential realm of T. C. Nicholas. Instead, Mick set about tackling the volcanic rocks and the geomorphology of the eastern Lake District. He subsequently gained his

Fig. 35 – Left to right, G.H. Mitchell, T.C. Nicholas, W.B.R. King and S.E. Hollingworth. Taken on Cunswick Scar, N.W. of Kendal during the INTERNATIONAL GEOLOGICAL CONGRESS XVIII Session – Great Britain A2 Excursion N.W. England, August 1948. (Reproduced by kind permission of Murray Mitchell).

PhD at Liverpool and a Diploma of Imperial College, before becoming a demonstrator at the latter institution. On joining the Geological Survey of Great Britain in 1929, he was thus well placed to work in that organisation's Cumbria office, but following Survey tradition, he was set to map elsewhere. During a distinguished career that followed with the Survey, he became an expert on coalfields in the English Midlands and Yorkshire. Latterly, he was firstly District Geologist of the South Lowlands field unit in the Survey's Scottish Office and then its Assistant Director in charge of the Survey's work in Scotland (Fig. 35).

Mick believed that the key to the interpretation of the complex and difficult Lake District volcanic rocks lay in systematic and careful field mapping of the rocks and their structure, and in setting up a lithostratigraphical succession. This same methodology is at the heart of the recent work by the British Geological Survey and has formed the basis of other important contributions by, for example, R. L. Oliver at Scafell and

M.J. Branney in Langdale. Mitchell's six-inch field maps, archived at the British Geological Survey, Edinburgh, are meticulously detailed and a testament to the excellence and quality of his field craft. He was an astute observer; for example, he was the first to find trace fossils in volcaniclastic sandstone beds at Lum Pot, in the Lickle valley, one of only two records of macrofossils in this sequence. (Recently, these have been described and illustrated as the earliest known terrestrial arthropod tracks and trails.)

Mitchell's early interpretations of the structure of the Borrowdale Volcanic rocks were naturally coloured by current thinking, particularly the influential ideas of J. E. Marr and J. F. N. Green. For many years, Marr and his co-workers at Cambridge had disputed the earlier interpretation of W. T. Aveline and his Geological Survey colleagues that the base of what is now known as the Windermere Supergroup represents an intra-Ordovician unconformity; they regarded it as a lag-fault. Green, on the other hand, accepted the unconformable relationship and related it to NNE-trending 'pre-Bala' folding and erosion of the volcanic rocks. Mitchell's major life work involved mapping the volcanic rocks adjacent to their boundary with the overlying Coniston Limestone across the whole district from Shap to Dunnerdale, with the exception of the Langdale–Grasmere area, surveyed by J. J. Hartley. The results are recorded in a remarkable sequence of research papers in which the evolution of his ideas can be traced: Kentmere (1929), Longsleddale–Shap (1934), then westwards to Coniston (1940), Dunnerdale (1956) and finally northwards to the Seathwaite Fells (1963).

The early work established the reality of the unconformity, and his structural interpretation accepted Green's pre-Bala folds, particularly in the ground north of the Garburn Pass, west of Kentmere. It also incorporated another of Green's influential ideas, again at variance with Survey views, that the Lake District rocks were isoclinally folded and disposed in great anticlinoria and synclinoria, thus preserving low sheet-dips, with a much thinner volcanic succession than implied by the Survey view of open folding. Mitchell initially tended to map sequences of tuffs and andesite as repetitions of the same units by isoclinal folding: a good example of this is on the ridge of Shipman Knotts, east of Kentmere. It must be remembered that this work predated the general use of sedimentary structures as 'way-up' criteria. Thus in his 'middle' period Mitchell often mapped natural terminations of volcanic units as fold closures. He gradually abandoned this approach; the last example is probably the termination of the thick andesite sill that makes Dow Crag, near Coniston. The concept of NNE-trending pre-Bala folds was also abandoned, probably as a result of mapping the pre-Coniston Limestone Ulpha syncline which trends E–W. Mitchell's last map, of the Seathwaite Fells, has a very modern appearance, with a far from layer-cake stratigraphy, and the structure is dominated by block faulting with some volcanic units thinning across faults, presaging current thinking on the evolution of these rocks (Figs. 36, 37 and 38).

In his Presidential Address to the Yorkshire Geological Society (1956, p.425) Mitchell expressed a desire to go back over some of his old ground to revise the structural interpretation. Unfortunately, that opportunity did not arise, but in the address he outlined his changing thoughts on the structure of the Coniston area as a result of his work in Dunnerdale. He also recognised then the implications for the thickness of the volcanic succession. Despite the differences in interpretation, his maps have proved of great value during the systematic resurvey of the Borrowdale Volcanic Group, recently completed by the British Geological Survey.

Mick kept abreast of the developments in volcanology during his work. He recognised early on the truth of Green's view that many of the fragmental rocks are flow breccias, produced by the break-up of the solidified carapace to lava-flows during eruption, and he developed criteria for separating them from pyroclastic deposits. Later, Mick was greatly impressed by the work of the New Zealander R. L. Oliver in the Scafell area, who recognised that streaky textures in some of the silicic volcanic rocks are similar to those observed in welded tuffs from his homeland. Mick soon recognised similar textures in his field area. Thus flinty rhyolites were reinterpreted as the products of 'nuées ardentes', and the terms 'welded tuff' and 'ignimbrite' entered Lake District literature. Many other features diagnostic of pyroclastic and sedimentary deposits remained generally unrecognised in ancient successions such as the Borrowdale Volcanic Group for many years after he completed his work. It has also recently come to light that many sheets mapped as lava flows are in fact shallow sills, having considerable implications for understanding the stratigraphy.

Mitchell's publication record, for which he won many plaudits, is impressive. His honours include: the Bigsby (1947) and Murchison (1964) medals of the Geological Society of London; the Sorby Medal of the Yorkshire Geological Society (1965); the Clough Medal of the Edinburgh Geological Society (1970). He was elected FRS (1953) and FRSE (1955), and made CBE in 1967. He was a very able communicator of his science, particularly enjoying field discussions; he was Field Meetings Secretary of the Yorkshire Geological Society (1935 to 1938) and President (1955-56). As President of the Geology Section of the British Association meeting in Dublin in 1957, his subject was naturally Ordovician volcanism in the British Isles.

Why should Mitchell be considered as one of the icons of twentieth century Lake District geology? In mapping such a considerable area he

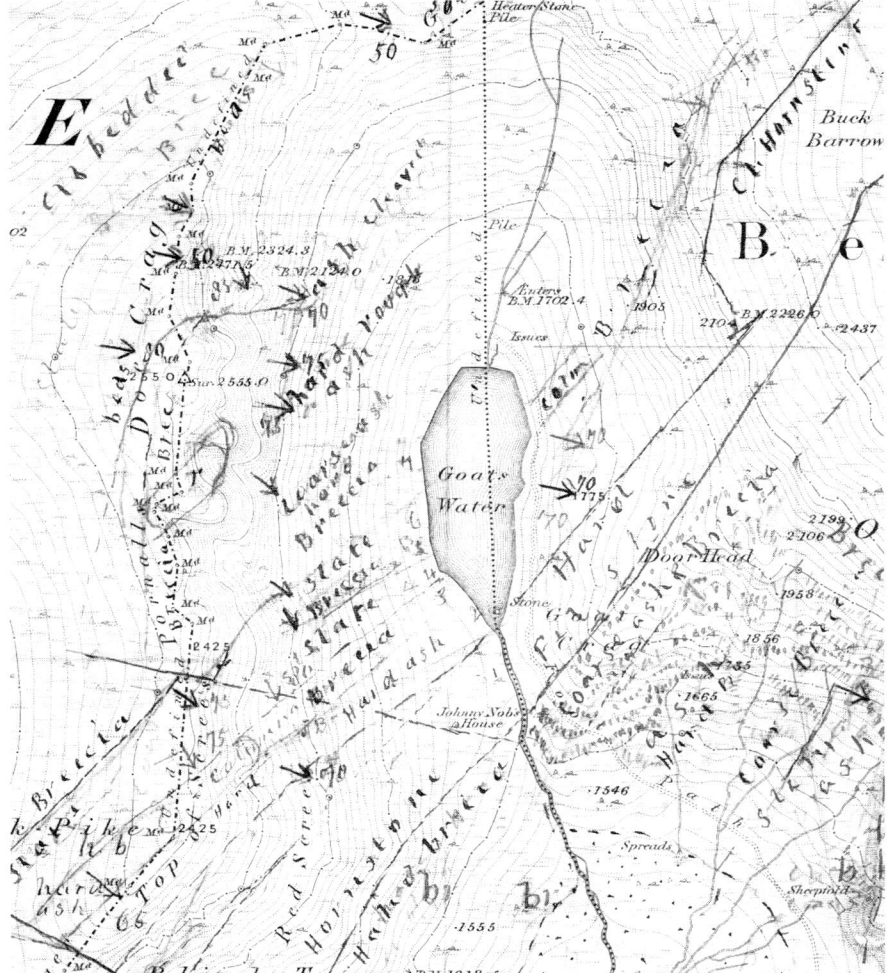

Fig. 36 – Made by W. T. Aveline pre-1882

Figs. 36. 37. and 38. Field slips of the Goat's Water area near Coniston showing the style and detail from three eras of geological mapping in the Borrowdale Volcanic Group.

Mitchell's quality field map contains abundant detail of the rocks, evidence of dip and dip direction of the strata, and careful linework. Comparison of the maps shows little difference in the ground interpretation of the outcrops of the main units, particularly the Paddy End 'Rhyolite'. Note in particular the shape of the north-eastern limit of the steeply dipping andesite sheet that forms the main rock face of Dow Crag, immediately to the west of Goat's Water. The andesite outcrop is surrounded by well bedded volcaniclastic rocks (interbedded tuff, lapilli-tuff and sandstone). Neither map shows evidence of the direction of younging.

It is remarkable that radically different interpretations of the structure of the area have arisen from essentially the same data collected. Mitchell 1940 interpreted the north-eastward termination of the andesite as the closure of an isoclinal fold, although later he altered this interpretation after mapping in the Dunnerdale and Seathwaite Fells. By contrast the recent Survey interpretation is that it is the termination of an andesite sill.

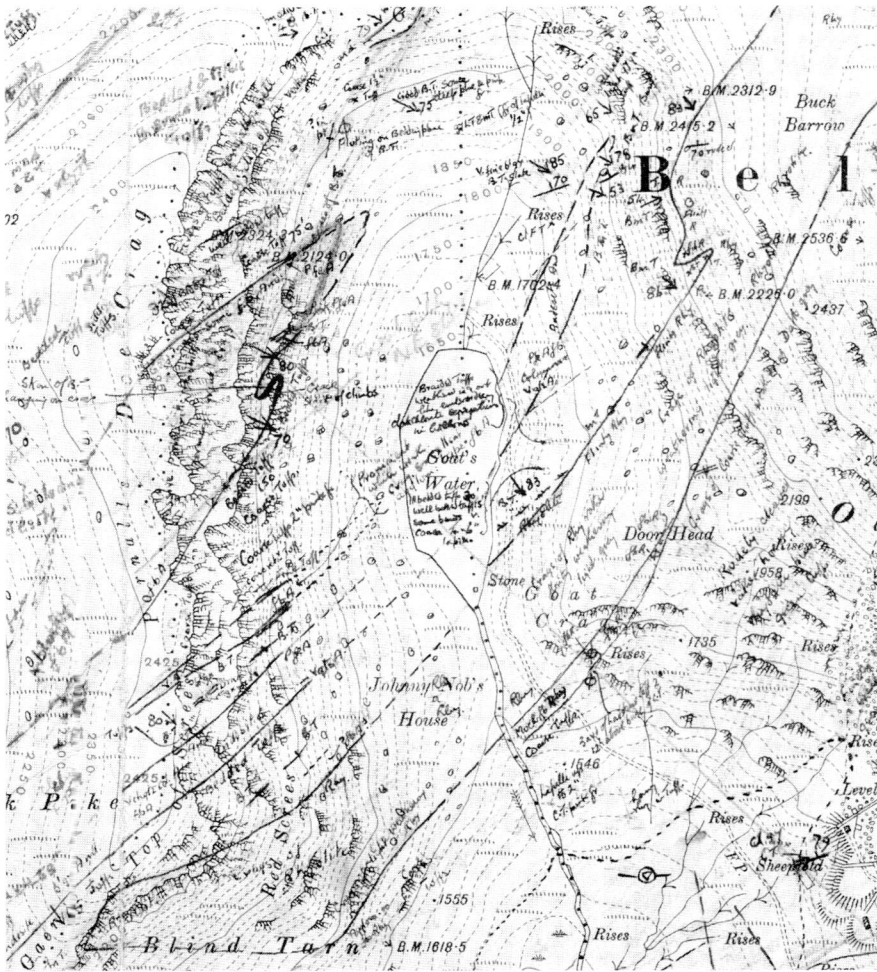

Fig. 37 – Made by G. H. Mitchell in 1938-1939

had an unrivalled knowledge of the geology of the Lake District. Though mostly known for his work on the volcanic rocks, including its petrography (1930), his early work on the Coniston Limestone (1925) and on the geomorphology of the eastern Lake District (1931) should not be forgotten. He was thus well placed to give an account of the geological history of the Lake District, as Presidential Addresses to the Yorkshire Geological Society in 1955 and 1956, in which he included a lithostratigraphical model of the volcanic succession. The paper was a worthy successor to Marr's classic

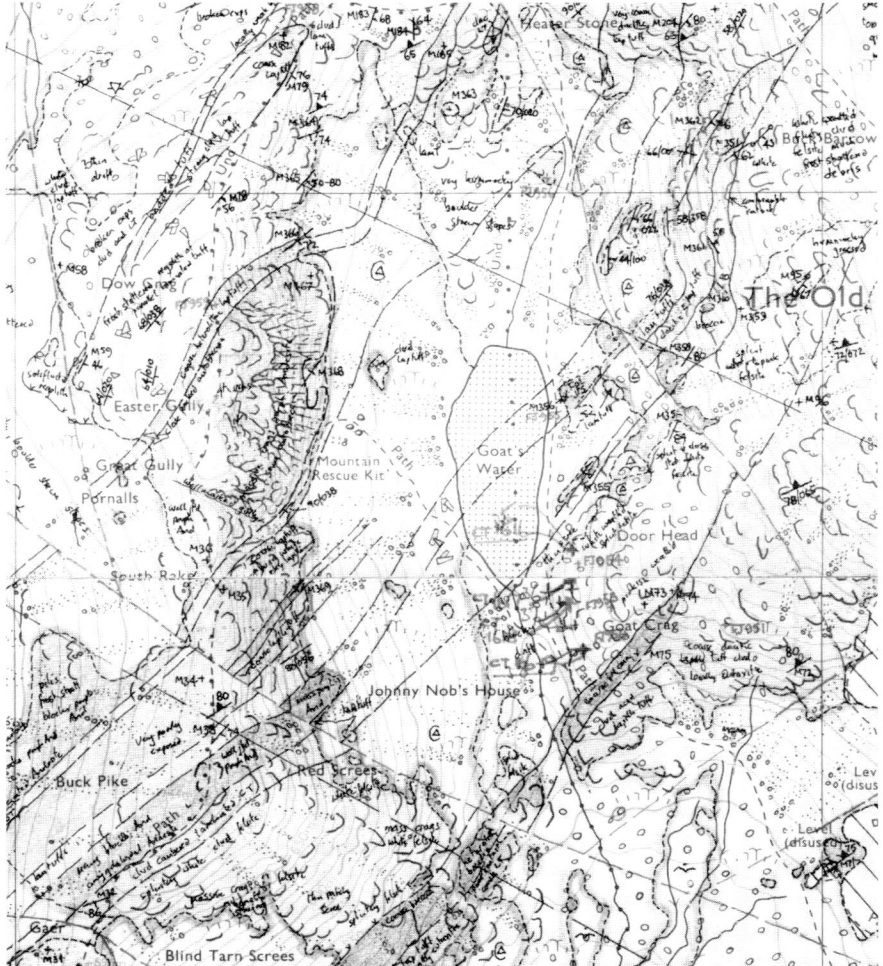

Fig. 38 – Recent map from the British Geological Survey (D. Millward) 1986.

Geology of the Lake District (1916) and remained the most authoritative account of Lake District geology for the next 20 years. However, unlike Marr and Green before him, Mitchell did not produce a novel interpretation that could be especially associated with him as a significant breakthrough in the development of the understanding of Lake District geology. To our knowledge, he did not travel to any modern volcano to examine its products, which would have been very beneficial. Also, his contribution to the volcanology of the Lake District rocks has to be seen in the context that during Mitchell's era volcanology was essentially an observational, rather than interpretative, branch of our science, and it remained so until the 1970s. His legacy then is that through detailed field mapping it is possible to understand and interpret such complex and difficult ancient subaerial volcanic successions. The recent lithofacies interpretations of the Borrowdale Volcanic Group owe much to his example.

BIBLIOGRAPHY

MITCHELL, G.H., 1925, The Coniston Limestone Series in the Kentmere district. *Geol. Mag.*, Vol. 62, 264-267.

1928, The pre-Glacial history of the River Kent, Westmorland. *Proc. Liverpool Geol.Soc.*, Vol. 15, 78-83.

1929, The succession and structure of the Borrowdale Volcanic Series in Troutbeck, Kentmere and the western part of Long Sleddale (Westmorland). *Quart.Journ.Geol.Soc.*, Vol. 85, 9-44.

1930, Notes on the petrography of the Borrowdale Volcanic Series of Kentmere (Westmorland). *Quart.Journ.Geol.Soc.*, Vol. 86, 1-8.

1931, The pre-Glacial History of the River Kent, Westmorland. *Proc. Liverpool Geol. Soc.*, Vol. 15, 78-83.

1931a, The geomorphology of the eastern part of the Lake District. *Proc. Liverpool Geol.Soc.*, Vol. 15, 322-338.

1934, The Borrowdale Volcanic Series and associated rocks in the country between Long Sleddale and Shap. *Quart.Journ.Geol.Soc.*, Vol. 90, 418-444.

1934, The Diatomaceous Earth deposit of Kentmere. *Proc.Liverpool Geol.Soc.*, Vol. 16, 142-149.

1940, The Borrowdale Volcanic Series of Coniston, Lancashire. *Quart.Journ.Geol.Soc.*, Vol. 96, 301-319

1956, The geological history of the Lake District (Presidential addresses for 1955 and 1956). *Proc.Yorks.Geol. Soc.*, Vol. 30, 407-463.

1956a, The Borrowdale Volcanic Series of the Dunnerdale Fells, Lancashire. *Liverpool and Manchester Geological Journal*, Vol. 1, 428-449.

1957, Ordovician volcanoes *(Presidential address to Section C of the British Association). Advancement of Science*, 14, 34-47.

1963, The Borrowdale Volcanic rocks of the Seathwaite Fells, Lancashire. *Liverpool and Manchester Geological Journal*, Vol. 3, 289-300.

1967, The Caledonian Orogeny in Northern England. *Proc.Yorks.Geol.Soc.*, Vol 36, 135-138.

1970, *'The Lake District'*. Geologists' Association Guides, No.2, 42pp

1972, (with F MOSELEY and others). Excursion to northern Lake District 30 August-5 September 1970. *Proc. Geol. Assoc.*, Vol. 83, 443.

The Physiographers

*P*hysiography is a term no longer in common use. Around the middle of the Twentieth Century the more precise, modern term, *geomorphology* took its place. In reality the two terms are not synonyms. *Physiography* had a broader connotation, frequently being used to cover the study of the physical features of the earth's surface, including considerations of climate and life forms. To some *physiography* was rather loosely synonymous with *physical geography*. Nevertheless, from the Nineteenth Century, many workers trying to explain the form of the Lake District landscape used the term *physiography*, so it is appropriate we stay with the older term for this section. None of the four people reviewed here would, I believe, have regarded themselves as *geomorphologists, – physiographers –* more likely, or possibly *physical geographers*.

The three previous sections of the book have illustrated how the study of Lakeland geology surged forward at an accelerating pace from the early beginnings in the first quarter of the Nineteenth Century. From the work of early local amateurs, the impact of the Survey geologists and the increasing tide of academic workers pushed forward the margins of our knowledge of the rocks, fossils, minerals and geological history at an ever increasing rate. The same cannot be said for studies of earth surface processes and landforms (*physiography or geomorphology* – whichever term we use). It can be argued that geomorphology was very much a neglected science. Geologists as such seem preoccupied with the rocks and what lay beneath the surface. Increasingly the literature became obsessed with the geological minutiae of rock, fossil and mineral lists and precise petrological and stratigraphical detail, with little regard to explanations of the surface morphology.

The reasons for this are not hard to find. In many ways all the factors that lay behind the growth and popularity of geology were reasons why geomorphology rarely gained attention. Geology has for centuries, and still does today, provide an outlet for collecting. Landform study cannot fulfil this in any similar way. Geology is also something that allows observations to be recorded on maps fairly easily. It was notable that the accelerated progress of the Survey geologists quickly followed the publication of the first detailed and accurate mapping of our country by the Ordnance Survey. There is always satisfaction to be gained by amateurs and professional alike, from the task of tracing outcrops, plotting them on maps, and producing a coloured-in map of the geology. Geomorphological mapping on the other hand was more problematical and was a very crude tool up until the late 1950's and 1960's. There was always a fundamental problem of whether to simply record the morphology of the surface, or make genetic judgements about landforms from the start and record them somehow in map form. Geology has a more immediate and practical economic credibility. Exploitation of economic mineral deposits and the acquisition of building and other materials required specific geological knowledge and led directly to economic activity and employment. Geomorphology, in the early days, had few economic spinoffs – only in relatively recent times has the science proved its worth in hydrology, in civil engineering and in environmental applications. Landscape and landform study was indeed an outdoor activity, something that potentially was an attractive thing to pursue in a scenically attractive area like the Lake District, but in reality it provided few precise activities. There was nothing to hammer or look at with a hand lens, little to measure and dating anything was very difficult. Very quickly the observer was into theorising with few opportunities to test his findings. The spectacular scenery of the Lakeland fells attracted the curious observer, but the drift covered areas of the lowlands of Cumbria or the flat Solway Plain sparked little enthusiastic enquiry.

Although physiographic studies languished in a state of some neglect compared with the progress made by mainstream geology, some early work did take place. Work in the Lake District very much mirrored patterns and trends being played out on the national and international stage. In the early nineteenth Century and before, the controversy between catastrophism and uniformitarianism ranged back and forth. Later in the Nineteenth Century, the battle between the diluvialists and the exponents of the glacial theory came to the fore. We have not been able to explore these debates in Lakeland terms fully in this book, but we have seen, for example, that doubts about the glacial theory were certainly held by workers like Jonathan Otley and even Clifton Ward. It was left to very late Nineteenth Century workers and people like J.E. Marr well into the Twentieth Century to achieve complete conversion to seeing Lakeland as a terrain shaped by cold climate processes in the very recent geological past. Gradually a number of other physiographic themes began to emerge and to direct thinking on landscape issues.

Once the stratigraphy and lithology of Lakeland rocks had been explained, considerations of the relationships between rocks and relief were raised. As early as 1848 Hopkins had drawn attention to the radial pattern of the drainage lines of the Lake District and posed the possibility that it had been initiated on a dome structure of relatively new rocks and superimposed on to the Palaeozoic inlier. From the late Nineteenth Century the fact that British physiographic studies were so hidebound within the guiding principles of the American physiographer W.M. Davis, led to an obsessive emphasis on seeing landscape evolution in terms of cycles of erosion and pursuing denudation chronologies. The concentration and separation of activity into University Departments of Geography and away from Departments of Geology clearly affected the paths of research. The work that was done was predominantly descriptive, deductive and focussed on the morphology of the landscape underpinned with very little knowledge of the mechanisms of surface processes.

Several of the early workers already reviewed in the three preceding sections were the true pioneers of physiography in Lakeland – Clifton Ward, J.E. Marr, J.G. Goodchild, F.M. Trotter and Bernard Smith. The work of the Survey geologists put on record many of the earliest observations of the landforms – particularly the glacial forms of the upland areas, the moraines, striae and erratic boulders. Elucidation of the Quaternary and Recent deposits of the district was within the remit of the Survey and it is to them that the credit goes of first mapping and describing these materials and establishing a suggested chronology. This was particularly important in lowland Cumbria. Clifton Ward devoted a considerable portion of the Memoir on the Northern Lake District to glacial phenomena and Goodchild and Trotter pioneered the interpretation of glacial events over many of the lowland areas. An inspired and very early physiographic paper was Bernard Smith's work on Black Coombe in 1906, which set the pattern for many later studies. Interestingly the fact that Smith did much of his physiographic work as a spare time personal leisure pursuit perhaps says something of how such studies were valued in these early days. The other major physiographic pioneer was J.E. Marr. Probably more than any one else he brought together, particularly in *'Geology of the Lake District'* *(1916)*, the current ideas on the radial drainage pattern, rocks and relief and on the glacial landforms. Many of his earlier papers also clarified thinking on the glacial origin of the lake and tarn basins.

There remain very few possible physiographers to be reviewed in this section. The significant advances in the field have come only in the last 40 years or so, and hence are outside the remit of this review. The outstanding personality was undoubtedly Thomas Hay, to whom we devote a substantial article. His work typifies the descriptive and deductive landform studies of his time. R.K. Gresswell's work is similarly significant in illustrating the descriptive phase of the 1950s, very much in the tradition of the 'geographer physiographer'. The short pieces on Arthur Raistrick and Frank Monkhouse are worthy of inclusion for specific reasons explained in the accounts – Raistrick somewhat in the Hay tradition, Monkhouse because of his strong Cumbrian connections and as a pioneer in popularising Lakeland landforms for the student.

15. Arthur Raistrick (1897-1991)
A Legendary Yorkshireman
Alan Smith

Arthur Raistrick was not a particularly significant figure in Lakeland geology, but his work on the glaciation of Borrowdale in the 1920's illustrates an important part of the history of physiographic research in Lakeland and warrants a short account. Raistrick was of course a Yorkshireman through and through. In his long life he became the pre-eminent figure of studies into the industrial archaeology, landscape history and the local geology of the Yorkshire Dales and North Pennines. A prolific writer, lecturer, researcher and passionate supporter of many causes and organisations he led an exceptionally full life.

Raistrick was born in the model industrial village of Saltaire, near Bradford, but his roots were in the Yorkshire Dales where he lived for most of his life. From Bradford Grammar School he went on to Leeds University. His career as a WEA lecturer and extra-mural tutor in the Universities of Newcastle, Durham and Leeds brought him into contact with a great range of people and activities. He developed an intricate knowledge of coal mining in the north of England and an understanding of miners and their communities. He became Senior Lecturer in geology in Newcastle, was a fellow of the Geological Society and was awarded their Lyell and Clough Medals for work on the Coal Measures.

His published work on the glaciation of Borrowdale stemmed from his thesis research submitted as part of his BSc. Hons. Degree at Leeds in 1923. It was very much the work of a young man at the start of his academic career. Its interest lies in the way it reflected current thinking into landform study at the time. It built directly on the work of J. Clifton Ward and J.E. Marr – the only two significant workers to have commented on the glacial features of Borrowdale by that date. Raistrick found it necessary, even in 1923, to go back to Ward's work and on the glaciation to re-examine three axioms that Ward posed – did the glaciating agent work from north to south, did it come from within or without the area and was the agent floating ice, a system of local glaciers or an unbroken ice cap? Raistrick appreciated the details of Ward's observations on glacial striations and confirmed support for ice movements from a central ice cap, at times moving across ridges disregarding the topography, but at other stages being confined to the valley routes. More strongly he emphasised that any notions of 'floating ice' that may be still lingering could not be supported in any way by the field evidence. He saw Marr's work as being of a general nature, focussed on the Lake District at the regional level, with few of the details of specific landforms worked out. He regarded Marr's 1916 book as giving "in charming manner the wider grasp of the district which is necessary before local detailed work".

Raistrick set about to remedy this by working on the local detail of Borrowdale. He traced at some length the movement of ice in the area as evidenced by striation directions and erratic trains. He spent considerable time describing and analysing the moraines, particularly the complex sequence at Rosthwaite where his observations on the stratigraphic sequence and contained clasts represents one of the first systematic studies of a morainic sequence in the Lake District. His work is also interesting in that it reflected the growing awareness of deglaciation and the work of meltwaters in shaping the landscape. He describes where he regarded pro-glacial lakes existed in Borrowdale as the ice downwasted and retreated. He was the first to invoke the then fashionable ideas of 'overflow channels' and aligned sequences conveying meltwaters from pro-glacial lakes along the western flanks of the Borrowdale valley and around the Newlands area. It is also clear he realised that this was a landscape shaped by different phases of glacial activity – referring to 'the maximum and subsequent glaciation' and 'corrie glaciers of the late phase'. He was also interested in clarifying the relationships between Lakeland and Scottish ice and in sorting out the stages of glaciation in the region. He went on to propound many of these same ideas on glaciation in his later writings on the Yorkshire Dales – a series of papers on Wharfedale, Swaledale and Airedale followed.

Raistrick's work in the Lake District was not highly innovative. He applied the ideas of the day and filled in some local detail. As an early physiographer his approach was largely descriptive but he questioned what he saw and demonstrated that he had 'an eye for country', which he illustrated with such formidable skill in his writings on the Pennine areas for which he is principally remembered. The impact of his early association with Lakeland can however, be detected in some of his later writings such as *"Teach Yourself Geology"*, where his book in this well known series includes many references to Lakeland examples.

From the Lake District, Raistrick went on to a life in the Yorkshire Dales of extraordinary productivity and diversity. His writings on the area were prodigious. His lecturing and field teaching touched the lives of vast numbers of people. His love of music, his devotion to Quakerism, a life-long relationship with the Labour Party and his association with the Ramblers Association, YHA, Holiday Fellowship, potholing and the National Parks movement were all part of his full life.

He died on April 9th 1991 at the age of 94.

BIBLIOGRAPHY

RAISTRICK, A., 1925, A preliminary note on the glaciation of Borrowdale. *Geol. Mag.*, vol. 62, pp 277-279

1925a, The Glaciation of Borrowdale, *Proc. Yorks. Geol. Soc.*, vol. 20, pp 155-181.

RAISTRICK, A. and BLACKBURN, K., 1932, Analysis of some Lake District Peats. *N.W. Naturalist*, pp 94-97.

1932a, Late Glacial and Post-glacial periods in the North Pennines. Part 11 The Post Glacial Peats. *Trans. N. Naturalists Union*, vol. 1, pp 79-103.

16. Thomas Hay (1873-1957)
Lake District Physiographer
Richard Clark

Thomas Hay (Fig. 39) was one of the more important writers on Lake District landscapes and landforms, publishing thirteen papers from 1926 to 1951. His work spanned the time from Marr to Hollingworth, Mitchell, Raistrick and their colleagues. Unlike these latter, he virtually confined his interest to the fell country. Physiography (Hay kept to the older term) changed during this period from a largely descriptive, deductive activity, towards a more experimental, numerate science and he contributed to that change in respect of this area.

Fig. 39 – Thomas Hay
(Reproduced by kind permission of Bridgitte Hay)

Though he read his papers at London meetings and published in national journals he was not latterly well-known beyond family and the circle of geologists operating in northwest England. He has been described as of rather reserved though genial disposition. In 1938 he received the Back Award of the Royal Geographical Society for promoting understanding of Lake District landscapes and for demonstrating analysis of glaciated

Fig. 40 – Moss Crag, Hay's home in Glenridding in the Ullswater valley. Now a guest house and tea room.

landscapes to members of interwar Arctic expeditions. Alongside his physical landscape papers there are twelve in the *Transactions of the Cumberland and Westmorland Antiquarian and Archaeological Society.* Now there are very few left who knew him and the circumstances of his rather unusual life have not previously been recorded.

A life of 'two halves'

Hay was born in 1873 of a Scottish Border family settled on Tyneside. He attended Newcastle Royal Grammar School, 1887 – 92, becoming captain of rugby XV and cricket XI. He read mathematics with distinction at St John's Cambridge, graduated in 1895 and became a schoolmaster. Two years later he took a London External B.Sc. After teaching in London and then in Stone, Staffordshire, he moved in 1899 to King Edward VI School, Chelmsford. By 1903 he was Headmaster at Midhurst, Sussex and in 1909 returned as Headmaster to Chelmsford. Following family holidays at the Dun Bull in Mardale he bought Moss Crag, (Fig. 40) the house in Glenridding which became the base for the exploration of lake shore, dale and fell in which he had been encouraged by Professor Marr and H.R. Mill.

In 1928, the year of his second landform paper, Hay retired from schoolmastering, unusually early for those days and with the reluctant permission from the Governors – though probably prompted by an independent-minded wife tiring of her role at the school. Twenty-five of thirty-three years in teaching had been in headship. The prospect of mostly lone excursions among the hills proved more attractive than some ten more years of school with little or nothing more to prove there. He left Glenridding in the close of the Second World War with great sadness and, again, probably at the behest of his wife whose family home in Nailsworth became available on the deaths of older sisters. Hay then wrote on the history and construction of Bannuttree House and on Cotswold landslips. His last Lake District note appeared in 1951 when he was 78. He died in November, 1957.

'Second half : in the Lake District '

David and Michael Hay told how their father 'read a tremendous amount – history, art, literature – he read and acquired a working knowledge of most things. As occasion demanded he taught French and Science – European literature too. Mathematics taught him orderly thinking but above all he was a keen observer'. 'He saw at once that a particular piece of ground, or the position of a boulder, was not quite right - something had happened'.

Observation went in harness with systematic knowledge. Citations show his reading included works in German and French, on the Alps, France, North America and the Arctic as well as a range of Lake District papers from Clifton Ward (1873) on fissures in bedrock to McConnell (1939) on planation surfaces. He also examined alpine landscapes in the company of Swiss geologists as well as joining excursions of British geological societies. Evidently he was a committed and well-prepared student.

His work was described as 'revealing delight in close argument and compact results – a sense of dynamic landscapes, processes at work – all landscape features to be read, to contribute to the story.' Nevertheless an accompanying lightness in style was not much evident in early papers except as flashes of special curiosity. In later papers he pushed for understanding, speculating as an amateur may where caution might otherwise counsel the professional.

His interests took in contemporary landscape processes, notably high magnitude-low frequency events such as major floods: he examined links between rainfall, discharge and their morphological consequences – what, when and where. But he persistently pursued certain major themes, especially the work of glacier ice, the effects of freeze and thaw of ground water, the formation and development of the high-level areas of rather subdued relief.

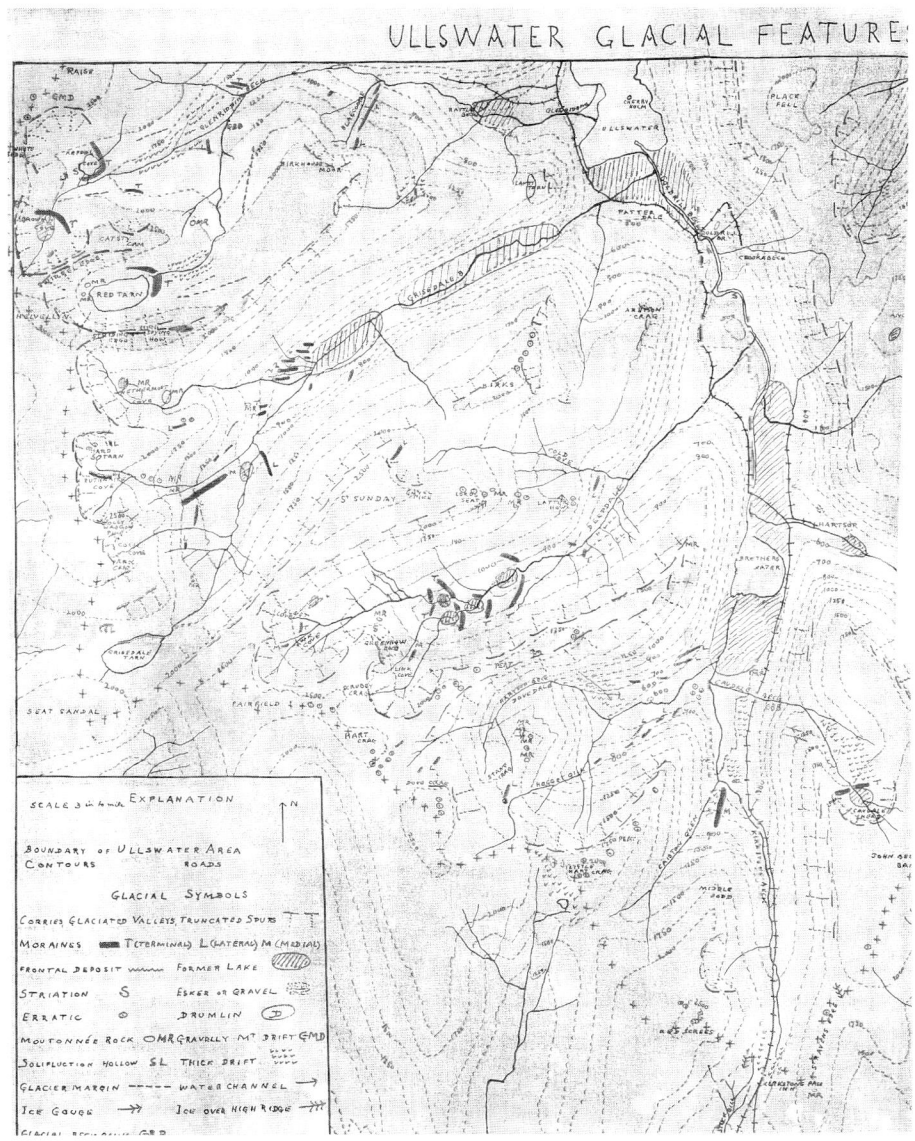

Fig. 41 – A portion of Hay's pysiographical map of the Ullswater area. He recorded details in the field on six-inch to one-mile (1 : 10,560) scale Ordnance Survey maps, frequently adding copious field note on the margins of the sheets. He then compiled 'fair copies' of the field data on to sheets like this

Rarely, after the early papers, was an article devoted to just one of these themes There was the habit of returning to topics with new observations, insights, and connections. Though his papers deal with many of the important aspects of Lake District landscape development there is no evidence he was drawn to the popular contemporary planation-level approach to landscape history of which Hollingworth was a prominent local exponent (Fig. 41).

Along lake shores

Early studies, started in school holidays, concentrated on comprehensive description and classification of lakeside landforms. He was encouraged in this by J.E. Marr and by H.R. Mill of the Lake District Bathymetric Survey. He was advised, too, by Phillip Lake (1865-1949), fellow Northumbrian and St John's scholar, Reader in the new Cambridge Geography Department and remembered by older generations for his 'Physical Geography', for long the standard text.

The ensuing papers (1926, 1928, 1930) remain the most comprehensive accounts of lakeshore forms. Interest in process is exemplified by attempts to explain the sometimes complex and apparently perverse planforms of lakeshore deltas. Among the sorts of feature that puzzled him were masses of waterlaid sands and gravels, their level tops some metres above present mean lake levels, 6m at the head of Ennerdale Water. Possible relations with old higher lake levels were mooted but in general there is little evidence for persistent higher levels. Impounding effects of residual ice masses were also considered. The Ennerdale features, as others, remain to be explained: they need not be linked to levels of the present lake but perhaps to events during loss of glacier ice.

The more interesting features he encountered along the shores owed more to the work of ice, frost, and rivers than to shoreline processes. Hay turned from the constraints of the lakes to broader prospects for his curiosity and to the themes and problems he then pursued to the end of his time in the Lake District.

Fells and dales

The first of the 'new' papers (1934) dealt with glacial landforms in the Ullswater area concluding, in complement to Marr (1916) and Clifton Ward (1875), that erosive ice crossed ridges up to c. 680 m O.D. and that the whole area had been ice covered. He thought that at the end of the last major glaciation dwindling valley glaciers became separated from upland ice masses that sustained a 'Highland Glaciation'. His evidence for the latter and for the intervening ice-free ground is not convincing but no substantial alternative account exists of the end of the latest glaciation in the upland.

He considered there was evidence for two glaciations on the basis of variation in till character and the local presence between tills of water-sorted sands and gravels. At that time such widely known tripartite sequences were usually taken to demonstrate loss of ice before a second ice advance. The till-gravel-till exposure at Rattlebeck, Glenridding, important in Hay's argument, may have only local significance but, nevertheless, is a fine example of such a succession.

The presence of esker-like features among the drumlins of the lower Ullswater area was seen as indication of stagnation in previously active ice. The Ullswater drumlin tract, with the neighbouring Matterdale tract, adjacent to the field of drumlins from southern Vale of Eden round to the coast between Silloth and St Bees, shows that the ice-sheet conditions which led so widely to drumlin formation extended well into the hill country. Hay recorded that moulding of bedrock by moving ice extended to the scale of whole hills but he did not comment on the repetitive parallel grain of drift drumlins and the moulded rock-hills that stood above the drift or overlooked the drumlin zone from its flanks. Their directional conformity raises questions of contemporary formation, thickness of moving ice and, importantly, relative rates of rock erosion and drift deformation during episodes of drumlin formation.

In the heart of the fells, in the neighbourhood of uppermost valley-head moraines, Hay acutely recorded 'fascinating high-level marginal lines which reveal the old locations of the edge of a stream of ice - seen in certain lights or when the ground is covered in snow'. These trimlines can consist of the most subtle change in slope angle or debris coarseness, easier to see across a valley than underfoot. Though he mapped some associated valley head moraines and knew the 'marginal lines' matched old glacier limits he did not use them to plot the successive limits of valley-head glaciers. Almost fifty years were to pass before Sissons (1980) mapped the maximum extents of the many Lake District valley glaciers he ascribed to the short severe Loch Lomond Stadial that concluded the Pleistocene.

Hay recognised the similarity of hummocky moraines in the Scottish Highlands, Torridon for example, and in Lake District dale heads but never overtly associated them with a discrete late episode of glacier formation. Nevertheless, he did record that the apparent chaos of hummocks could be caused by gullies ' breaking up the orderly array of ridges into a disorderly patchwork of more or less isolated mounds, plateaux and ridges.' The ' orderly array of ridges' marks out, as do marginal lines, successive ice margins. Hay, like Manley (1959), was content with general indications of glacier sites rather than plotting the successive margins of individual glaciers. That has been a task for this decade (e.g. Bennett 1990, Bennett and Boulton 1993)

In the 1934 paper Hay distinguished between ordinary 'real scree' and what he termed 'great taluses', the localised collection of huge angular boulders he associated with joint patterns that 'help the slow forces – in loosening and discharging' the massive blocks and with sites 'where local cliff ice or a combe [corrie] glacier – brought down local short-distance erratics'. On a visit to the Dolomites he discriminated between an inner hillfoot 'real scree' on Sasso Beacie and an outer zone of angular, unabraded, unstriated large local boulders which, arranged in a mass of arcuate ridges and furrows, he took to be the moraines of a hillside or 'wall' glacier (1935). He applied this interpretation to Lake District great taluses as at Auterstone near Ullswater, though his Dolomite example was more probably a rock glacier site below a massive rockfall. At that time dynamics of rock glaciers and rockfall were little known. The Auterstone and many other Lake District great taluses were probably from rockfalls, some within the limits of and thus post-dating the last glaciers.

In the 1930s work by Carl Troll and other continental geologists on periglacial processes was penetrating Britain: Hollingworth and Raistrick as well as Hay became interested. Patterned ground resulting from orderly segregation of finer and coarse particles into nets, circles and stripes attracted attention. Hay (1936) proposed an explanation of sorted stripes. The essential problem was not the maintenance but initiation of sorting. Hay said stripes, lateral separations of coarse and fine particles, became fixed only where a subsurface set of downslope corrugations had become stable and that this happened where vegetation had recently been disrupted and eroded. He cut trenches which showed coarser debris occupied the furrows and fines covered the intervening ridges, though whether coarser stripes facilitated run-off and the furrows formed beneath them or the furrows came first was not determined.

Sorting remains problematic even though the general dependence on heave by ice-crystal growth in moisture-retentive fine material is accepted. Werner and Hallet (1993) produced patterns by computer simulation of sorting in a notionally unsorted mixture of variously sized particles. They assumed the ice-crystal process and some random local variation in coarse-fine proportions in the original mix. Hay (1937) had said 'assemblages of small particles may become the focus of collection [sorting] and its operation a 'self-reinforcing process'. Werner and Hallet wrote of self-organisation from local feedback – over fifty years, and computers, later.

The 1937 paper also recorded the first British examples of sliding (gliding) blocks, longer known in continental Europe. These are the surface boulders which slide down hillsides – as some still do in hard winters – with bow waves of turf and soil and furrows behind showing distances most recently moved. That paper dealt especially with the 'continued struggle' especially over c 730 m O.D. 'between – downslope movement of materials, and especially frost effects and solifluction – tending to destroy the vegetation ' and the plants 'continually trying to repair the damage and to regain ground from which' as Hay assumed 'it had been temporarily ousted'. Hay noted the incorporation of peat in some frost-generated landforms, the present circumstance having replaced one of greater soil and vegetation stability though he did not discuss how and when that change may have come about.

In 1942 Hay considered several types of upland landform, just four of them noted here. More evidence was presented on high altitude movement of glacial erratics on the western fells near the ice shed. He emphasised influence of lithology on development of high altitude block-fields and the particular susceptibility of Ennerdale granophyre, and noted presence of glacial erratics in blockfields. He thought, with Marr (1916), that blockfields might survive having been under an ice-sheet and thus 'cannot be used as evidence of the amount of sub-aerial weathering since' though he was quite clear that blockfields resulted from 'vigorous frost-working on massive rocks with well-marked joints'. Distribution and development of blockfields and the possible survival of included erratics from earlier glaciations have been, and are, used in argument over extent and effect of ice cover in North America, Scandinavia, Scotland and elsewhere. As far as is known, the potential of clay mineralogy to shed some light on type, humid temperate or periglacial, and occasion of weathering has not been applied to Lake District summit blockfields.

In a first British record of stone flats, Hay described how frost-riven blocks at suitable sites tend to 'level themselves out in a flat spread'. Stone flats, level layers of surface stones usually underlain by finer material, are formed in places that have experienced freeze-thaw cycles. High altitude Lake District sites include shallow seasonal pools. Site characteristics vary, and so might the formative processes. At Hartside (756 m O.D.) north of Helvellyn the surface stones were 'wonderfully consistent in size – only one layer of these bigger stones on top – below them a layer of small fragments, and below this fine black soil.' Incorporation of organic material in the sorting and spreading implies Holocene formation of that stone flat.

As he assumed, perhaps from present bareness and mobility, that scree is still significantly accumulating, so he thought that adjacent to the

Hartsice stone flat the 'little stream of surface stones working their way down the live rock edge, moved by solifluction' meant that in time the 'remaining live rock will disappear.' But the movement of debris, if demonstrable, does not itself show that frost-riving of outcrops remains vigorous. Similar processes were described from near Helvellyn Man (925 m O.D.) and at that height evidence for some present-day frost action is stronger. The combination of frost-riving and solifluction tends to produce 'greater uniformity in outline and so to increase the appearance of subdued relief'. Here he was outlining the progression of what Peltier (1950) later termed the periglacial cycle of landscape development – and he was also implying the continuing Lake District problem: what are the relative contributions to subdued summit-level relief in the fell country of pre-Quaternary temperate processes, prolonged Pleistocene periglacial episodes (cf. Boardman, 1992), erosion by ice and, perhaps, Holocene environments.

'Several narrow but deep fissures occur across the top' of Helm Crag, Grasmere 'not quite parallel to the run of the mountain edge' with gaping fissures and great holes one like a 'huge rough cauldron'. Clifton Ward (1873) had thought earthquake shocks a more probable cause of fissure opening than recent faulting or rock failure on steep slopes. Hay looked at the 'great cracks in the flat ground' at the top of a high, near vertical face in a Threlkeld micro-granite quarry and concluded they had developed due to removal of the buttressing rock: by that token 'oversteepening of the east side of Helm Crag led to its subsequent instability.' The interplay of master joint or fault alignments, slope steepening by ice erosion, isostatic response to rapid loss of ice cover and continuing tectonic adjustments makes singular cause difficult to isolate but it is worth noting that among historically recorded local earthquakes (Melville 1986) are those associated with rockfalls.

Not all reaches of major ice-outlet valleys have been oversteepened. Hay noted valley sides where 'slope of the live rock is nearly in the same straight line as the slope of scree lying at its foot – here is one continuous slope in profile.' He saw attainment of uniform rock slopes at about scree angle as a first stage of that 'long process [by] which the mountain acquires a more subdued form.' Any projecting crags would be 'gradually reduced until a continuous [uniform] slope covers a wide area.' This was an early British recognition of an important stage in development of slopes where scree did not accumulate thickly above slope foot. Well after Hay's time in the Lake District it was described as a 'remarkable new geomorphological law' and the straight rock-cut, scree angle, hillsides were termed Richter slopes after an early continental geomorphologist. Such slopes are widespread in the Lake District.

Quite straight valley sides occur in both narrow V and broad-bottomed valleys. Some of the Richter slopes carry evidence of glacial erosion but if their general straightness was achieved in periglacial environments it may well have survived the most recent general glaciation rather little modified. Not all the abraded and plucked rock surfaces were subsequently removed in the brief but severe Loch Lomond Stadial. Clearly there is more to learn of how the dales acquired the detail of their shapes.

Of the three topics in the 1943 paper, freeze-thaw processes and sorted stone stripes, how asymmetric forms may be produced by moving ice, and the value of U and V valley cross-sections in discriminating between fluvial and glacial influences, the last is not touched on elsewhere. Hay noted the difficulties experienced on the north Pennines, certainly glaciated, in determining that fact from the shapes of local valleys, and also that certain Lake District dales have both wide open 'U-shaped' and constricted 'V-shaped' reaches though, patently, the whole valleys had discharged ice. Henri Onde (a continental geologist) had asserted that both valley forms could result from ice erosion reflecting difference in valley long profile steepness and thus the likely rates of ice movement. Hay resolved to test the relationship by measurement and concluded from his Lake District sample 'the fact that the V-shaped valley – where inclination is steep – has sufficed – owing to the swifter flow of ice – for the passage of ice which on a more gentle slope needed a U-shaped bed for its transit implies that a valley cannot be classified as non-glaciated simply because it is V-shaped,'

There was a last brief note in 1951 but two 1944 papers were the last substantial Lake District contributions. The first (a) returned to several old topics, high altitude ice transport, the Rattlebeck exposure, but particularly to valley moraines. Hay had commented in 1942 that moraines 'do not occur in our main valleys with anything like the frequency expected'. That led to the view that where 'morainic matter was deposited it must often have been exposed to very destructive influences'. He assumed, reasonably, that declining valley glaciers, immobile or still active, would leave spreads or ridges of moraine. The arcuate moraines at Rosthwaite, Borrowdale, had long been known. Hay ascribed this rare case of survival, as he saw it, to The How, one of two ice-abraded rock bosses projecting through the drift – presumably part of a more extensive rock bar separating valley basins with lower rockhead. There, 'braided streams could wander' eroding moraines: 'if there had been no How there might have been no moraines', that is, no protection from erosion.

No systematic search by Hay or subsequently for other moraines of the main glaciation is known. Sporadic observation suggests the few other moraine ridge sites down-dale from the valley heads are protected by rock bosses, spurs, or lie out of reach of rivers. Where valley-floor rockhead is low, some moraine could have been buried under younger deposits. Enough evidence remains to suggest that some Loch Lomond Stadial glaciers extended significantly beyond the limits mapped by Sissons (1980) or that some valley glaciers were active quite late in the decline of the preceding general ice cover, conceivably both.

The 1944 (b) paper is a wide-ranging discussion of the shapes of the Lake District mountains. Hay was about seventy then and retained his compact yet discursive style, implying, pointing rather than explicitly unraveling all his argument, expecting the reader to take both point and significance. He noted that in the Southern Uplands 'the rounded forms of the mountain tops are - ascribed to ice action by Scottish geologists' while the 'small parts of Lakeland with rounded summit land' were thought by Marr to be 'a remnant of the preglacial surface practically unaltered by ice action' How can two such divergent interpretations be true of the two areas situated so close together – that they experienced practically the same later history?'

He recognised contrasts in intensity of ice erosion in and adjacent to the Lake District fells. While erosive ice had sufficient power to reshape hills marginal to the main fells there were areas within the central fells that seemed little affected by ice erosion. He outlined the decline in intensity of modification northwards from the ice-shed area along the Helvellyn ridge to beyond Raise, the northermost place 'where ice action has had much influence on the summit land'. Presaging by thirty years Clayton's (1974) classification of glacial landscape by degree of alteration Hay identified :

'foothills where the rounded form is very noticeable – they have been subjected to heavy ice attack,

great valleys show the effects of ice action in their U-shape – truncated spurs – and hanging valleys,

rugged land between the valleys – up to the summit areas – the whole the result of the plucking action of the ice,

summit land – mainly rugged and irregular – the direct result of plucking and removal of blocks,

parts of the summit areas have a gently sloping surface – like elevated downs – Marr interpreted [them] as relics of the preglacial surface,

combes or corries and cliff walls – most face some point between north and east'.

By now his views on the summit surfaces were somewhat complex. He knew evidence pointed to ice-erosion having occurred close to the ice-shed, the top of Great Gable for example, but also to survival of summit block fields through glaciation. The inhibiting notion that thinner ice over high crests would everywhere and always be cold-based and thus erosively ineffective, field evidence to the contrary, was to come later.

Retrospect

Hay's Lake District physiography was but one part of his 'second half': there was Hay, local historian. It is to be considered in the context of its time. The discursive, essay-style was not displaced by the formal almost stereotyped structure of scientific papers until well after the Second War. Possibly professional papers of his time were more often controlled in construction than some of Hay's but comparisons with those by his contemporaries and immediate successors on similar topics might show choices of word and phrase to be the more obvious differences.

The essential quality, noticeable even in the earliest papers, was curiosity – the recognition that there was something needing to be understood and thus, as teacher, to be explained. His papers sustain much of their value and are still cited, as by Ballantyne and Harris (1994), Gurney (1995) and in Boardman (1997). They are a record of things seen, questions posed, answers proposed. It is still appropriate to read Hay, as Marr, for a perspective on what has been said and thought about local landscapes and, importantly, for what there may be still to do.

Nonetheless, two important regrets persist. Had Hay been encouraged to seek locational relationships among landforms and their likely associated processes, and to explore their order in time his conclusions might well have been much more significant. As it was, forty or fifty years were to pass before some of his topics were taken significantly further: some have not been.

The second regret is that in the years just after the Second War, when his work was fresh and known, more was not made of the opportunities it revealed. In the next twenty or so years only some eight Lake District landscape papers appeared, on such diverse topics as scree (Andrews 1961, Caine 1963), sorted stripes (Caine 1963), glacial troughs (Linton 1957), district glaciation (Gresswell 1952, 1962, Walker 1966), planation surfaces (Parry 1960) and Late Glacial moraines (Manley 1959). Younger students seem to have been given confining topics, established scholars didn't take understanding very much further. There were no integrating studies on broad scales and none that pulled together a range of landform types, distributions and processes. There are parts of the fell country Hay didn't mention and to all intents and purposes they remain unstudied, notwithstanding the more recent resurgence in glacial and periglacial studies. Much remains to be done.

BIBLIOGRAPHY

HAY, T._ 1926, Delta Formation in the E. Lakes. *Geol. Mag.* , Vol. 63, pp. 292-301.

1928, The shore topography of the English Lakes. *Geogr. J.* Vol. 72. pp 38-57

1928a, Glenridding Flood of 1927. *Geogr. J.*, Vol. 73, pp 90-91

1930, Further notes on the shore topography of the English Lakes. *Geogr. J.*, Vol. 75, pp 324-344.

1934, The Glaciology of the Ullswater area. *Geogr. J.*, Vol. 84, pp 136-148.

1935, Scree with Great Boulders, *Geogr. J.*, Vol. 85, pp 372-373.

1936, Stone Stripes. *Geogr. J.*, Vol. 87, pp 47-50.

1937, Physiographical Notes on the Ullswater area. *Geogr. J.*, Vol. 90 pp 426-445.

1942, Physiographic Notes from Lakeland. *Geogr. J.* Vol. 100, pp 165-173.

1943, Notes on glacial erosion and stone stripes. *Geogr. J.*, Vol. 102, pp 13-20.

1944 Rosthwaite Moraines and other Lakeland notes. *Geogr. J.*, Vol. 103, pp 119-124.

1944a, Mountain Form in Lakeland. *Geogr. J.* Vol. 103, pp 263-271.

1951, Stone lines in Boulder Clay and sliding blocks. *Geogr. J.*, Vol. 107 pp 367-368.

17. Ronald Kay Gresswell (1905-1969)
A Physiographer and Teacher
Richard Clark and Alan Smith

Ronald Kay Gresswell spent all his life in the Southport area of Merseyside. He was born there on 13th October 1905 and died there on the 3rd January 1969. His work however, took him further afield, to many parts of North West England, other areas of Britain and particularly to Scandinavia where he established many contacts and became well known in the geographical and geological communities.

Because of poor health as a child he was educated privately, but he developed a remarkable range of interests that equipped him well for his early work as a private tutor and coach. During the 1930's he developed an interest in his local coastal area, for the pursuit of which he was awarded an MA degree of the University of Liverpool in 1936 and which led ultimately to the publication of perhaps his best known work, his book on *'The Sandy Shores of South Lancashire'*, in 1953.

Fig. 42 – R. K. Gresswell (tall man, standing at back on the right, in University blazer), alongside The Lieutenant-Governor of the Isle of Man, Sir Ronald Garvie at the opening of the Autumn Extra-Mural School in the Isle of Man, September 1965.

Following the Second World War he was invited to undertake the teaching of geomorphology in the Department of Geography in the University of Liverpool and he remained there as a Special Lecturer (part-time) for the rest of his life. In the early 1950's he started extra-mural teaching at which he excelled. In 1962 he became a lecturer jointly in the Department of Geography and Adult Education and Extra-Mural Studies (Fig. 42).

Gresswell's contribution to research on Lake District physiography consists of three substantial papers, all on landforms and processes in south west Cumbria. He concentrated his attention on the low Silurian terrain and coastal areas of Furness, but extending up into the Coniston, Langdale and Grasmere areas of Lakeland proper. It was fortunate he was attracted to this area for otherwise there would have been little written on its physical landscapes. His first paper, published in 1952 was simply called 'The Glacial Geomorphology of the South-Eastern part of the Lake District' and covered the Windermere Basin from upper Langdale and Dunmail Raise down to the Kent Estuary. His final paper published in

1962 on the Glaciology of the Coniston Basin pursued and developed similar themes to the west. Neither has been supplanted.

The 1952 study employed a simple chronology of the most recent glaciation, a stage in which ice cover attained greatest thickness and extent, and later stages, which attracted most of the paper's attention, when ice cover had declined to a set of valley glaciers. Gresswell described the 1952 paper as concerned 'with the valley glaciations and associated lowland ice-sheets subsequent to . . . the Main Irish Sea glaciation'. He saw that as an episode in the Newer Glaciation. Following it was a Scottish Re-Advance in which ice reached the Fylde, building a terminal moraine at Kirkham and moulding drumlins between the high fells and that moraine. Next was a Highland Re-Advance, which in Gresswell's study area was manifested by valley glaciers that, according to site description, also formed drumlins. There was a final Cirque Glaciation of marginal significance to the study area. The Scottish Re-Advance as interpreted by Gresswell was perhaps more related to that envisaged by Trotter (1929) than the more restricted one expounded later by Huddart (Huddart 1971a and b, Huddart et al 1977). More recently Vincent (1985) noted that, although it was then thought Lake District ice of the Newer Glaciation (Late Devensian Dimlington Stadial as by then designated) had stagnated and wasted quickly, there are moraines which mark positions of temporary margins of a dwindling ice cover. He cited only four terminal moraines, those identified by Gresswell, adding 'these outer moraines represent some as yet undated stage' between maximum glaciation and onset of the Windermere Interstadial.

As the papers, now showing their years, have sustained their authority it is pertinent to consider how conclusions were reached and to what extent they were justified. That not all seem well-founded is not wholly consequent upon later developments in understanding of ice sheets and of British glacial chronology. In the 1952 paper Gresswell proposed the occurrence after decline of a more continuous ice cover, of a set of contemporary glaciers in valleys from the Langdales and round Grasmere in the high fells to a 'small local Gilpin glacier' in the east. The Gilpin valley has very little land over 200m above sea level and its present annual precipitation hardly exceeds 1600 mm. The large Langdale catchment extends in places to over 900m with 4000mm mean local precipitation. That is an unlikely conjunction. Formation of a local Gilpin glacier would imply conditions leading to a Lake District ice cap and ice sheets extending well beyond.

Gresswell's evidence for the set of valley glaciers was based on *roche moutonnees.* drumlins, kames and features regarded as terminal moraines. Alignments showed directions of ice movement, but these conform with ice movement directions derived from evidence between the proposed valley glaciers. No evidence for glacier margins other than terminal was given. Thus there is inadequate testimony to glacier area, thickness and surface slope which would support assertions about glacier diffluence and locations of outer limits. Drumlins and kames tend to be more abundant in, rather than, between local valleys. *Roche moutonnees* have a similar distribution but to a lesser extent. All could be explained in context of a complete ice cover, which would have its areas of thicker ice, greater erosion and meltwater concentration. Differentiation of glaciation stages depended very much on a small number of features taken as having formed by and at fronts of separate active valley glaciers.

Gresswell was exercised to explain the narrow steep-sided Backbarrow valley followed by the River Leven as it exits from Windermere. Rather like the Duddon, Crake and Kent, the Leven reaches tidewater from a more open valley by way of a narrow valley, gorge like in part. In a common context there may well be shared elements in explanation. The particularity at Backbarrow is that low ground continues south from Windermere by Ayside, with a nearby sill in drift at c 70 m, to the seaward end of the Cartmel peninsula. The Cartmel route had been seen as the former and 'natural' way for drainage from the Windermere valley. The Backbarrow route Gresswell supposed to have been incised in stages, first as a meltwater channel, then by a branch from the Windermere valley glacier, and then the lowest 12m were cut by the postglacial river so lowering the level of Windermere. Wilson (1987) returned to the Backbarrow question showing that the sill rockhead lay 4 –9m below the surface, well above the present exit from Windermere. He also discounted the idea that late discharge of water from the Windermere basin passed by the Cartmel route. Gresswell thought that his Windermere valley glacier had continued south that way with the drumlins along it being formed at that time. Overall the apparently anomalous Backbarrow valley may be better understood in terms of progressive denudation on a long established drainage route, in an influential structural-lithological setting.

The central theme of the 1962 paper is also the identification and description of discrete valley glacier sites. Again, these range from those nourished in the high fells, here round Coniston, to very small, local glaciers as at Scathwaite Beck, Colton and Bouth. The same points about disparity of environments for generating glaciers arise. There is the same lack of evidence for glacier margins. And there are propositions of valley glaciers, which from the given indications of extent could have only a certain maximum surface altitude and ice thickness, being sent in diffluence over cols which demand a greater ice surface height and thickness to a degree that would have necessitated more extensive ice cover than indicated. It is also difficult to reconcile account of a Torver glacier in the greater Scottish Re-Advance with that of a Coniston glacier in a lesser Highland Re-Advance with its set of South Lakes valley glaciers. This paper too, identified terminal moraines of the Coniston glacier at Nibthwaite and of a Rusland glacier at Haverthwaite, both cited by Vincent (1984). The latter, of drift mounds some perhaps ice-moulded, lies on and among glaciated rock knolls at the end of a spur separating ice routes, the Rusland valley route seeming the major one. The mounds lie on the path of ice that moved along the line of the spur rather than down Rusland valley and do not really extend across the valley.

The Nibthwaite mounds may then be the stronger candidate to be considered terminal moraine. Even so, it must be asked whether drift mounds among rock mounds at the down-valley end of a rock basin are a sufficient testimony to the former existence and frontal position of an active valley glacier.

Although he invoked an extended sequence of glacial stages for much of his territory, Gresswell interpreted events in Low Furness more parsimoniously. Two suites of glacial drift occur there, one extensive with material derived locally, a second around Barrow with erratics from West Cumbria and southern Scotland. Gresswell's mapping included north-south drumlins of the first suite. He regarded these adjacent drifts as products of contemporary confluent ice sheets. Contacts between the two, which include the margin of the second drift cover cutting across the drumlin alignments of the first and its tills and outwash overlying the first suite in the area west of Roosebeck, show a diachronous relationship. Scottish ice moved east over part of the area no longer occupied by active Furness ice. It remains to be determined whether there are landforms and deposits in the uplands that correlate with the incursion of 'Scottish' ice into the Barrow area. Gresswell's proposed Coniston glacier would be a candidate.

In studying glacial landforms in the South Lakes area Gresswell observed and mapped carefully, using many categories of classification. His is still the only reasonably comprehensive landform mapping of that terrain. The texts expound what he considered most in need of explanation albeit in the light of models of glaciation to which the landforms could have suggested alternatives. He did though, identify and deliberate upon the interesting and critical localities. He broke extensive ground and broken ground is easier to work than an untilled field.

His 1958 paper was of a different nature. It dealt with the filling by sediments of the coastal valleys from the Duddon to the Kent as sea levels rose from their Late Pleistocene low stands to the maximum of the mid-Holocene transgression. That was an important topic and the paper a pioneering one, though soon to be overtaken. As well as its broad range of landform mapping and analysis, it used sub-surface data from bores and geophysical survey and also evidence of vegetation history from pollen analysis. It drew attention to and partially explained the long deep north-south coastal valleys, most not associated with major rivers.

This paper belongs to the post-war generational transition in geography from a discursive treatment of physiography – rather like an historian's – to the incorporation of more rigorous field examinations in reports increasingly structured as scientific papers. In its rather leisurely, not particularly incisive style, it is rooted in the former, contrasting sharply with contributed appendices in scientific mode. Explanation tends to be one-dimensional with little appraisal of contending possibilities. Even so, for anyone seeking to know what has been recorded and thought about these valleys the paper is not just valuable but essential. Later work on the same topic has constrained itself much more to the infills. Gresswell took a broader view.

Throughout his life Gresswell was a teacher. He was a keen field worker and a superb photographer. He loved landscapes and the outdoors. He had the ability to interpret what he saw in simple and popular terms and the skill to illustrate his lectures and writings with first class photographs. All this enabled him to become an influential exponent of his subject at every level, from the local to the international, from the beginner to the professional academic. Year after year he led groups of people on fieldwork in Britain and in Norway, and his students quickly became his friends. Many people from modest backgrounds were converted to an interest in physical landscapes by his talks, excursions and writings.

In the late 1950's and early 1960's he turned his knowledge and experience in education into a series of books for school use. Three simple school texts on *Beaches and Coastlines, Rivers and Valleys* and *Glaciers and Glaciation* appeared in 1957 and 1958. This was followed by *Geology for Geographers* in 1963. His largest book was *Physical Geography*, an 'A level' text published in 1967. In all of these books his own photographs and diagrams played a very important and original part. Not only did his photographic collection illustrate features in locations like Cumbria or Scandinavia, but he made a point of collecting together first rate pictures of textbook geological features. He generously allowed others access to his collection – examination of Frank Monkhouse's *Principles of Physical*

Geography for example shows many Gresswell pictures including several from Cumbria. They were colleagues in the Department of Geography in Liverpool for a time.

He continued writing right up to the time of his death. He had also become involved in consultancy work, a report on coastal protection in south-west Lancashire and Wirral in connection with the studies being undertaken to consider the possibilities of a Dee barrage lay unfinished when he died at the beginning of 1969.

BIBLIOGRAPHY.

GRESSWELL, R.K., 1952, The glacial geomorphology of the south-eastern part of the Lake District. *Lpool and Manchr Geol. J.* Vol. 1, pp 57-70.

1958, The post-glacial raised beaches in Furness and Lyth, north Morecambe Bay, *Trans. Inst. Brit. Geogs.* Vol 25, pp 79-103.

1962, The Glaciology of the Coniston Basin, *Lpool and Manchr Geol. J.*, Vol. 3, pp 83-96.

18. Francis J Monkhouse (1915-1975)
Lakeland Geographer
Mervyn Dodd and Fred Lawton

Frank Monkhouse (Fig. 43) was born in Cumbria and educated at Workington Grammar School, where Herbert White, a former Treasurer of this Society, taught him and found him to be a quite exceptional pupil. He read Geography at Cambridge where he obtained a good degree. Before the Second World War he enjoyed and successfully taught geography at Wakefield Grammar School. His career was both interrupted and enhanced by that war. He was drafted to the Intelligence Division of the Naval Staff where he

Fig. 43 – Frank Monkhouse

worked on the production of the highly regarded Admiralty Handbooks. In 1946 he was appointed as a Lecturer in the Department of Geography at Liverpool University, also teaching in the Department of Education where he supervised students on practice, critically but kindly. While at Liverpool University he became the Chief Examiner in Geography for the Cambridge Syndicate 'A' level, reorganising the examination of physical geography and encouraging the development of practical examinations. In 1954 he became Professor of Geography at Southampton University, a post he held until he took early retirement in 1966.

Early retirement allowed him to develop a new, equally busy career. He and his wife settled in and modernised Crag Farmhouse, Ennerdale, a return to his beloved Lake District, which a kindly reviewer of one of his books likened 'to a Herdwick returning to his heaf'. During retirement he worked as a visiting professor at American Universities, travelled widely, lectured extensively and enjoyed rock climbing. Together with J. Williams he wrote *Climber and Fell Walker in Lakeland* in 1972. In its way this was an unusual book. Besides the 'usual' history of rock climbing and accounts of individual climbs there was quite a long chapter, actually 'a mild dose of physical geography', as one reviewer put it. This related rock climbing to rocks and structures, and very interestingly wrote of rock climbing as applied geology, or in his case 'geology at his fingertips', with convincing references to the changing effects of differences in rock characteristics on individual pitches. His death in 1975 was sudden, while he seemed still to be a fit man at the height of his intellectual powers.

He was a man of wide interests and many parts, a talented amateur sportsman in his youth. Simply, he never had enough time, nor the inclination, to become and remain a dedicated researcher. Early in the Second World War he had at least three articles about the history of mining in the North Pennines published in respected journals like the *Transactions of the Cumberland and Westmorland Antiquarian and Archaeological Society*. His most respected piece of research was the monograph *The Belgian Kempenland*, published in 1949. This was regarded as one of the very best contributions to regional geography. In 1952 he was joint author of *Maps and Diagrams*, a long running university textbook. Much the most important and the most successful of his textbooks was *The Principles of Physical Geography*, well suited to the needs of A level and first year University students. This first appeared in 1954 and the much-revised 8th edition was published in the year of his death. His other magnum opus was his authoritative *Regional Geography of Western Europe*, the University level text appearing in 1959 and the intermediate (A-Level) text in 1964. He also found time to write in 1960, the concise but very effective *The English Lake District*, the first volume in the British Landscapes through Maps series, published by the Geographical Association. His *Dictionary of Geography* was for long the basic reference and authority on geographical terminology.

His greatest scholarly strength lay in his writings in regional geography. He was a craftsman in this art of regional description and explanation, using geology and physical geography as part of the background to the area's economic development with its historically changing landscapes, natural and human. His material was supremely well organised, showing great skill in deductive and inductive reasoning, using a wealth of pertinent, well chosen examples. He had an easy style, with a judicious mixture of long and short sentences. His writings were always eminently readable. Terms were briefly and clearly explained, jargon avoided and in many respects he was a master of geographical synthesis. He retired when human geography started to change. He was not interested in the "young turks" insistence on models and scientific method with mathematical measurement of every phenomenon, irrespective of whether it was suitable or the feature had any significance.

His *Principles of Physical Geography* appeared when the initial post-war expansion in the numbers of A-Level Geography students was beginning. It was so much more appropriate for this niche market than the competitors, which were either trivial or unnecessarily erudite. It was so much better illustrated by well-drawn, apposite, simple diagrams and well printed photographs. His clarity of thought and expression made many a difficult concept far easier to understand. Wherever suitable he used most convincingly examples from Cumbria. The relationship of drainage patterns to structure, glacial and periglacial landforms and most notably the different types of lakes with their different histories were sympathetically illustrated in this way. A particularly memorable example was his description of how lakes came and went in the Kentmere valley. His *The English Lake District* was a very effective introduction to Lakeland rocks and landscapes. These two books played a major part in stimulating geographical studies in Cumbria and a wide range of field courses in Lakeland. Thus, rather like Edgar Shackleton in Lakeland geology, his great contribution is as an academic populariser and an inspiration to study of the physical and human landscapes of Cumbria.

Frank Monkhouse was outgoing, an extrovert who respected others. A fellow Lecturer at Liverpool University wrote of him . . . "as a congenial colleague and a wise counsellor whose judgement could always be relied upon", and "as a great enthusiast in all he did". I remember him coming to talk to A-Level students at Whitehaven Grammar School when I taught Geography there. There was no question of him charging a fee, as he knew well enough local schools had insufficient funds to pay the fee he could command. He was highly organised, graphic, relaxed and riveting in an easy conversational style, striking an instant rapport with his audience. Such were his considerable personal skills, undeniable kindness and integrity.

Fred Lawton adds his own personal recollection of Frank Monkhouse from 1973.

"On a rather damp January day with visibility down to 30 feet, four friends and I decided to walk up Fleetwith Pike. In the group was Frank whom I had met for the first time a week earlier. There was not any real enthusiasm in the party due to the weather, but Frank urged everyone to carry on. He also suggested that all would be well at 1500 feet when we would emerge into brilliant sunshine. There was a great deal of good humoured scepticism to this remark, to which Frank responded by accelerating his pace until he disappeared into the mist muttering about the company he kept. Half an hour or so later, a shout from above stating in unequivocal terms that there was indeed brilliant sunshine at that level and not, as pessimistically forecast by that unbelieving group following behind.

The rest of the day continued above cloud level and in sunshine with temperatures well above normal. In fact it was warm enough to scramble on the crags of Little Round How before walking onto Haystacks.

Throughout the day Frank was extremely good company (contrary to the impression I may have given earlier), stopping to explain in layman's terms, how to interpret the landscape both geologically and geographically and describing the phenomenon of a Brocken Spectre which we had witnessed that day.

On subsequent walks in the mountains he was always a very friendly and informative companion, but I shall never forget that earlier meeting and especially his interpretation of the weather pattern and his 'prediction' which provided such a memorable day".

BIBLIOGRAPHY

MONKHOUSE, F.J.,1956, The Lakeland Landscape, Jubilee Volume, *Journ.of the Fell and Rock Climbing Club of the English Lake District*, Vol. 17, No.3, pp 1-16.

1960, *The English Lake District*, (A description of the Ordnance Survey One-Inch Tourist Map of the Lake District). The British Landscape through Maps, No. 1, Geographical Assoc., Sheffield 19pp., 2nd Edit., 1972, 24pp.

MONKHOUSE, F.J. and WILLIAMS, J., 1972 *Climber and Fellwalker in Lakeland*. David & Charles, Newton Abbot 214pp. (Chapter 1, The Climbers Landscape, pp.11-26).

Amateurs and Professionals

The six pioneers in this final section of the book are a very diverse group of men. For the most part they are Twentieth Century personalities, bringing us up to the immediate post Second World War period of the 1950's and 1960's. Each account records a unique life and a specific pioneering contribution to the field of Lakeland geology. Chronologically they form a group. Beyond that it has to be admitted that little more than editorial convenience justifies them being brought together in this last section.

Even in the Twentieth Century the amateur still had a role to play. Three of these accounts show how untrained, local enthusiasts could carve out a niche and make their mark on the geological scene. John Postlethwaite was very much a Victorian figure, being born in the year the young Queen came to the throne and gaining his geological experience in the Nineteenth Century. His work however, did not reach the public eye until the early Twentieth century. It is logical therefore to include him here – first in this section. Charles Edmonds and Edgar Shackleton were, similarly, amateurs whose enthusiasm for the subject led them to write and research into the local area, and to recruit others into the field. Both these men, as the accounts show, were not only significant figures in Cumbrian geology, but instrumental in founding the West Cumberland Geology Group (Fig. 44). In 1961 the Group was formally established as the Cumberland Geological Society.

R.H. Rastall, on the other hand, was the consummate professional - yet another Cambridge academic geologist who carried out much fundamental research work in the area. Similarly Sidney Hollingworth represents the professional side of geology in the district at this time. Initially a Survey Geologist, but later moving into academic work at University College London, the breadth of his researches in Cumbria is notable, spanning not only work on the bedrock geology, but also including some significant contributions on the geomorphology of the district. Lastly within this section we have J.F.N. Green, a highly independent and at times controversial figure.

Fig. 44 – A field meeting of the West Cumberland Geology Group in the late 1950's. Standing at the extreme right (in cap) is Charles Edmonds. Edgar Shackleton is standing in the middle of the group, towards the back (in trilby, tie and jacket).

19. John Postlethwaite (1840-1925)
Lakeland's Foremost Exponent on the Mines and Mining
Alan Smith

Fig 45 – Third edition of Postlethwaite's 'Mines and Mining in the Lake District' published in 1916.

Postlethwaite's *'Mines and Mining in the Lake District'* is one of the best known and widest read books to be written on Cumbrian geology. First published in a limited format in 1877, it was followed by a second enlarged edition in 1889. The third edition, revised and enlarged further in 1913 is the one most people know. Produced with a distinctive cover design and picture of Brandley Mine and with a choice of four colours (red, blue, green or brown) these are now treasured volumes (Fig.45). Its popularity was such that a modern reprint was very successfully published by the Cumbrian bookseller Michael Moon in 1975, fulfilling a quite remarkable continued demand for the work.

Postlethwaite the man behind the book is by comparison a little known and rather enigmatic figure. Little known too are his early published papers on Cumbrian geology between 1882 and 1897.

John Postlethwaite (Fig. 46) was born at Birkrigg in the Newlands Valley, near Keswick in 1840. At that time Newlands was an active mining area, with the Yewthwaite mines bearing galena, cerussite, blende and iron pyrites within sight of his home, and the rich Goldscope and Barrow mines short distances away. His father was Under-Manager at the Force Crag mine in Coledale, again close at hand. From the age or four he was befriended by the miners and the lads in the mine, many of whom in those days were only seven or eight years old. At an early age we know he had a passion for diverting streams, making miniature mill races and driving model water wheels.

Fig. 46 – John Postlethwaite

He attended the small school in the Newlands Valley and later the village school in nearby Braithwaite and eventually Crosthwaite School in Keswick. Mines and mining were in his blood from his earliest days, so it was not by chance that after his school days his first job was at the Thornthwaite mines where he worked in the joiners shop as well as on the dressing floor. Later he joined his father at the Brandley mine at Brandlehow on the western shores of Derwentwater. Here he worked underground and later was superintendent of the dressing floors. Brandley was a difficult mine to work, pumping was always a problem, the high salinity of the water prevented it being used in the boilers. In 1864 the mine was in decline. John was attracted to look for employment to the

Cockermouth, Keswick and Penrith Railway (CK & P), then under construction, and seen as a worthwhile career for an ambitious young man of 24. He was appointed junior clerk in the accounts office six months before the railway opened. He progressed to be responsible for stores and later took charge of the accounts department for about 30 years. In all he worked for the railway company for 50 years, seeing it eventually pass into the hands of the great London, Midland and Scottish (LMS) combine.

Coming to geology from this relatively humble background and very much as an untrained amateur in the science, his achievements were impressive. Such an early and powerful association with Lakeland mines, miners and minerals stayed with him throughout his life and were at the core of his geological interests. Perhaps more importantly, his conversion to geology as an academic pursuit and the impetus to write and publish, probably came from his friendship with James Clifton Ward. Ward had been posted to Keswick as the Survey geologist in 1869. They lived close to each other in the town, Ward in Blencathra Street and Postlethwaite almost round the corner in Eskin Street. Both were active members of the newly formed Keswick Literary and Scientific Society in the 1870's. Both men had much to gain from their friendship. Ward, the professional geologist involved in mapping the Keswick area, is known to have put great store on talking to local miners and those involved in the mining industry. The similarity between the material in Ward's field notebooks, still preserved in the British Geological Survey archives at Keyworth, Nottingham, and many sections of Postlethwaite's book is striking. This is particularly seen in the sections covering the mines and mineralised areas. For Postlethwaite, contact with a professional geologist like Ward, in a small town like Keswick, must have been a godsend. It seems likely in particular, that it was Ward that prompted Postlethwaite's interest in fossil collecting. The two men were also associated with the fairly short-lived Cumberland and Westmorland Association for the Advancement of Literature and Science. It had a branch in Keswick, but met in several other centres in the County in the period after 1876. This proved a channel for Postlethwaite to publish four of his earliest geological papers. It was here that he also came into contact with another professional geologist, J.G. Goodchild, who not only edited the Transactions of the Association but also collaborated with Postlethwaite in a paper on trilobites in 1886.

All Postlethwaite's published work can be traced back to these early influences of his mining background, his contact with Ward and Goodchild and the opportunities that existed within a short distance of his home in Keswick. He developed an early passion for searching for fossil remains in the Skiddaw Group rocks around Keswick. Adam Sedgwick had announced the first fossil finds in the Skiddaw Group in 1848 and for the next few decades the ground was diligently searched by many local enthusiasts, Postlethwaite amongst them. He spent much of his leisure time working on Randel Crag (NW of Skiddaw summit), on Carlside Edge and Barf and in Hodgson How Quarry at Portinscale. His first two published papers record in great detail the current state of knowledge about graptolite and trilobite finds in the Skiddaw rocks. Both are comprehensive accounts describing with great precision the morphology, state of preservation and classification of the finds. He frequently refers to prized specimens in his own cabinet, but also in the cabinets of two other Keswick enthusiasts, a Mr. P. Harrison and Mr. W. Kinsey Dover, the latter clearly having a cabinet of the finest specimens of all. He acknowledges the help of Goodchild in identifying some of the finds and several of the best specimens were handed over to Goodchild who drew them in great detail – the Goodchild drawings figuring particularly in their joint paper on trilobites published in 1886. Many of these fossil finds have now found their way into some of the prime museum collections in the country, particularly the British Museum, the Fitzwilliam Museum in Cambridge and locally in the Keswick Museum. In a very recent popular book, 'Trilobite', by Richard Fortey he reminds us of the importance of these early finds by Postlethwaite, stressing how rare trilobites are in the Lake District rocks but how much of our understanding of the early geological history hinged on the identity of these primitive creatures. (p 150).

Postlethwaite took the opportunity to write up and have published material he must have gleaned during his working life. His paper on the 'Mineral Springs near Keswick', published in 1886 clearly stems from his early knowledge of the saline waters experienced at Brandley Mine, Derwentwater in the very early years of his life. Likewise, his 'Notes on some railway cuttings near Keswick' connect with his employment with the CK & P Railway Company. In that paper he was intrigued by exposed sections of two separate clays in the glacial drift, which he interpreted as representing two distinct periods of glaciation in the district. His 1890 papers on the metallic and mineral deposits of the Skiddaw area and on the Borrowdale plumbago point to his continued interest in mineralogical investigation.

In 1892 and 1893 he published two papers on the Dioritic Picrite and Diabase intrusive rocks of the Bassenthwaite area. His intention here was to describe these intrusive masses in greater detail than Clifton Ward had been able to do in his initial Survey work. He spent time tracing the outcrops on the ground in great detail and extracted a series of specimens from the intrusions which he had chemically analysed by Professor T.G. Bonney. He acknowledges the help of Bonney in very fulsome terms and records the fact that the professor 'for want of time' allowed him to incorporate his notes and analyses into his paper. Again, this is a pointer to the fact that Postlethwaite had established his credibility with the academic community and was clearly known by the professionals. By the time these later papers were published he had become a Fellow of the Geological Society of London. His paper on 'The Cleaved Ashes and Breccias of the Volcanic Series of Borrowdale' was also done in collaboration with T.G Bonney.

The third edition of *'Mines and Mining in the Lake District'* published in 1913 was an accumulated work. It was the summation of material collected from his working life, his researches and his local fieldwork. He was 73 years of age when it appeared. Its main contribution was the detailed record of the mines and quarries of the district, their working and their history. This material has stood the test of time. It also contained a general appraisal of the rocks and structure of the Lake District, much of it following the late Nineteenth Century work of the Survey geologists. This was soon eclipsed by Marr's *'Geology of the Lake District'* published in 1916. Postlethwaite's work on the palaeontology of the Lake District was also presented in the book, most of the material having appeared in his early papers. The book contains valuable plans, sections and diagrams of the mines and it is illustrated with a number of hand drawn maps. These seem to be very much a trademark of Postlethwaite, drawn in a style that suggests he enjoyed doing the work. Not only are they detailed, but they are embellished with ornate lettering and in the case of his 1891 paper on 'The Cleaved Ashes and Breccias of the Volcanic Series of Borrowdale' by a very elaborate cartouche. In view of this it is surprising that he almost always relied on other peoples drawings of fossils, J.G. Goodchild and someone with the initials E.H.

Following the publication of the third edition of *'Mines and Mining in the Lake District'* in 1913 the Geological Society of London presented him with the Lyell Geological Fund in recognition of his work. He continued to live an active life in retirement in Keswick. He was for many years President of the Cumberland Nature Club and was involved with the Fitz Park Trust in Keswick. Apart from his geology he had some reputation in shooting, and was a prize marksman in the local area. He died in September 1925 at the age of 85.

BIBLIOGRAPHY.

POSTLETHWAITE, J., 1883, Graptolites of the Skiddaw Slates. *Trans. Cumb. & West. Assoc. Adv. Lit & Sci.* No. 8, pp37-67.

1885, Trilobites of the Skiddaw Slates. *Trans. Cumb. & West. Assoc. Adv. Lit. & Sci.* No. 10. pp 71-80.

1886, The Mineral Springs near Keswick. *Trans. Cumb. & West. Assoc. Adv. Lit. & Sci.* No. 11, pp 142-5.

1889, *Mines and Mining in the Lake District.* Samuel Moxon : Leeds. xi + 101 pp. (This was the second edition of this work. The first edition was published in 1877, the material having been first presented to the Keswick Literary and Scientific Society in 1874. Where the first edition was published is obscure).

1890, The Deposits of Metallic and other minerals surrounding the Skiddaw Granite. *Trans. Cumb. & West. Assoc. Adv. Sci. & Lit.* No. 15, pp 75-86.

1890, The Borrowdale Graphite on Plumbago: its mode of occurrence and probable origin (Abstract), *Quart. Journ. Geol. Soc.,* Vol. 46, Rep. of Proceedings, pp 124-5.

1891, The Cleaved Ashes and Breccias of the Volcanic Series of Borrowdale. *Trans. Cumb. & West. Assoc. Adv. Lit. & Sci.,* No. 16, pp 41-53. With an Appendix by T.G. BONNEY, On the structure of some Volcanic Ash from the Borrowdale Series. Pp 53-54.

1892, The Dioritic Picrite of White Hause and Great Cockup. *Quart. Journ. Geol. Soc.,* Vol. 48, pp 508-513.

1893, An intrusive sheet of Diabase and associated rocks at Robin Hood, near Bassenthwaite. *Quart. Journ. Geol. Soc.,* Vol. 49, pp 531-535.

1895, Notes on some railway cuttings near Keswick. Quart. Journ. Geol. Soc., Vol. 51, p 493.

1897, *The Geology of the English Lake District, with notes on the minerals.* T. Bakewell : Keswick, Guardian Office, 78 pp. Republished in 1906 by G. and T. Coward, Carlisle. 90 pp

1903, The Geology of the English Lake District., *Trans. Fed. Inst. Min. Eng.* (N. Eng. Inst), Vol. 25, pp 302-330.

1913, *Mines and Mining in the Lake District,* 3rd. Edition. W.H. Moss : Whitehaven, 164pp. (A reprint edition of this 3rd Edition was published by Michael Moon : Beckermet, Cumbria 1975, under the title *Mines and Mining in the English Lake District* with a new biographical sketch of the author by E.H. Shackleton.

20. Richard Heron Rastall (1871-1950)
Lakeland Petrologist
Alan Smith

R.H. Rastall was in every way the archetypal Cambridge bachelor don. His college was his home and his life was focused on his geological work. Coming from the Cambridge School of Geology, where he was taught by Marr and Harker, he carried on the long tradition of interest in Lake District rocks with a series of fundamental and detailed research studies in the early part of the Twentieth Century. His varied geological interests and expertise, however, went far beyond Cumbria, with generations of students, for example, being introduced to geology through his textbooks.

Fig. 47 – R. H. Rastall

Richard Heron Rastall (Fig. 47) was born near Whitby in North Yorkshire in November 1871. He was educated privately and first studied agriculture with a view to managing the family estates around Grosmont and Ruswarp in Eskdale. He taught at Tamworth Agricultural College for a short time. He had a childhood interest in geology, clearly being influenced by the rich fossil localities of the Whitby district. He was nearly 30 years of age when he went to Cambridge in 1899 to read Geology, obtaining a double first in the Natural Science Tripos in 1903. He was awarded the Harkness Scholarship and in 1906 elected to a Fellowship at Christ's College. He remained in Cambridge until 1942.

In the Lake District Rastall's work was primarily concerned with the petrology and metamorphism of the igneous rocks. In his early post-graduate period he was clearly directed by Marr to investigate the Buttermere and Ennerdale Granophyre intrusion, which was the subject of his first detailed paper in 1906. This area had remained untouched since Clifton Ward had described the intrusion in the Survey Memoir 30 years earlier. Inspired by the new petrological techniques he had learnt under Harker at Cambridge, he produced the first really systematic examination of this intrusion. He concluded this was an excellent example of an acid magma which had crystallized under the peculiar set of conditions that give rise to the perfect development of granophyre structure. He saw these conditions as being intermediate between those of the plutonic and the true hypabyssal rocks. He demonstrated that there were marginal patches of more basic material, evidence he believed of partial differentiation of the magma before intrusion. Additionally there was development of peculiar rock types as a result of re-mixing of previously differentiated partial magmas.

It was at the same time as he started this work in Buttermere, in the summer of 1903, that he and Bernard Smith, a fellow post-graduate at Cambridge, explored the tarns on the nearby ridge-top of Haystacks and produced a joint paper on their origin in the *Geological Magazine*.

Rastall's best known Lakeland work was his paper on the Skiddaw Granite, published in 1910. Like the Buttermere-Ennerdale Granophyre paper it was based on detailed field work and intense petrological work on a large number of specimens. Not only did this work describe the composition and petrological character of the intrusion, and its general structural and tectonic relations, more importantly it illustrated for the first time the detail of the metamorphism of the country rock. He refined the mapping of the intrusion, showing it to be much more restricted in outcrop than Clifton Ward had portrayed it on the Survey map of 1876. He concluded that the intrusion was one of large volume, may be a laccolithic form and that the temperature of intrusion was not very high.

Arguably his most pioneering geological work was in directing attention to the significance of accessory minerals in rocks. In the Lake District his paper of 1915 with W.H. Wilcockson was a detailed exposition of the techniques of separating and identifying accessory minerals. It demonstrated the importance of using bulk, powdered samples and subjecting them to magnetic and chemical tests, rather than relying upon small samples of rocks in thin section. Detailed results were produced for the six major intrusions in the Lake District (Skiddaw, Shap, Eskdale, Threlkeld, Armboth and Buttermere-Ennerdale). Rastall went on to do pioneering work on accessory minerals in sedimentary rocks, notably in the Jurassic iron ores.

Between the two World Wars Rastall's work took him away from Lake District subjects. He devoted his attention to a wide range of topics, notably tectonics and underground structures of southern and eastern England, the rocks of Yorkshire and the genesis of tin and tungsten ores. He worked in South Africa and in the tin mining areas of Malaya.

Rastall will be remembered by many for his textbooks. First published in 1910 Lake and Rastall's *Textbook of Geology* ran to five editions. When the fourth edition was approaching exhaustion Philip Lake generously made over all author's rights to Rastall, who then proceeded to completely re-write and enlarge the book as the fifth edition in 1941. Eight reprints followed up until 1964, fourteen years after his death. Hatch and Rastall's *Petrology of Sedimentary Rocks* was almost equally successful, running to two editions and a later revision. *Agricultural Geology, Geology of Metalliferous Deposits* and *Physico-Chemical Geology* were less well known, but nevertheless substantial works.

Rastall's final contribution to Lakeland geology came close to the end of his career in 1940 and 1941 with three further papers. The first examined the Ore Deposits of the Skiddaw District, and the other two, the petrology of the Threlkeld intrusion. The Ore Deposits paper related to further laboratory work he was able to complete on specimens collected years earlier from the Skiddaw area, with an attempt to draw comparisons with the mineralisation of the Alston Block. He reached what he called an inescapable conclusion that the copper-lead-zinc veins of the northern Lake District were of Caledonian age and were in all probability connected with the intrusion of the Skiddaw Granite. At Threlkeld he focused on two aspects of the intrusion, the xenoliths and a rather unusual carbonate rock he had first found in 1925. The xenoliths paper is often quoted even today and remains an important work because of its relevance to the Skiddaw Group/Borrowdale Volcanic Group junction controversy. Unfortunately the detail he provided was less than comprehensive, the paper providing inadequate illustration and no record of whether there was a contained cleavage.

Rastall's work on Lakeland rocks was of a pioneering nature. His papers remain essential reading even today for fundamental and detailed observations made from classic field collection and laboratory examination of specimen material. His contribution to the science of geology went much wider than that. He taught generations of students at Cambridge and contributed much to university life. He is recalled as one of the earliest undergraduate car owners, motoring being a life long pleasure. He was converted early in life to the Roman Catholic faith and was a very influential figure in Catholic activities in the University. He had a reserved and shy manner and his true warm hearted and affectionate nature was revealed to very few. He spent a lonely retirement on his family estate in North Yorkshire, where he died on February 3rd 1950.

BIBLIOGRAPHY.

RASTALL, R.H., 1906, The Buttermere and Ennerdale Granophyre. *Quart. Journ. Geol. Soc.,* Vol.62, pp 253-274.

1910, The Skiddaw Granite and its Metamorphism. *Quart. Journ. Geol. Soc.,* Vol. 66, pp 116-140.

1940, Xenoliths at Threlkeld, Cumberland. *Proc. Yorks. Geol. Soc.* Vol. 24, pp 223-232.

1940a, A Carbonate Rock at Threlkeld. *Proc. Yorks. Geol. Soc.* Vol. 24, pp 232-234.

1941, The Ore Deposits of the Skiddaw District. *Proc. Yorks. Geol. Soc.,* Vol. 24, pp 328-343.

RASTALL, R.H., and SMITH, B., 1906, Tarns on the Haystacks Mountain, Buttermere, Cumberland. *Geol. Mag.,* Vol. 42, pp 406-412.

21. John Frederick Norman Green (1875-1949)
An Independent Mind

Margaret Bennett

John Frederick Norman Green was educated at Bradfield College and Emmanuel College, Cambridge, where he studied Mathematics and Natural Science. In 1896, after university, he joined the Colonial Service. He was a member of the British Delegation to the Paris Peace Conference in 1919 and became an Assistant Secretary in 1920. He showed great interest in the Colonial Geological Survey throughout his career, retiring in 1933.

Green joined the Geologists Association in 1904, was President 1918-1920 and became an Honorary Member in 1940. He became a fellow of the Geological Society in 1908, was awarded the Lyell Medal in 1925 in recognition of the value of his research, and became President of the Society in 1934. He left an impressive series of researches on Wales, the Lake District, the Highlands of Scotland, and river deposits in Southern England. Green belonged to that group of geologists, both amateur and professional, who believed there is no substitute for in depth fieldwork and accurate mapping.

His first published work, in 1908, was on the St. David's area where he looked at the problem of succession. This was an area that had been bitterly contested by rival groups of theorists. Green mapped the whole area in detail, on six-inch maps. He covered both the coast and inland areas. The resulting maps clearly demonstrated that the basal Cambrian onlaps different lithological horizons in the Precambrian. The maps also highlighted and clarified the complicated relationships between the St. David's Granite and the surrounding rocks.

Green subsequently turned his attention to the Lake District, publishing nine papers between 1912 and 1921. First he became interested in the junction between the Skiddaw Slates and the Borrowdale Volcanics, which were mapped at the time as faults. His work kept him in London, so he studied the Geological Survey's six-inch maps at their Jermyn Street office. He doubted the interpretation that had been put on these maps. The area between Millom in the west and the Duddon in the east was comparatively free from major intrusions, appeared to be undisturbed by folding and was most easily accessible from the south.

He gave his first paper on the Lake District, The Older Palaeozoics of the Duddon Estuary, to the Geological Society in 1912. His work clearly showed that the succession could be traced, without a break, from the Skiddaw Slates into the volcanics without any sign of the great faults shown on many older maps. It met with so much animosity that the Society declined to publish it in the Journal and Green had to have it published privately. He next turned his attention to the junction between the Borrowdales and the overlying Coniston Limestone, maintaining that the junction was an unconformity. This directly challenged the work of Professor Marr and the Cambridge school who had interpreted the junction as a series of faults. Green then attempted to prove that the volcanic succession was not as thick as many supposed by applying the succession he had worked out to the rest of the Lake District.

In 1915 his paper The structure of the eastern part of the Lake District was published in the *Proceedings of the Geologists Association*, and The Garnets and streaky rocks of the English Lake District in the *Mineralogical Magazine*. The age of the chief intrusions of the Lake District followed in 1917 along with The Mell Fell Conglomerate and The Skiddaw Granite: a structural study again in the *Proceedings of the Geologists Association* in 1918.

"The Vulcanicity of the Lake District" (1918) and "The Geological Structure of the Lake District" (1919) were Presidential Addresses to the Geologists Association. In these he suggested that much of the vulcanicity had been of a submarine kind and that many of the rocks then considered to be explosion breccias were actually flow breccias; that subsequent folding had exaggerated the thickness of the sequence; and that rhyolites belonged almost exclusively to, and clearly indicated, the upper parts of the volcanics.

His work on the great intrusions and on the garnets and associated streaky rock caused fierce debate, which was always conducted in a friendly manner on his part. He was always ready to acknowledge help received from the work of others. His work tended to over simplify, in particular on structural matters, but it was the stimulation and starting point for a tremendous amount of patient mapping by many workers in and around the English Lake District.

The Second World War confined Green's work to the South of England where he investigated the Weald Clay and continued publishing papers up to 1948, the year before he died.

In Cumbria and the Lake District he is best remembered for his work questioning the early interpretation of the rocks and for his role in stimu-lating others to look more closely, and with an open mind, at the rocks and structures.

BIBLIOGRAPHY

GREEN, J.F.N. 1912, *The older Palaeozoic Succession of the Duddon Estuary*. Hayman, Christy and Lilly Ltd.,London, Privately published 8vo., 23pp.

1915, The structure of the Eastern part of the Lake District. *Proc. Geol. Assoc.*, Vol. 26, pp 195-223.

1915a, The Garnets and streaky rocks of the English Lake District. *Min. Mag.*, Vol. 28, pp 207-217

1917, The age of the chief intrusions of the Lake District. *Proc. Geol. Assoc.*, Vol. 28, pp 1-30.

1918, The Mell Fell Conglomerate. *Proc. Geol. Assoc.*, Vol. 29, pp 117-125.

1918a, The Skiddaw Granite, a structural study. *Proc. Geol. Assoc.*, Vol. 29, pp 126-136.

1919, The vulcanicity of the Lake District. *Proc. Geol. Assoc.*, Vol. 30, pp 153-182.

1920, The Geological Structure of the Lake District. *Proc. Geol. Assoc.*, Vol. 31, pp 109-126.

1921, Long excursions in the Lake District. *Proc. Geol. Assoc.*, Vol. 32, pp 123-138.

22. Charles Edmonds (1885-1964)
A Man of Many Parts
Mervyn Dodd

I met Charles Edmonds in 1962 when he and Edgar Shackleton were joint leaders of a Society excursion. He was in his late 70's at the time and set the scene geologically rather than taking us to the outcrops, as he was not in the best of health. He was articulate and concise, a model of accuracy and precision. In later conversation with him I appreciated how tolerant he was of a keen but all too ignorant new member, being ready to explain basics simply and clearly.

Charles Edmonds (Fig. 48) was a man of many parts. A very competent amateur geologist, trade union organiser, Labour Party County Councillor,

Fig. 48 – Charles Edmonds

Chairman of Cumberland County Council Education Committee for many years, a J.P. – these were the main aspects of a very full and active life. Another interesting aspect, beside his dialect poetry, is the play in Cumbrian dialect he wrote and produced in 1921 at Cockermouth for his trade union, then the Cumberland Iron Miners' Federation. Yet his only formal education was in the village school at Bigrigg, his birthplace.

His working life began in the village post office in Bigrigg, delivering mail to the iron ore 'bosses', before becoming an iron ore miner. By 1919 he was already an active Labour Party member, being elected then to the Cumberland County Council, of which he remained a member until his death. He became an Alderman in 1934. In his later working life he became the fulltime county organiser for the General and Municipal Workers' Union. Like Lord Adams of Ennerdale he negotiated long and hard for the iron ore miners. He was a member of the group which campaigned successfully for the recognition of silicosis and pneumoconiosis as industrial diseases caused by use of compressed air drills without dust suppressors, winning compensation for affected miners.

Also in 1919 he was co-opted onto the Cumberland County Council Education Committee, remaining a member until his death. From 1937 to 1961 he was its Chairman, and was an employers' representative on the Burnham Committee which controlled teachers pay. As expected, he was a member of many of the Education sub-committees and, interestingly, laid the foundation stone of Whitehaven College in 1957. In 1954 the University of Durham gave him an honorary M.Sc for his services to education. The local library in Egremont was named the Charles Edmonds Library in his memory as a tribute to his dedicated work for local education.

As an amateur geologist his particular expertise was in the Carboniferous Limestones of West Cumberland. Before he wrote his considerable paper The Carboniferous Limestone Series of West Cumberland (1922) he had long discussions with Dr Vaughan and his co-workers at the University of Bristol who had recently established the palaeontological zonation of the limestones of the Avon Gorge. His article was the first serious discussion of the local limestones since Kendall (1885), who had concentrated on describing the succession. Edmonds' work was based on fieldwork begun in 1910, concentrating on the palaeontology, relating the fossils of Garwood's 'life zones' and Stanley Smith's index fossils. This allowed him to correlate West Cumberland limestones with those of the North Pennines. He pointed out the generally shallow water nature of the local limestones, with intervening sequences showing emergence. Interestingly also he noted how the limestones formed ridges with the hollows between containing clastic rocks His paper lacked the photographs and maps normal to modern papers. In their place were appendices listing the fossils of individual formations together with the age ranges of rugose corals present and a particular useful list of the exposures of the various formations. In 1924 he helped, as the only amateur amongst the professionals then mapping the area for the Geological Survey, to lead a week-long excursion to West Cumberland reported in 1925 in the *Proceedings of the Geologists' Association* Vol. 36, Part 1.

His detailed knowledge of the limestones of West Cumbria was recognised by the Geological Survey workers and the memoir of Whitehaven and Workington contains a number of acknowledgements recognising his expertise in this area "our work (on the Carboniferous Limestone) merely confirms that of Edmonds". Further recognition is recorded in the naming of two corals – *Nemistium edmondsi* (the type genus and species) and *Orionastraea edmondsi* from the quarries at Eskett and Clints respectively.

His collection also provided the type material figured in the formal description by Bisat (1924) of *Gastrioceras* (now *Cancelloceras) cumbriense* collected at Bigrigg, and which is the emblem of the Cumberland Geological Society. He was also involved in educating the public about the decline of iron ore mining in Cumbria, writing a long series of quite authoritative, demanding articles in February and March 1924 for the Whitehaven News, which stimulated many questions from readers to which he replied. In the late 1920s he was elected to membership of the Geological Society of London and the Geologists' Association. In 1929 he was awarded the Lyell Fund by the Geological Society of London. In 1936 he was an invited guest at the International Geological Congress where he had been commissioned to read a paper on the limestones of West Cumberland. He visited Russia twice! What amazed him on his second visit was that Russia was then producing 600-700 graduate geologists annually, making him think that the UK, even then, was training far too few.

The opening of the Whitehaven office of the Geological Survey in 1920 must have been 'manna from heaven' for him, a place where he could relax from the stresses of his public life. The professional geologists, led initially by Bernard Smith and then by Tom Eastwood, kept open house to interested amateurs. Many a time Charles Edmonds and his son were there, happily talking geology. Tom Eastwood in particular encouraged him, giving him many of the maps, papers and books that formed part of Charles' collection. At that time he rubbed shoulders with Dixon, Trotter and Hollingworth, who were working locally for the Survey. In later years when he had meetings to attend in London he often made time to visit the Geology department of University College to chat with 'Syd' (Hollingworth) or Eric Robinson.

Before the Cumberland Geological Society was established he and Edgar Shackleton between them led all the occasional excursions of the rather small West Cumberland Geology Group. Edgar wrote of Edmonds' encyclopaedic knowledge of almost every quarry between Millom and Alston Moor, to which he must have travelled by train, bus, bicycle or on shanks' pony. His observational skills certainly impressed Edgar. Charles Edmonds was the first President of our Society in 1962 and its original Honorary Life President in 1963. He was inspirational, yet a very unassuming and relaxing person with whom to be. No wonder then, that both his son and granddaughter became professional geologists.

Edgar Shackleton, who knew him well, wrote an appreciation of him (published in the Society Proceedings 1964, Part 1) on which I have drawn heavily in this article. In the same year Edgar suggested the Society establish a prize in his memory, which became a reality in 1965. Since then it has been awarded every second year or so, – a fitting memorial to a rather special person.

BIBLIOGRAPHY

EDMONDS, C., 1922, The Carboniferous series of West Cumberland. *Geol. Mag.*, Vol. 59, pp 74-83 117-131.

23. Sydney Hollingworth (1899-1966)
An Exemplary Field Geologist
Eric Robinson

When reviewing the progress of Geology, there is a tendency to say that the present lacks the great figures who shaped our science in the heroic years of the 19th century – the polymaths who knew no specialisms but were content to call themselves 'geologists'. Against that, it may only be a matter of time before a time perspective gives due credit to Sydney Hollingworth (Fig. 49) for the range and diversity of the work he achieved in his life. What is even more of a recommendation must be the influence which he had on so many of the 'specialists' of our generation as a teacher able to infect students with some of his enthusiasms. This present occasion is an opportunity to list and analyse a fraction of his contributions

Fig. 49– Sidney Hollingworth

Born in Northampton and educated at the Northampton Grammar School in the years up to the First World War, he was called up for military service, wounded and discharged to take up his studies at Clare College, Cambridge. Taught by Rastall and Harker he achieved a First Class Degree and the Harkness Prize, but as important, from those distinguished researchers, he gained his first insights into Lake District geology in a

Department run by J.E. Marr. At the end of those student years, 'Hollie' as everyone tended to call him, went on a continental journey through a Germany under Allied occupation and just recovering from economic devastation in company with a fellow graduate, Tilley. There was a strange contrast in the character of the two which makes one wonder why they struck up the notion of the joint expedition, but a diary which Hollie kept gives an early insight into his character which was to continue into his later life. Their objectives were to take in as much of the Rhineland and Eifel volcanic rocks, and, if possible, to meet and talk with petrologists in the German universities. Their itinerary was full and one which would constitute a first rate excursion at the present time. Notes and records of a wide range of volcanic rocks and minerals prove that Hollie was quite comfortable with the finer points of rock classification and field identification of hand specimens, thanks to the grounding acquired from the Lab work instigated by Harker. Humanity emerges in the careful record of the food, beer and cigarettes consumed at meal times and in the hours of rest.

When they went to the famous quarries at Niedermendig, the well-known source of Roman millstones for the legions, he relates,

"across country to Herschenburg with basalt tuffs on upper trachyte tuffs around a basalt dyke with melilite on the SW side. Day very hot; met a man on the way with whom I conversed under difficulties using a mixture of English, French and German. From Herschenburg to Nieder Tissen where I consumed a pork chop with two fried eggs, salad, and innumerable fried potatoes, two cigars, three glasses of beer. I passed on cheerily towards Laacher. Collected a little schist on the Drachsbusch Hill; consumed three more beers and a cigar at Maria Laach . . . having been walking a good four hours . . . a beer at Niedermendig and another at the station restaurant and a packet of chocolate and a cigar.."

Although this was 1921 when he was twenty-two, this was a pattern which continued through later life; he was never an ascetic as any of his students at University College could affirm.

Returning from the unlikely continental journey with Tilley, he joined the Geological Survey and was sent to the Lake District, a move which was to focus his whole life as a geologist. In the first instance, he was being asked to scrutinise and make decisions on field relationships which had been written upon by his Cambridge teachers, J E Marr, and Alfred Harker. Most of his decisions hinged upon accurate field mapping which proved to be his forté whatever he had to deal with. Nowhere is this better demonstrated than in his work on Carrock Fell where he built upon work done by Rastall, defining metamorphic mineral zones and consequently, was able to outline the limits of the Skiddaw Granite and more especially, the complex which is the gabbro intrusions. It remained work of which he was proud throughout his life.

No greater contrast could be found than in the work which he did with F M Trotter on the glacial deposits of the Lake District and the Vale of Eden in particular. Glacial cover excited few Survey officers at the time, compared with the challenge of solid geology units, but Hollie was inspired by Dwerryhouse and Lamplugh and soon became absorbed in the mapping of drumlin distributions and orientation. As he and Trotter worked closer and closer to the Pennine Escarpment and the Cross Fell Inlier, he became aware of the drainage channels which notched the slopes and, in places, cut in and out of the solid outcrops. The work was published by the Geological Society in their journal in 1931, and remains a classic in the literature of glacial geomorphology and field mapping. In the pattern of Geological Survey work, it might be said that it gave respectability to time and effort devoted to 'superficial' Geology when there was a natural impatience to get to grips with the 'solid' units beneath that cover.

A similar willingness to pay attention to what often seem unrewarding sequences led to Hollie identifying evaporite cycles within the red rocks of the Permo-Trias of the Vale of Eden with the appreciation that such cycles could provide a framework for correlation across the Pennines and into the Irish Sea in the absence of palaeontological evidence, ideas first floated in the Brampton Memoir (1932), expanded in the *Proceedings of the Geologists' Association* (1942), and rounded off in the work of one of his research students, Henry Meyer (1965).

Like all who worked for the Survey, duties in Cumberland required him to tackle the correlation of the Upper Limestone Group and Millstone Grit of North East and West Cumberland, with its unique tradition of numbering from top to bottom. A task he shared with F M Trotter, it brought him into contact with the acknowledged local experts and was the beginning of a life-long friendship with Edgar Shackleton and Charles Edmonds. Such friendships and the diversity of the Geology made the ten years spent in the Whitehaven Office years which he remembered with much satisfaction when he converted to being an academic geologist. In part, it was the separateness of the location and the spirit which was engendered in the company of colleagues such as Tom Eastwood and Bernard Smith, but as much it was the diversity of the geological experiences which came his way for which he was always grateful. With Trotter, in a short paper in the *Geological Magazine*, he set down the notion of the Alston Block as an influence upon local stratigraphy in the Carboniferous and a tectonic entity in subsequent structural history (1928). His work on the glacial deposits was later extended into the Cheshire Basin and continued by his research student, Arthur Whiteman, one of several who followed his example by working for the Geological Survey.

Wartime saw him transferred to work seeking to exploit our mineral resources. Working from the West Midlands and, later, Cambridge, this work took him back to his native Northamptonshire and the Ironstone Fields of the Middle Jurassic. With J H Taylor and G A Kellaway, he came to understand the nature of superficial ground movements in areas of valley slope and the distortions which large-scale superficial structures can cause in predicted thicknesses and total reserves. Again, this resulted in an elegant and well-draughted paper presented to the Geological Society and subsequently incorporated in the Memoir for Kettering, Corby and Oundle (1963). As a direct result of this work, gulls and valley bulges became recognised structures in field mapping in all parts of the World.

The Geological Society played a large part in the Hollingworth life and in his contribution to Geology. Joining as a junior Survey officer in 1922, he rose to being Secretary between 1949 and 1956, and President in 1961-62. He was one of the founders of the Engineering Group in his belief that Applied Geology was a vital element in the health of Geology in general (something he credited to the influence of Tom Eastwood from those Whitehaven years). Through the Society, he found a way of maintaining his contacts with all those active in the many aspects of geology which appealed to him. Always a social animal, the atmosphere of a good London club was for him to be found in Burlington House. The Society and its circle became still more important to him when in 1946, he became the Yates-Goldsmid Professor of Geology at University College London in Gower Street. A radical place in its 19th century foundation, it had a post-War atmosphere of academic freedoms which allowed Hollie to work out his best strategies for teaching while other ex-Survey colleagues inherited traditions which were far less comfortable. Never a great lecturer, Hollie scored triumphs by vastly increasing the amount of fieldwork involved in all courses throughout the three years of study. Handling the small classes of students of the post-war years (all UC students were deemed Honours Students, there were no Pass Degree classes until much later), he naturally took them to his favourite ground of Carrock Fell (Fig. 50) and the Cross Fell Inlier, and later, North Wales. Back in Gower Street, he linked up with S.W. Wooldridge to make geomorphology a main plank of all Geology degree courses and became recognised in that field at World

Fig. 50 – Carrock Fell excursion 1960, with Prof. sitting surrounded by five students who went on to be members of the Norwegian teams in the years that followed. Left standing, Peter Jones, seated Len Freddi, Mervyn Jones, Bunny Brown. In front, Oliver Holmes and Dai Lewis.

level. One of the benefits to students from this fame became regular visits by the South African Lester King, who had much in common with Hollie in his enthusiasm for the subject, but the added virtue that he could give first-rate lectures from which good notes could be taken. While all agree that lectures by Hollie were 'difficult' as they were often delivered to the blackboard or screen, field classes were a different matter as he instructed in the keen observation which was the basis for his field mapping. Equally winning was his informality away from College and on the fell-sides in all weathers. Students were allowed to buy the drinks and learnt that a constant supply of cigarettes was expected (Hollie often produced a packet containing but one cigarette as if to underline a predicament).

Looking back on the years between 1954 and 1966, Hollie initiated several ambitious research projects overseas, which usually involved both undergraduates, research students, and members of the staff at UCL. A large area of Norwegian Caledonides straddling the Arctic Circle was a long-term commitment culminating in a remarkable map draughted with skill by Maurice Wells. Over the years, the work involved Reg Bradshaw, Maurice Wells, Roye Rutland, Robin Nicholson, Keith Ackermann and Brian Walton, all of whom went on to individual work on related topics in structural geology and petrology. Roye Rutland was one of the students of the early Hollingworth years, proceeding smoothly from graduating to being an active member of the Sulitjelma project which saw the completion of a map which resolved a key area of the Norwegian Caledonoides across the Arctic Circle. The work continued for almost five seasons of fieldwork with the Professor doing his fair share of the logistics for the safe crossing of upland glacier fields. His role included establishing friendly relationships with the mining interests in Sulitjelma, and with Norwegians sharing his interests in geomorphology and glaciation (a reprise for that early work on Edenside and the Brampton Memoir years).

Fig. 51 – Breakfast porridge in the hut on Sokumvatn, Norway in the summer field season of 1953. (Photography by Finn Berg, kindly supplied by Roye Rutland.

When with the working party, he was famous (?) for his porridge making, a service captured by the local mainstay, Finn Berg, who was also a skilled photographer (Fig 51). The summary of the mapping, the work of some fourteen geologists, was a mosaic so tall that the mounting board curved in its upper quarter to allow the spectator to take it all in.

Norwegian gabbros must have invited comparisons with many years of wrestling with the enigmas of Carrock Fell. Almost all the students who went on to join the Norwegian teams had all been initiated by Prof. in the becks of Mungrisdale working out from the Mill Inn. Again, it is Roye Rutland who tells that, when he met with Kingsley Dunham and Peter Cooke, when he (Roye) was Director of the Australian Bureau of Mineral Resources, it was Hollingworth field excursions which was the subject of their reminiscences. Such was the Lake Dsirtict tap-root of Hollingworth geology.

His ability to recognise the potential in students was one of Hollie's strengths, best illustrated in another ambitious mapping project developed in northern Chile. The aim was to map the volcanics of the Andean chain adjacent to the northern Atacama Desert but linking such pure geology with the economic geology of the copper and sulphur deposits, which are the commercial driving force in the Chilean economy.

He himself worked closely with George Muller, an Hungarian geologist who had come to London in wartime, but became Professor in Santiago in the early 1950's. The other members of the party were 2nd year Geologist, John Guest, and 2nd Year Geography student, Ron Cooke, who at the time had done Ancillary Geology. John was to study the volcanics, Ron to undertake the desert geomorphology. Both have subsequently become leaders in their chosen field in their own right. (John moved from terrestrial volcanoes to lunar craters and then planetary surfaces, as they became available through NASA; Ron has made deserts his speciality). All his students acknowledge his help but what is equally clear must be Hollie's ability to identify true talent.

One approach which he adopted in the training of his students was to persuade them to become Junior Associates of the Society, simply so that they would have the opportunity to attend the Wednesday evening meetings and listen to the leaders of our science debating. With the old arrangements of benches lengthwise along the meeting room, "debate" was the procedure followed, the papers being followed by questions and answers in a fashion which added greatly to the interest and understanding of the occasion. This was Hollie's chance to probe and explore a presentation, sometimes with a slightly mischievous purpose without being either unfair or unkind.

Given his birthplace in Northampton and his purchase of his retirement home in the Northamptonshire village of Flore, it might have been expected that Hollie would buried there. In fact, after cremation, his ashes were taken by geologists involved in the Chilean research project, and scattered on an elevated ridge on the edge of the Atacama Desert. Close to the spot, stands a cross bearing a brass plaque (Fig. 52). The history of this circumstance is best told by John Guest in a recent reminiscence of working in Chile with Hollie;

"Driving across the desert to San Pedro, one crosses a mountain range, the Altos de Purilactis. From the crest of this range there is a stunning panorama of the High Andes, the great slope of massive ignimbrite surface rising up to the Puna surmounted by the cones of andesitic volcanoes, most of which top about 6,000 m. This was my field area. When Prof. and I drove to the field area, he would stop at that particular vantage point to admire the scene. Many times he expressed the desire that when he died, his ashes should be spread at this site, his favourite view in the world. He also expressed this wish to his wife . . ."

John has subsequently visited the spot and reports that the cross

Fig. 52 – *Geomorphologist's Paradise. The Hollingworth Cross raised by the Chilean Geological Survey as their tribute. (Photograph kindly supplied by John Guest).*

survives where it was placed by Chilean colleagues, but further adds another form of record which any geologist would appreciate.

John adds,

"the name of Hollingworth will remain in geological history because the Servicio (Geological Survey in Chile) has ramed an important rock unit exposed near his cross, the Hollingworth Gravels. The unit is Miocene in age and consists of gravels thought to have formed during an interval of pedimentation in the evolution of the Andes. To name this unit in this way was a very gracious and touching act by our longstanding geological friends in Chile."

Hollie had a wicked sense of humour betrayed by a twinkle in the eye ably caught in the photograph which accompanies his obituary in the first part of the *Quarterly Journal of Engineering Geology* (1967), a publication which he had greatly encouraged. Interestingly, in this quizzing role, Hollie was following almost exactly the approach of George Bellas Greenough, a founder of University College London in 1829, and referred to in a history of the Society as a consistent 'Objector General' at their meetings.

Probably the best summary of his scientific life was given by Hollie himself when responding to the award of the Murchison Medal in 1965:

"In reflecting, as one does on such an occasion as this, I appreciate not least that our science can still honour the "general practitioner". Having an inclination towards pastures new (I am almost a one-paper-per-topic geologist) gives little opportunity for that popular and even elevating pastime of recantation".

Recantation ? The irony is that such thoughts would never have been in his mind. Much of his geology was done on the backs of envelopes or refined through lengthy discussions in one of his favourite pubs. If there were 'corrections' or reinterpretations, he probably took as much satisfaction from the thought that he had provoked the response which moved understanding forwards. Our science has need of such facilitators. In his life, Hollie made a substantial contribution which ought to be recognised.

BIBLIOGRAPHY

1929, The evolution of the Eden drainage in the south and west. *Proc. Geol. Assoc.*, Vol.40, pp 115-138.

1931, Claciation of Western Edenside and Adjoining areas and the Drumlins of Edenside and the Solway Plain. *Quart. Journ. Geol. Soc.*, Vol.87, pp 281-357.

1934, Some Solifluction phenomena in the Northern Part of the Lake District. *Proc. Geol. Assoc.*, Vol. 45, pp 167-188.

1935, Coastal Plateau (Correspondence). *Geol. Mag.*, Vol. 72, p. 48.

1936, Platforms in the Lake District. *Rep. Brit. Assoc. Trans. Sects.*, pp 348-349.

1937, The Gypsum deposits of the Vale of Eden. *Rep. Brit. Assoc. Trans. Sects.*, p.355.

1937a, High level erosional platforms in Cumberland and Furness. *Proc. Yorks. Geol. Soc.*, Vol.23, pp 159-177.

1938, The recognition and correlation of high-level erosion surfaces in Britain: a statistical study. *Quart. Journ. Geol. Soc.*, Vol.94, pp 55-84. (Lake District results, pp 69-70).

1938a, Carrock Fell and adjoining areas. *Proc. Yorks. Geol. Soc.*, Vol. 23, pp 208-218.

1942, The correlation of Gypsum-Anhydrite Deposits and the associated strata in the North of England. *Proc. Geol. Assoc.*, Vol.53, pp 141-151.

1951, The influence of Glaciation on the Topography of the Lake District. *Journ. Inst. Water Engs.*, Vol. 5, pp 485-496.

1954, The Geology of the Lake District – a review. (With contributions by ROSE, W.C.C. and OLIVER, R.L. and FIRMAN, R.J.). *Proc. Geol. Assoc.*, Vol.65, pp 385-402.

1969, The Rocks and Scenery. Chapter 3 in *'The Lake District National Park Guide'*, No. 6, H.M.S.O., pp 11-19.

24. Edgar Howard Shackleton (1903-1991)
Founder and President of the Cumberland Geological Society
Tom Shipp

Edgar Howard Shackleton was a quite remarkable person. The writer, as one who came to know and respect Edgar through the last 30 years of his long life, was greatly impressed by his infectious enthusiasm and encyclopaedic knowledge, largely self-taught. He was a prolific lecturer and writer, communicating his opinions on geology, botany, north country life, dialect and literature through the media of books, magazine articles, newspapers, evening classes and meetings in the field. His speech betrayed his origins; he was born at Great Harwood (Snotty 'arrod as he termed it) in East Lancashire just after the turn of

Fig. 53 – Edgar Shackleton

the 20th Century. Soon after the outbreak of the First World War he left school at the age of twelve to start work in a Lancashire cotton mill, and at fourteen commenced a textile engineering apprenticeship, attending evening classes in Blackburn where his favourite subjects were geology and botany. This seems to have marked the end of his formal education, but not of his enthusiasm for geology, for he was soon involved with the newly formed East Lancashire Regional Group of the Geologists' Association as its secretary (Fig. 53).

By the mid-1920s Edgar had married and moved to Windermere, earning a modest living as a lecturer and mountaineering guide. One of his climbing clients of those days later reached the exalted rank of Lord Chancellor! By 1934 he had found rather more security as a local repre-sentative with Hoover Ltd., soon becoming area supervisor for the region from Whitehaven to Penrith.

During the Second World War he was drafted into ordnance work at Drigg, manufacturing materials for explosives, and he remained in West

Fig. 54 – Edgar Shackleton (centre) in conversation with Sir Kingsley Dunham (Director British Geological Survey) (left) July 1983. Photographed at a Cumberland Geological Society field excursion, Winder Mine Tip, Frizington.

Cumberland, joining the United Steel Company at Workington, officially as an instrument engineer and perhaps less officially as a geological adviser on such matters as faulting and drainage in local iron ore mines, assessment of clays and refractory sandstones, and the mineralogy of imported ore supplies, many from India, from which he collected and documented several rare manganese minerals.

It was at about this time that he met up with the late Charles Edmonds, a miners' union organiser from Cleator Moor, with an unrivalled knowledge of the stratigraphy of Carboniferous Limestone in West Cumberland. Together they instituted Workers' Educational Association classes in geology, attracting and enthusing a group of people to form a West Cumberland Geology Group which in 1961 formally became the Cumberland Geological Society (Fig. 54).

During the following two decades he led this Society as its President, contributing lectures, field excursions and written articles to its activities. He was also prominent as a lecturer in the weekly programmes organised by the Newcastle University Department of Adult Education for summer visitors to the Lake District. He served on the Regional Committee of the

British Association for the Advancement of Science and also gave valuable service to the Lake District Naturalists' Trust, his particular concern being for the conservation of valuable geological sites (pre-empting RIGS). Of his publications, *The Carboniferous Limestones of West Cumberland* (1962), *Lakeland Geology* (1966) and *Geological Excursions in Lakeland* (1975) have been republished several times, and reflect his enthusiasm for geological matters.

Fig. 55 – The former home of Edgar Shackleton in Lincoln Road, Hensingham, Whitehaven.

In 1980 he was awarded the Cumberland Geological Society's Charles Edmonds Prize, whilst in 1981 due to failing health he relinquished active Presidency, the Society conferring upon him the title of Honorary Life President in recognition of his unique involvement in its development.

He was further honoured by being awarded the R. H. Worth Prize of the Geological Society of London in 1981, in recognition of his many contributions to the science of geology.

Throughout the years he contributed generously from his collection of rocks, fossils and minerals to universities, museums and other educational institutions. His modest home in Hensingham, (Fig. 55) was almost a private, lovingly tended geological museum in its own right. It is particularly gratifying that much of his geological collection is now held by the West Cumbria Mines Research Group in Egremont.

Edgar Shackleton died at Whitehaven on 14 March 1991. The Society mourned the passing of a generous and knowledgeable benefactor and leader whose views, however idiosyncratic, were always worth acknowledgement and discussion. Those closest to him miss his unaffected friendship and inspiration.

The following passage taken from the concluding section of his final book *Geological Excursions in Lakeland*, summarises Shackeleton's geological and personal philosophy very well and expresses the way he saw his efforts to popularize the subject and share his knowledge and experience:

'In conclusion may I say I have tried to give my reader a picture of Lakeland geology over the years and how various workers have tried to resolve the many problems that beset the subject. Where I have offered opinions of my own it must be remembered that they are the ideas of a completely amateur geologist whose only excuse for them is a deep and lasting interest in the subject, and our lovely Lakeland, that has never left me all the days of my life. No one in a subject like geology can claim infallibility, even more so in a complex area like ours. What I do ask is that you will try and visit each area described and see for yourself such evidence as is available, remembering too that a second visit is often more illuminating than the first!

One thing is quite certain. What you see and what you can get from what you see is dependent to a large extent on experience, and that comes and can only come from following the dictum of the great French geologist Nicolas Desmarest – " Go and see ! " If my humble efforts at guidance can bring pleasure and enjoyment as well as a little understanding of a great field of human endeavour on a none too simple subject I shall be well content.'

BIBLIOGRAPHY

SHACKLETON, E.H., 1962, Granite and Granitisation. *Proc. Cumb. Geol. Soc.,* Vol. 1, No. 1, pp 1-16.

1963, Jonathan Otley, *Proc. Cumb. Geol. Soc.,* Vol. 1, No. 2, pp 5-8.

1963a, *The Limestone Series of West Cumberland,* 47 pp, Cumberland Geological Soc. Whitehaven

1966, *Lakeland Geology.* Dalesman Publishing Co. Clapham 128 pp.

1966a, Robert Harkness. *Proc. Cumb. Geol. Soc.,* Vol. 2, pt. 1, pp 19-23.

1969, Henry Alleyne Nicholson. *Proc. Cumb. Geol. Soc.,* Vol. 2, pt. 3, pp 105-107.

1969a, Erosion at work: some recent Lake District Changes. *Proc. Cumb. Geol. Soc.,* Vol. 2, pt. 3, pp 115-116.

1971, Adam Sedgwick. *Proc. Cumb. Geol. Soc.,* Vol. 3, pt. 1, pp 33-36.

1973, The Story of Lakeland Geology. *Proc. Westmorland Geol. Soc.,* Vol. 1, No. 1, pp 3-4

1975, *Geological Excursions in Lakeland.* Dalesman Publishing Co. Clapham, 125pp

Postscript

Each one of these accounts of the 25 pioneering Lakeland 'Rock Men' stand on their own as separate evaluations of the individuals life and work. Together, however, they do paint some of the broader picture of how Lakeland geology began to be built up over the last 200 years. The picture revealed is incomplete. Many other significant figures played their part, but we believe we have made a contribution by bringing all this material together under one cover. Perhaps we may have misread or misinterpreted some people, but very much like the pioneers we have been writing about, this book is the product of many individuals, amateurs and local enthusiasts, as well as trained professionals.

The accounts span around 150 years of work. Starting with Jonathan Otley whose writings appeared just before 1820, we have reviewed contributions up until the 1960's. Clearly our decision to include only the deceased means that much Twentieth Century material must remain to be evaluated in the future. The book covers much of what is best described as the formative years of Lakeland geology.

It is fashionable at the present time to talk about 'learning curves'. To push a geological analogy, the upward curve of progress we have witnessed is rather like viewing the long profile of a river but in reverse - that is from mouth upwards to source. The early Nineteenth Century showed a very low growth gradient but steepening slightly as the century progressed. Small irregular steeper section mark significant advances. In the Twentieth Century the gradient continues to steepen. but only after about 1960 (the point where the book stops) does the gradient really take off and reflect serious growth. Much more has been done in the last 50 years than in the preceding 150.

The accounts have revealed some consistent themes. Most striking of all has been the part played by amateurs and local enthusiasts. Right from the earliest days of Otley, Ruthven and Bolton there has been a place for local people with local knowledge and the enthusiasm to go out into the field, collect, measure, observe and pose questions and record what they found. The tradition was continued by Postlethwaite, Edmonds and Shackleton. The part that local groups and societies can play in this process must also be remembered. Since those early days workers found gatherings of likeminded individuals not only a place to exchange ideas and views, but also a place to publish their findings. We have seen examples of this back in the Nineteenth Century when *The Cumberland & Westmorland Association for the Advancement of Literature and Science* enabled Clifton Ward, Goodchild and Postlethwaite to make their local observations available in print. Even earlier Otley had used *The Lonsdale Magazine* in a similar way. Since then, *The Cumberland & Westmorland Antiquarian & Archaeological Society, Carlisle Natural History Society* and *the Barrow Naturalist Field Club* have all been outlets for local work. The Cumberland Geological Society has continued this tradition with annual programmes of winter lectures and summer field excursions and more importantly the production of volumes of *Proceedings*, which allows space for publication of original writing with a strong preference for Cumbrian material. Also within the County The Westmorland Geological Society and The Furness Geology Group provide similar facilities. Geology is very much alive and thriving in the County and long may this important tradition continue.

The importance of individuals acting as mentors and guides to others and passing on the geological tradition has also played a part in the process of geological discovery. The personal contacts between Sedgwick and Otley, Ward and Postlethwaite or Edmonds and Shackleton have all been alluded to. The majority of the pioneering work has come from the professional geologists. The Lake District has obvious attractions for academic study with its wide variety of rock types and the challenging nature of its geological complexity. The contribution from the University of Cambridge School of Geology to the district has been quite remarkable, starting with Sedgwick and continuing throughout the whole period. No less than nine of the 'Rock Men' were graduates of that University and four were staff members of the Geology School. Nowhere else can the handing down of the Lakeland tradition from tutor to student be shown to have been more effective. Contact between the professional Survey Geologists and the local men was another important aspect of the development of ideas. Cumbria has always suffered from it relative remoteness and never having had a University nor base of Higher Education, reliance on outsiders has always been necessary. The value of a Survey Regional Office in Whitehaven for a short period in the 1920's has been highlighted.

It is interesting to try to evaluate just how far Lakeland geology had progressed from the early work of Otley around 1820 until the early 1960's when the last of our pioneers finished writing. Clearly a great deal of very detailed work on the lithology and characteristics of the main rock types had been completed and good inventories of the fossil finds and mineralogy compiled. The whole County had been mapped professionally by the Survey at least once, but the initial surveys dating from the late Nineteenth Century remained the only systematic record for much of the Lower

Palaeozoic inlier of the central Lake District. The lack of up to date Survey maps at popular scales (one inch to one mile or 1:50,000) was a constant source of frustration for visiting geologists, students or local enthusiasts. It is probably true to say the quality of material available for lowland Cumbria on the other hand, was better than for the Lake District. This was due to the fact that the Survey material was newer and in general the geology was more straightforward.

In 1954 and 1956 two very useful summaries of the position of Lakeland geology appeared. Both are useful milestone papers evaluating where research on the district stood at the time and sufficiently close to the end of the pioneers period to warrant re-reading in this context. Both focus particularly on the core area of the Lower Palaeozoic inlier of the Lake District. The former, S.E. Hollingworth's *The Geology of the Lake District – a review,* highlights the amount of work still to be done and the need for co-ordinated effort to infill the gaps in the mapping of the Lower Palaeozoics. The 1956 paper was G.H. Mitchell's Presidential Address to *The Yorkshire Geological Society* which was published as a 56 page booklet under the title *The Geological History of the Lake District.* It was, in his words "an attempt to summarize present knowledge of this interesting area". The level of uncertainty that still existed about the nature, succession and structure of the rocks is a striking feature of Mitchell's summary. The main divisions were still seen as the Skiddaw Slate, The Borrowdale Volcanic Series, The Coniston Limestone and the Silurian System. Detailed stratigraphies for the Slates and the volcanics were still being debated, with much detailed mapping awaiting completion. Ideas on the palaeogeographical conditions during the Palaeozoic were equally uncertain. Different interpretations of the relationships between the Slates and the Volcanics existed and work to clarify details of the Coniston Limestone and Silurians was still pending. The petrological detail available on the intrusive rocks was fairly extensive, but the age of most of them was still not clear. Similarly the age of the mineralisation was still a matter to be argued. Neither the Hollingworth nor the Mitchell papers were totally retrospective. They both refer to on-going research and ideas that were beginning to emerge on the Skiddaw and Borrowdale Groups in particular. Attempts were being made to unravel the Skiddaws and establish a sequence. The work of Oliver (1954, 1956) on the Borrowdales was instigating new thinking on the nature of the vulcanism and new ideas on the structural relationships were beginning to be put together.

The harsh reality was that by the late 1950's things had only just started to move since the late 1930's. The interruption of the war years and the dearth of work in the 1950's meant that Lakeland geology had been in limbo. Taking it forward even from the late 1950's, it is noticeable how long it took for many of these ideas to reach fruition and even more noticeable, how long it was before much of this thinking reached the popular literature. Even looking at some of the last contributions from our pioneering 'Rock Men' it has to be noted how for the student, or interested amateur seeking good general introductions to Lakeland geology what was at hand well into the 1960's was largely 1930's material. For example in the official Lake District National Park Guide published in 1969, the general account of the geology by Hollingworth (admittedly printed three years after his death) refers to little substantially new material. Edgar Shackleton's book *Lakeland Geology* published in 1966, which cornered the popular market and was one of the first books written in the style of a field guide contained practically nothing of the new thinking that was emerging.

Finally, and briefly, projecting all this forward to consider where we are today in 2001, some 40 years+ on from where our 'Rock Men' finished, brings us to a totally different order of things. Progress in the last few decades has been truly staggering. The upward curve of progress has surpassed everything achieved by our 'Rock Men'. One thing above all else has changed things – that is the advent of the theory of global plate tectonics. Formulated in the 1960's this changed the way we look at the Lake District and it has given us a framework in which to place the geological history. Technology has given us better and improved means of analyzing rocks, dating fossils and recognizing microfossils. More accurate ways of dating material by radiometric and other methods now exist. Our knowledge of what lies at depth beneath the Lake District has been vastly extended, so that we know more about the deep structures and have a good picture of the granitic batholith beneath our region and the relations between the intrusive masses we see exposed at the surface. The Lower Palaeozoic inlier has now been re-mapped in some detail and the stratigraphy clarified with new Group/Supergroup, Formation and Member names. Our understanding of both the sequence and palaeogeographical detail of the Skiddaw Group and the Borrowdale Volcanic Group in particular, has seen detailed work and new interpretations. New Survey maps offering new interpretations are now available for most of the district.

In the geomorphological field, after the dearth of work early in the Twentieth Century serious advances in our knowledge of the district have similarly been achieved. The advent of palynology and other sophisticated dating techniques have powered a revolution in Quaternary and Holocene stratigraphy. Field studies on earth surface processes have led to a greater understanding about landform evolution. Work has become more analytical with more precise measurement of phenomena and computer analysis and modelling lifted the level of scientific research. We now have work being done on hydrology and fluvial processes in the Lake District, on the periglacial features and on slope processes – all comparatively new fields.

New 'Rock Men', and women, are at the present time continuing the endless pursuit of unravelling the geology and landscape of this fascinating region. There is much yet to do. At some stage in the future, hopefully not as far on as the next Millenium, someone will evaluate the work of the current pioneers.

Notes & References

1. JONATHAN OTLEY

The correspondence between Otley and Sedgwick is contained in WARD, J.C. 1877, Jonathan Otley, the Geologist and Guide. *Trans. Cumb. & West. Assoc. Adv. Lit. & Sci.* No. 11, pp 125-169

I am indebted to David Oldroyd (personal communication) for the information regarding the possible whereabouts of a geological map drawn by Otley.

Thanks are due to Keswick Museum for allowing access to their Otley collection.

2. ADAM SEDGWICK

This paper was first published in *'Comparative Planetology, Geological Education, History of Geology' : Proceedings of the 30th International Geological Congress*, vol. 26 VSP Int. Sci. Publ., Zeist, The Netherlands 1997. The author greatly acknowledges the permission of the publishers to reproduce the paper.

References.

BOLTON, J., 1869. *Geological Fragments Collected Principally from Rambles among the Rocks of Furness and Cartmel.* D Atkinson, Ulverston, and Whittaker and Co., London

CLARK, J.W. & MCKENNY HUGHES, T.S. (Eds), 1890. *The Life and Letters of the Reverend Adam Sedgwick.* Cambridge University Press, Cambridge.

ÉLIE DE BEAUMONT, L. 1831. Researches on some of the Revolutions of the Surface of the Globe; Presenting Various Examples of the Coincidence between the Elevation of Beds in Certain Systems of Mountains, and the Sudden Changes which have Produced the Lines of Demarcation Observable in Certain Stages of the Sedimentary Deposits. *Phil. Mag.* 10 (New Series), pp 241-264.

HOOYKAAS, R.1970. *Catastrophism in Geology, its Scientific Character in Relation to Actualism and Uniformitarianism.* North Holland, Amsterdam.

OTLEY, J. 1820., Remarks on the Succession of Rocks in the District of the Lakes. *Lonsdale Mag.* 1, pp 433-435.

1823, *A Concise Description of the English Lakes, the Mountains in their Vicinity, and the Roads by which they may be visited: with remarks on the Mineralogy and Geology of the District.* Keswick, London and Kirkby Lonsdale.

PHILLIPS, J., 1873. Sedgwick, *Nature.* 7, pp 257-259

RUDWICK, M.J.S., 1985. *The Great Devonian Controversy*. Chicago University Press, Chicago and London.

SECORD, J.E., 1986. *Controversy in Victorian Geology: The Cambrian-Silurian Dispute,* Princeton University Press, Princeton.

SEDGWICK, A., 1831, Address to the Geological Society. Delivered on the evening of 18th of February 1831, by the Rev. Professor Sedgwick, M.A., F.R.S. &c on Retiring from the Presidents Chair. *Proc. Geol. Soc. Lond.,* 1, pp 281-316.

1836, Introduction to the General Structure of the Cumbrian Mountains; With a Description of the Great Dislocations by which they have been separated from the Neighbouring Carboniferous Chains. *Trans. Geol. Soc. Lond.,* 4 (series 2), pp 47-68 (Read Jan 5th, 1831).

SPEAKMAN, C., 1982, *Adam Sedgwick: Geologist and Dalesman 1785-1873.* Broadoak Press/The Geological Society of London/Trinity College Cambridge, Heathfield.

TODHUNTER, I., 1876, *William Whewell: An Account of his Writings.* 2 Vols. Macmillan & Co., London, Vol. 1 p 32.

TORRENS, H.S., 1994, Joseph Harrison Fryer (1777-1855); Geologist and Mining Engineer in England 1803-1825 and South America 1826-1828: A Study in failure, in S. Figueiroa and M. Lopes (Eds), *Geological Sciences in Latin America: Scientific relations and Exchanges,* INHIGEO, Campinas, pp 29-46.

3. JOHN BOLTON

NORMAN, T. N., 1961. *The geology of the Silurian Strata in the Blawith area, Furness.* Unpublished Ph.D thesis, University of Birmingham.

ROSE, W.C.C. and DUNHAM, K.C., 1977, *Geology and hematite deposits of South Cumbria.* Inst. of Geol. Sciences, HMSO, xii + 170pp.

4 JOHN RUTHVEN

The original work on John Ruthven was done by the late Toby Butler of the Westmorland Geological Society. This account has been re-drafted from material compiled by Toby and recorded in the *Westmorland Geological Society Proceedings* No 26 1998. I am indebted to the WGS for the loan of the Ruthven map which is now in their Library collection by kind permission of Toby's widow.

I also indebted to Murray Mitchell for drawing my attention to Ruthven's *Description of his Geological Map* and for providing a copy. I was not aware of the existence of this booklet when the original article in *Proc. Cumb. Geol. Soc.* Vol. 6, pt 3, pp 329-331 was published, nor I believe was Toby Butler when he compiled the original material.

Acknowledgement is due to Kendal Museum for locating and loaning the watercolour of Ruthven that is reproduced as Fig.10.

5 ROBERT HARKNESS

GEIKIE, A.,1878. *Nature* Oct l0th, p.628.

GOODCHILD, J.G., 1883. Professor Robert Harkness, FRS, FGS, *Trans. Cumb. Assoc. Adv. Lit. & Sci.* No. 8, pp 145-188

OBITUARY, 1878., Professor Robert Harkness. FRS, FGS, *Geol.Mag.* V, pp 574-576.

OBITUARY, 1878., *Min.Mag.* II, pp 153-154.

SHACKLETON, E.H., 1966., Robert Harkness, FRS, FGS. *Proc. Cumb. Geol. Soc.,* Vol. 2 pp 19-22.

7. J.E. MARR

Notes.

1. Indeed, according to Marr (1883, 27), Barrande had gone wrong because of the British geologists! The Survey officers had been inclined to construe all graptolite-bearing black shales as Llandeilo. Accepting this, Barrande had supposed that certain rocks that were seemingly stratigraphically younger than Llandeilo (on other palaeontological grounds) <u>were</u> Llandeilo simply because they contained graptolites. It was on this assumption that the notion of "precursorial" forms in colonies was developed. It is interesting that Barrande named his "colonies" after those who opposed his theories. So one of them was designated *"Colonie Marr"*. I understand that it was situated on the slopes of a hill called "Smutny" near the town of Zdice in Bohemia.

2. Evidence in the Hughes archive, recently donated to the Cambridge University Library, reveals that Hughes's Sedgwickian ideas lay behind his resignation from the Survey, though there were other factors also involved, and some official dissatisfaction with his performance. He made apparently inflated travel allowance claims, and wanted to be in the London office for periods longer than his superiors thought warranted

3. Today, the contact in the quarry is rather overgrown, but the boundary is seen quite well by a small waterfall in Ash Gill itself, nearby.

4. Subsequently, the retiform *Dictyonema pulchellum* (Hall) (Tremadoc) has been found by Adrian Rushton (1985) at Trusmadoor in the northern Uldale Fells.

5. The conflation of Eycotts and Borrowdales went back to the time of Otley and Sedgwick and was also made by Nicholson, who may indeed have had an unhelpful hand in the development of Marr's structural theory of the Lake District. Correspondence between Nicholson and Lapworth, preserved at Birmingham University, reveals that in 1883

Nicholson supposed that the Drygill Shales formed a unit at the base of the Eycott Series; and that the Eycotts ran all the way from St John's Vale, though Borrowdale, over Honister, and on to Ennerdale! It seems possible that some erroneous structural ideas, never published by Nicholson, passed from him to Marr in the field or in correspondence.

6. Such a fault system is rather rare in the theoretical armoury of the structural geologist. But see for example: Soper and Anderton (1984).

7. Upstream, near Chapel Stile, there are some unimpressive deposits, possibly related to what Marr saw and described.

Acknowledgements.

I am grateful to Michael Dorling, of the Sedgwick Museum, for permission to reproduce material from Marr's field notebooks. Not long before he died in 1999, the late John Thackray, archivist at the Geological Society and the Natural History Museum, London, very kindly made available to me his transcript of his interview with T.C. Nicholas in 1975, for which I am most grateful. Thanks also to the Keeper of the Lapworth Archive at Birmingham University for allowing me to consult correspondence there from Nicholson to Lapworth; and to the Cambridge University Library for allowing me to consult the McKenny Hughes papers. My correspondent Dr Josef Haubelt of Prague has provided information about the location of "Colonie Marr". A good many friendly Lakeland geologists have also assisted me in my on-going project of writing a book on the history of geological research in the Lake District. Specifically, I am indebted to Angus Lunn for his careful reading of the paper and his critical comments thereon; and to Chris Thompson for his editorial work. Also, needless to say, no one can get anywhere in the study of the history of Lakeland Geology without utilising Alan Smith's two notable bibliographies SMITH, R.A., *A Bibliography of the Geology and Geomorphology of Cumbria*. Cumb.Geol.Soc. Vol. 1 (1974), Vol. 2 (1990). The help of all is greatly appreciated.

References

DAKYNS, J.R., 1869, Notes on the Geology of the Lake District, *Geol. Mag.*, dec. 1, Vol 6, pp 56–58.

FIRMAN, R.J., 1954, Note on the Metasomatic Changes in the Rocks Adjacent to the Shap Granite, *Proc. Geol. Assoc.*, Vol. 65, pp 412–414.

GREEN, J.F.N., 1911, *The Older Palaeozoic Succession of the Duddon Estuary,* Hayman, Christy and Lilly Ltd, London (published privately).

GREEN, J.F.N., 1915, The Structure of the Eastern Part of the Lake District, *Proc. Geol. Assoc.,* Vol. 26, pp 1–30.

HARKER, A. and MARR, J.E., 1891, The Shap Granite and Associated Igneous and Metamorphic Rocks, *Quart. Journ. Geol. Soc.,* Vol. 47, pp 266–328 and plate.

HARKER, A. and MARR, J.E., Supplementary Notes on the Metamorphic Rocks around the Shap Granite, *Quart. Journ. Geol. Soc.,* Vol. 49, pp 359–371 and plate.

HARKNESS, R., 1863, On the Skiddaw Slate Series With a Note on the Graptolites by J.W. Salter Esq., F.G.S., A.L.S., *Quart. Journ. Geol. Soc.* Vol. 19, pp113–140.

HICKS, H., 1876, Appendix to Marr (1876), pp 135–139.

HORNY, R. and TUREK, V., 1999, *Joachim Barrande (1799–1833): His Life, Work and Heritage to World Palaeontology,* National Museum, Prague (in English and Czech).

LAPWORTH, C., 1879 On the Tripartite Classification of the Lower Palaeozoic Rocks, *Geol. Mag.,* dec 11, Vol. 6, pp 1–15.

MARR, J.E., 1876, Fossiliferous Cambrian Shales near Caernarfon, *Quart. Journ. Geol. Soc.,* Vol. 34, pp 134–135.

1878, On some Well-Defined Life-Zones in the Lower Part of the Silurian (Sedgwick) of the Lake District, *Quart. Journ. Geol. Soc.,* Vol.34, pp 871–885.

1880a, On the Cambrian (Sedgw.) and Silurian Beds of the Dee Valley, as Compared with those of the Lake District, *Quart. Journ. Geol. Soc.,* Vol. 36, pp 871–885.

1880b, On the Predevonian Rocks of Bohemia, *Quart. Jour. Geol. Soc.,* Vol.36, pp 591–619.

1883, *The Classification of the Cambrian and Silurian Rocks.* Being the Sedgwick Prize Essay for the Year 1882, Deighton and Bell, Cambridge; George Bell and Sons, London.

1892a, The Coniston Limestone Series, *Geol. Mag.,* dec. 111, Vol. 9, pp 97–110 and plate.

1892b, Further Remarks on the Coniston Limestone, *Geol. Mag.,* dec. 111, Vol.9, pp 443–447.

1892c, On the Wenlock and Ludlow Strata of the Lake District, *Geol. Mag.,* dec.111, Vol. 9, pp 534–541.

1894, Notes on the Skiddaw Slates, *Geol. Mag.,* dec 1V, Vol. 1, pp 122–130.

1900a, Notes on the Geology of the English Lake District, *Proc. Geol. Assoc.,* Vol. 16, pp 449–483.

1900b, Long Excursion to Keswick, Monday, August 20th to Saturday, August 25th, 1900, *Proc. Geol. Assoc.,* Vol.16, pp 526–531.

1900c, *The Scientific Study of Scenery*, Methuen & Co., London.

1902, Exhibit of Specimens from a Metamorphosed Metalliferous Vein in Basic Andesites near the Shap Granite. *Quart. Journ. Geol. Soc.,* Vol. 58, pp lxxx–lxxxii.

1903, *Agricultural Geology*, Methuen & Co., London.

1905, Anniversary Address: The Classification of the Sedimentary Rocks, *Quart. Journ. Geol. Soc.,* Vol.61, pp lxi–lxxxvi.

1909, *Westmorland,* Cambridge University Press, Cambridge and London.

1910, *Cumberland,* Cambridge University Press, Cambridge and London.

1915, The Ashgillian Succession in the Tract to the West of Coniston Lake, *Quart. Journ. Geol. Soc.*, Vol. 71, pp 189–204.

1916, *The Geology of the Lake District and the Scenery as Influenced by Geological Structure,* Cambridge University Press, Cambridge, London, and Edinburgh.

1924, Notes on the Glaciation of the Coniston Fells, *Geol. Mag.*, Vol. 61, pp 264–269.

1929, *Deposition of Sedimentary Rocks*, Cambridge University Press, Cambridge and London.

MARR, J.E. and NICHOLSON, H.A., 1888, The Stockdale Shales, *Quart. Journ. Geol. Soc.,* Vol. 44, pp 654–732 and plate.

MARR, J E., and ROBERTS, T., 1885, The Lower Palaeozoic Rocks of the Neighbourhood of Haverfordwest. *Quart. Journ. Geol. Soc.*, Vol. 41, pp 476-491 and map.

MITCHELL, G.H., MOSLEY, F., FIRMAN, R.J., SOPER, N.J., ROBERTS, D.E., NUTT, M.J., and WADGE, A.J., 1970, Excursion to the Northern Lake District 30th August-5th September 1970, *Proc. Geo . Assoc.* Vol. 83, pp 443-470 and plates.

MURCHISON, R., 1872, *Siluria: A History of the Oldest Rocks in the British Isles and other Countries.* 5th Edition, John Murray, London.

NICHOLSON, H.A. and MARR, J.E., 1887, On the Occurrence of a New Fossiliferous Horizon in the Ordovician Series of the Lake district. *Geol. Mag.*, Vol. 4 (dec 111), pp 35-38.

1891, The Cross Fell Inlier, *Quart. Journ. Geol. Soc.*, Vol. 47, pp 500-529 and plates.

NICHOLSON, H.A., 1868, *Geology of Cumberland and Westmorland.* Robert Hardwicke, London.

OLDROYD, D.R., 1990, *The Highlands Controversy; Constructing Geological Knowledge through Fieldwork in Nineteenth Century Britain.* The University of Chicago Press, Chicago and London.

1991, The Archaean Controversy in Britain: Part 1 – The Rocks of St. David's. *Annals of Science,* Vol. 48, pp 407-452.

1999a, Evidence that disappears: John Marr *et al.* and Lakeland Geological Sites. *The Geologica Curator.* Vol. 7, pp 17-25.

1999b, Early Ideas about Glaciation in the English Lake District: The Problem of Making Sense of Glaciation in a Glaciated Region. *Annals of Science*, Vol. 56, pp 175-203.

RUSHTON, A.W., 1985, A Lancefieldian Graptolie from the Lake District. *Geol. Mag.*, Vol. 122, pp 329-333.

SEDGWICK, A. and SALTER, J., 1873, *Catalogue of the Collection of Cambrian and Silurian Fossils Contained in the Geological Museum of the University of Cambridge.* Cambridge University Press, Cambridge.

SOPER, N.J., and ANDERTON, R., 1984, Did the Dalradian Slides Originate as Extensional Faults ?. *Nature,* No. 307, pp 357-360.

UNITED KINGDOM NIREX LIMITED, 1997, *Sellafield Geological and Hydrogeological Investigations: The Quaternary of the sellafield Area.* (Report No S/97/002), Nirex, Harwell.

WARD, J C., 1876, *The Geology of the Northern part of the English Lake District.* Mem. Geol. Surv. 12 + 132 pp.

9 EDMUND GARWOOD

(Account by Murray Mitchell)

A fuller account of Garwood's work is given by Hudson (1950).

Mr Iain Burgess is thanked for his improvements to a draft of this contribution.

References

GARWOOD, E.J., 1907, Notes on the faunal succession in the Carboniferous Limestone of Westmoreland and neighbouring portions of Lancashire and Yorkshire. *Geol. Mag.,* dec. 5, Vol. 4, pp 70-74.

1913, The Lower Carboniferous succession in the north-west of England. *Quart. Journ. Geol. Soc.,* Vol. 68, pp 449-586.

GARWOOD, E.J. and GOODYEAR, E., 1924, The Lower Carboniferous succession in the Settle District and along the line of the Craven Faults. *Quart. Jour. Geol. Soc.,* Vol. 80, pp 184-273.

GARWOOD, E.J. and MARR, J.E., 1895, Zonal divisions of the Carboniferous system. *Geol. Mag.,* dec. 4, Vol. 2, pp 550-552.

GEORGE, T.N., JOHNSON, G.A.L., MITCHELL, M., PRENTICE, J E., RAMSBOTTOM, W.H.C., SEVASTOPULO, G.D. and WILSON, R.B. 1976, A correlation of Dinantian rocks in the British Isles. *Geological Society of London, Special Report* No.7, 87pp.

HILL, D., 1938, A monograph on the Carboniferous rugose corals of Scotland. *Monograph of the Palaeontographical Society of London,* Part l, pp l-78.

HUDSON, R.G.S., 1950, In Memoriam Edmund Johnston Garwood 1864-1949. *Proc. Yorks. Geol. Soc.,* Vol. 28, Part 1, 1-4.

HUDSON, R.G.S. and DUNNINGTON, H.V., 1945, The Carboniferous rocks of the Swinden Anticline, Yorkshire, with a redefinition of the boundary between Tournaisian and Viséan in England. *Proc. Geol. Assoc.* Vol. 55, Part 4,. pp 195-215.

RAMSBOTTOM, W.H.C., 1973, Transgressions and Regressions in the Dinantian: a new synthesis of British Dinantian stratigraphy. *Proc. Yorks. Geol. Soc.,* Vol. 39, Part 4, 567-607.

VAUGHAN, A., 1905, The palaeontological sequence in the Carboniferous Limestone of the Bristol area. *Quart.Journ.Geol.Soc.,* Vol. 61, pp 181-307.

10 JAMES CLIFTON WARD

Acknowledgements.

I wish to acknowledge the help of Professor David Oldroyd, of N.S.W. Australia who kindly provided me with a short unpublished entry on J.C. Ward he has recently prepared for the National Dictionary of Biography. I am also appreciative of personal conversations with David about Ward and other early Lakeland geologists.

I also wish to acknowledge the help of George Bott of Keswick. His small booklet 'Sponsored Talk - Keswick Lecture Society 1869-1968', (published by Ferguson Bros. Printers Ltd , Keswick, May 1971, 72pp) is a useful background history to Ward's involvement with the local scientific community in Keswick.

Volumes 1 and 2 of the Minute Books of the Keswick Lecture Society have also been made available to me by the Cumbria Record Office in Carlisle Castle.

11. JOHN GOODCHILD AND FREDERICK TROTTER.

References.

BUCKLAND, W., 1840-41, On the evidences of glaciers in Scotland and northern England. *Proc. Geol. Soc.,* Vol. 3, pp 332-337.

CARRUTHERS, R. G., 1953, *Glacial drifts and the undermelt theory.* Harold Hill, Newcastle upon Tyne.

CROLL, J., 1871, On the transport of the Wasdale Crag blocks. *Geol. Mag.,* Vol. 8, pp15-20.

DAKYNS, J.R., TIDDEMAN, R.H. & GOODCHILD, J.G., 1897 *The geology of the country between Appleby, Ullswater and Haweswater.* Mem. Geol. Surv.

EASTWOOD, T., 1953, *British Regional Geology: Northern England,* 3rd edn. H.M.S.O.

GOODCHILD, J.G., 1875, The glacial phenomena of the Eden valley and the western part of the Yorkshire-dale district. *Quart. Journ. Geol. Soc.,* Vol. 31, pp 55-99.

1887, Ice work in Edenside and some of the adjoining parts of North Western England. *Trans. Cumb. & West. Assoc. Adv. Lit. & Sci.,* No. 12, pp 111-167.

GREGORY, J.W., 1909, Obituary notice of John George Goodchild, born 26th May 1844, died 21st Feb. 1906. *Trans. Edinb. Geol. Soc.* Vol. 9, pp 331-350.

HOLLINGWORTH, S. E., 1931, Glaciation of western Edenside and adjoining areas and the drumlins of Edenside and the Solway plain. *Quart. Journ. Geol. Soc.,* Vol. 87, pp 281-357.

HUDDART, D., 1991, The glacial history and glacial deposits of the north and west Cumbrian lowlands. In Ehlers, J., et al. (eds). *Glacial deposits in Great Britain and Ireland.* Rotterdam, pp 151-168.

HUDDART, D., TOOLEY, M.J. & CARTER, P.A., 1977, The coasts of north-west England. In Kidson, C. & Tooley, M.J. (eds) *The Quaternary history of the Irish Sea.* Geol. Journ., Special Issue 7, pp 119-154. Liverpool.

KENDALL, P.F., 1902, A system of glacier lakes in the Cleveland Hills. *Quart. Journ. Geol. Soc.,* Vol. 58, pp 471-571.

OBITUARY, 1906, John George Goodchild, F.G.S. *Geol. Mag.,* Vol. 3, pp 189-190.

OBITUARY, 1907, John George Goodchild (1844-1906). *Min. Mag.,* Vol. 14, pp 271-2.

OBITUARY, 1907, John George Goodchild. *Quart. Journ. Geol. Soc. Lond.*, Vol. 63, pp lxv-lxvi.

OBITUARY, 1968, F.M. Trotter, *Proc. Yorks. Geol. Soc.* Vol. 37, pp 101-3.

OBITUARY, 1969, Frederick Murray Trotter, *Proc. Geol. Assoc.* Vol. 80, pp 126-7.

OBITUARY, 1969, Frederick Murray Trotter (1897-1968). *Proc. Geol. Soc.*, Vol.126, pp 133-5.

ROSE, W.C.C. & DUNHAM, K.C., 1977, *Geology and haematite deposits of south Cumbria,* Geol. Surv. Econ. Mem.

TIDDEMAN, R.H., 1872, On the evidence for the ice-sheet in north Lancashire and adjacent parts of Yorkshire and Westmorland. *Quart.Journ.Geol.Soc.,* Vol. 28, pp 471-491.

TROTTER, F.M., 1929a, The glaciation of eastern Edenside, the Alston block and the Carlisle plain. *Quart. Journ. Geol. Soc.*, Vol. 85, pp 549-612.

1929b, The Tertiary uplift and resultant drainage of the Alston block and adjacent areas. *Proc. Yorks. Geol. Soc.*, Vol. 21, pp 161-180.

TROTTER, F.M. & HOLLINGWORTH, S.E., 1932a, *The geology of the Brampton District.* Mem. Geol. Surv.

1932b, The glacial sequence in the north of England. *Geol.Mag.*, Vol. 69, pp 374-380.

(A comprehensive list of references on the work of J. G. Goodchild is contained in Gregory, 1909)

12. BERNARD SMITH

Reference

L.J. Wills, 1937, Obituary notice on Bernard Smith, *Quart. Journ. Geol. Soc.* Vol. 93 Proceedings pp cvii-cix.

An obituary notice also appeared in 'Obituary Notices of the Royal Society of London' No. 6. Vol. 2 pp 239-249 January 1938 by W.G. Fearnsides.

14. G.H. MITCHELL.

Acknowledgements

Biographical details are from Sir James Stubblefield's account of G H Mitchell in the *Biographical memoirs of Fellows of the Royal Society* (Volume 23, 1977).

We are grateful to Mr Murray Mitchell for his advice and comments.

THE PHYSIOGRAPHERS

Reference

Hopkins, W., 1848, On the elevation and denudation of the district of the Lakes of Cumberland and Westmorland. *Quart. Journ. Geol. Soc.*, Vol. 4, pp 70-98.

16. THOMAS HAY

This paper was originally published in *Proceedings of the Cumberland Geological Society*, 1998, Vol. 6 part 2 pp 171-182.

Acknowledgements

The late David and the late Michael Hay, sons of Thomas Hay, generously provided information about his background and life. John Hay, his grandson, gave access to his field maps and photographs. Their help is much appreciated. Miss Barbara Moon of Glenridding, friend of the Hay family, gave valuable assistance at the start of this study.

Thanks are also due to Dr Peter Wilson and to referees for constructive comment.

References

Andrews, J.T. 1961 The Development of scree slopes in the English Lake District and central Quebec – Labrador. *Cahiers Geogr. de Quebec* No. 5, pp 219 - 230.

Ballantyne, C.K. and Harris, C. 1994 *The Periglaciation of Great Britain*, Cambridge, Cambridge University Press.

Bennett, M.R. 1990 The deglaciation of Glen Croulin, Knoydart, *Scot J Geol*, Vol. 26, pp 41 - 46.

Bennett, M.R. and Boulton, G.S. 1993 Deglaciation of the Younger Dryas or Loch Lomond Stadial ice-field in the northern Highlands, Scotland, *J. Quat. Sci.*, Vol. 8, pp 133 – 145.

Boardman, J. 1992 Quaternary landscape evolution in the Lake District – a discussion. *Proc. Cumb. Geol. Soc.* Vol. 5, pp 285-315.

Boardman, J., ed., 1997 *Geomorphology of the Lake District: a Field Guide*, British Geomorphological Research Group, Oxford.

Caine, N T. 1963 The Origin of sorted stripes in the Lake District, Northern England. *Geogr. Ann. A*, Vol. 45, pp 172 - 179.

Caine T.N. 1963 Movement of low angle scree slopes in the Lake District, Northern England. *Rev. Geomorph. Dynamique* Vol. 14, pp 171 - 177.

Clayton, K.M. 1974 Zones of glacial erosion. In Brown, E.H. and Waters, R.S. eds *Progress in Geomorphology Spec. Publ. Inst. Brit. Geogr.*, No. 7, pp 163 - 176.

Gresswell, R.K. 1952 The Glacial Geomorphology of the South-Eastern part of the Lake District. *Liverpool and Manchester Geol. J.*, Vol. 1, pp 57 - 70.

Gresswell, R.K. 1962 The Glaciology of the Coniston Basin. *Liverpool and Manchester Geol. J.* Vol. 3, pp 83 - 96.

Gurney, S.D. 1995 *Large sorted stone stripes of the Staple Tors area, Dartmoor, south-west England: examples of relict patterned ground.* Univ. Reading Dept. Geogr. Discussion Paper 33, 32 pp..

Linton, D.L. 1957 Radiating valleys in Glaciated lands. *Tijdschrift van het Koninklijk Nederland Aardrijkskundig Gemootschap.* 74, pp 297-312.

Manley, G. 1959 The Late-Glacial Climate of North-West England *Liverpool and Manchester Geol. J.* Vol. 2, pp 188-215.

Marr, J.E. 1916 *The Geology of the Lake District*, Cambridge, Cambridge University Press.

McConnell, R.B. 1939 Residual erosion surfaces in Mountain Ranges. *Proc. Yorks Geol. Soc.* Vol. 24, pp 76-98.

Melville, C. 1986 Historical Earthquakes in Northwest England. *Trans. Cumberland and Westmorland Antiqu. and Archaeol. Soc.* Vol.86, pp 193-209.

Parry, J.T. 1960 The erosion surfaces of the South-Western Lake District, *Trans. Inst. Brit. Geogrs,* Vol. 28, pp 39-54.

Peltier, L.C. 1950 The geomorphic cycle in periglacial regions as it is related to climatic geomorphology, *Annals, Assoc. Amer. Geogrs*, Vol. 40, pp 214-236.

Sissons, J.B. 1980 The Loch Lomond Advance in the Lake District, Northern England. *Trans. Roy. Soc. Edinb.* Vol. 71, pp 13-27.

Walker, D. 1966 The Glaciation of the Langdale Fells. *Geol J.* Vol. 5, pp 208-215.

Ward, J.C. 1873 On Rock Fissuring. *Geol Mag.* Vol. 10, pp 245-248.

Ward, J.C. 1875 The Glaciation of the Southern part of the Lake District and the Glacial origin of the Lakes of Cumberland and Westmorland. *Quart. J. Geol. Soc.,* Vol. 31, pp 152-166.

Werner, B.T. and Hallet, B. 1993 Numerical simulation of self-organized stone stripes. *Nature* No. 361, pp 142-145.

19. JOHN POSTLETHWAITE.

I am indebted to Michael Moon, Bookseller, Lowther Street, Whitehaven for permission to quote from the biographical sketch of John Postlethwaite, written by E.H. Shackleton in the 1974 Reprint Edition of *'Mines and* Mining *in the English Lake District'* and for permission to repro-duce the picture of Postlethwaite in that book as Fig. 46.

Reference

Richard Fortey, 2000, Trilobite ! Eye Witness to Evolution. Harper Collins p 150.

22. CHARLES EDMONDS.

References

BISAT, W. S., 1924, The Carboniferous goniatites of the north of England and their zones. *Proc. Yorks. Geol. Soc.,* Vol. 20, pp 40-124.

KENDALL, J. D., 1885, The Carboniferous Rocks of Cumberland, North Lancashire and Furness. *Trans. Fed. Inst. Min. & Mech. Eng.,* (N. Eng. Inst.), Vol. 34, 125-236.